CPA Exam

FOR

DUMMIES®

A Wiley Brand

CPA Exam
FOR DUMMIES
A Wiley Brand

by Kenneth W. Boyd

FOR DUMMIES
A Wiley Brand

CPA Exam For Dummies®

Published by: **John Wiley & Sons, Inc.,** 111 River Street, Hoboken, NJ 07030-5774, www.wiley.com

Copyright © 2014 by John Wiley & Sons, Inc., Hoboken, New Jersey

Published simultaneously in Canada

For general information on our other products and services, please contact our Customer Care Department within the U.S. at 877-762-2974, outside the U.S. at 317-572-3993, or fax 317-572-4002. For technical support, please visit www.wiley.com/techsupport.

Wiley publishes in a variety of print and electronic formats and by print-on-demand. Some material included with standard print versions of this book may not be included in e-books or in print-on-demand. If this book refers to media such as a CD or DVD that is not included in the version you purchased, you may download this material at http://booksupport.wiley.com. For more information about Wiley products, visit www.wiley.com.

Library of Congress Control Number: 2014934808

ISBN 978-1-118-81373-7 (pbk); ISBN 978-1-118-81379-9 (ebk); ISBN 978-1-118-81362-1 (ebk)

Manufactured in the United States of America

10 9 8 7 6 5 4 3 2 1

Contents at a Glance

Table of Contents

Introduction

So you're interested in becoming a CPA, huh? Good for you! A CPA certification opens all kinds of doors for you professionally that are closed to accountants without this certification. Let me warn you, though: The CPA exam is challenging. You're going to need to organize and study an enormous amount of data. Lucky for you, *CPA Exam For Dummies* makes studying for the exam easier.

About This Book

I took the CPA exam myself and passed it in the early '90s. Passing all four sections took me multiple tries. I really struggled, and I now know why. I didn't think through the process of creating and implementing a plan of study. I just dove in with no real plan of attack. I wrote this book, in part, to provide that attack plan for you.

I struggled for another reason, too. The test-prep material I used was comprehensive, covering all the topics that were on the exam in detail. What I needed was a text that explained the most frequently tested topics using examples that I could understand.

This book explains concepts by providing examples you may already understand. When my kids learned to tie their shoes, a friend of ours explained that you take the two shoestrings and "make them into elephant ears." Because our kids could visualize an elephant's big, floppy ears, the kids could make the loops to tie their shoes. They understood elephant ears, and that helped them with the shoe-tying concept. (At least two of our three children still know how to tie their shoes!)

When people ask me about test-preparation material, I explain that there are lots of great books, videos, and online resources out there. You can find some great material on the web for free. What's missing, I believe, are tools to explain these complex ideas in a simple way. I hope that you get that clear explanation out of reading this book.

I wrote *CPA Exam For Dummies* so that each chapter can stand on its own. If you're like me, you may glance at the table of contents of a book to find a specific topic. This book allows you to find that topic, read about it, and come back to the book later.

This book is your tool to understand and successfully complete the CPA exam, so you'll see frequent references to "you" rather than "me." Also, keep in mind that companies sell both products and services. You'll see examples using both throughout the book. Some companies are manufacturers, and some are retailers. Instead of making a product, retailers typically buy inventory and sell it.

Also note that in accounting, you'll find situations in which two or more terms mean the same thing. Here are some of the synonymous terms that you find in this book:

- *Cost of sales* has the same meaning as *cost of goods sold*.
- *Sales* and *revenue* mean the same thing.
- *Indirect costs* has the same meaning as *overhead costs*.

✔ *Predetermined, budgeted,* and *planned* all mean the same thing.

✔ *Audit report* and *audit opinion* are used interchangeably.

✔ *Net income* is also *profit,* for the purposes of this book.

Foolish Assumptions

I had to make some assumptions about you, the reader. As I wrote the book, here's what I assumed:

✔ **You're able to follow basic arithmetic and algebra.** Some of the items you need to calculate appear in the form of equations. The CPA exam often provides numbers that you need to plug into a formula. One number in the formula isn't provided, so you use algebra to solve for the missing value.

✔ **You have a beginner's level knowledge of how a business works.** You understand that sales less expenses equals profit. You're aware that a business needs to have capital (cash, equipment, and so forth) to operate.

✔ **You're taking a serious look at studying for and taking the CPA exam.** This book is intended for the reader who has some interest in business or accounting and is considering adding to his or her skills by taking the CPA exam.

✔ **You may have taken some of the tests for the exam and not passed.** You may have several test-preparation books and resources already. You need a method to plan your study, and you need key exam concepts explained more clearly.

✔ **You're willing to read, pause, and assess what you've read.** Learning the concepts for the CPA exam takes some effort. It's not the sort of thing you can rush through. Although the text makes it easy to find information, understanding what you read takes some effort. Given the volume of information on the exam, you'll likely need to go over the concepts several times to commit them to memory.

Icons Used in This Book

To make this book easier to read and simpler to use, the book includes some icons that can help you find and fathom key ideas and information.

This icon appears whenever an idea or item can help reinforce your understanding of a concept. A Tip may make it easier to remember a topic.

Whenever you see this icon, you know the information that follows is so important that it's worth reading more than once.

Pay attention to the Warning icon to avoid pitfalls on the CPA exam.

Beyond the Book

Your purchase of this book includes one month of free access to CPAexcel. CPAexcel is a great online resource to study for the exam. The site includes questions and detailed answer explanations for hundreds of practice questions. After your free trial period, you can sign up to use CPAexcel at a discounted rate. For more info on what CPAexcel has to offer, how to access your free one-month subscription, and more, check out the Appendix.

This book also comes with some access-anywhere goodies on the web. Check out the free Cheat Sheet at www.dummies.com/cheatsheet/cpaexam for on-the-go access to the most helpful and important info about the exam. For some free articles and other tidbits, head to www.dummies.com/extras/cpaexam.

Where to Go from Here

This book is organized so that you can go wherever you want to find complete information. Need to know about the regulation test, for example? Head to Chapter 14. If you want to know about the prerequisites for taking the CPA exam, start at Chapter 3. You can use the table of contents to find broad categories of information or the index to look up more specific things.

If you're not sure where you want to go, you may want to start with Part I. It gives you all the basic info you need to understand the CPA exam and points to places where you can find more-detailed information.

Part I

Getting Started with the CPA Exam

getting started with
the exam

In this part . . .

- ✔ Find out what it takes to become a CPA — and why all the work is worth it.

- ✔ Become familiar with the structure of the exam and what types of skills it tests.

- ✔ Find out how to register for the exam and what to expect when you arrive on test day.

- ✔ Put together a study plan that works around your busy life to ensure that you're as successful as possible on the exam.

Chapter 1

So You Want to Become a CPA

In This Chapter

▶ Considering the benefits of a CPA designation

▶ Mulling over what a CPA does

▶ Weighing the CPA credential with other designations

A certified public accountant, or CPA, is a valuable credential in the world of accounting and finance. To gain the credential, a candidate must pass the CPA exam. Before you put in the work to prepare for the exam, though, make sure you understand the CPA designation.

In this chapter, you discover the added responsibilities that may come with a CPA designation. CPAs have a higher level of expertise and responsibility than non-CPA accounting professionals. As a result, many senior-level accounting positions require a CPA. Next, you go over the type of work that CPAs perform. The designation allows you to work in a variety of accounting positions. Finally, you look at a comparison of the CPA credential to other designations in the accounting profession.

Added Responsibilities with a CPA Designation

A CPA designation can allow you to advance your career beyond those people who simply earn an undergraduate degree. That's because the CPA exam tests you on a set of skills that are more specific than you find in an undergraduate business program. Also, the sheer amount of information tested makes passing the exam a real accomplishment. In this section, you see some of the additional responsibilities that come with a job that requires a CPA credential.

Many successful people in business, government, and the not-for-profit world started out as CPAs. That may be because CPAs understand how an entire entity works. An accountant has to understand each process within an organization, because he's responsible for posting the accounting transactions for those processes.

CPAs also generate the financial statements for the entity. To put together the statements, an accountant has to understand how the entire organization operates. It's the CPA who often must answer to stakeholders regarding the financial statements. Stakeholders include regulators, lenders, and investors, to name a few. Here are some typical issues that a stakeholder may bring up with a CPA:

> ✔ **Balance sheet and debt:** A potential lender to the company may want details on the amount of debt a business already owes to creditors. Some lenders compare the company's *total debt to total assets.* That ratio indicates the assets a company can sell to pay off debt, assuming that the company can't make payments of principal and interest.

You can compare this situation to using a car as collateral for a loan. If the car buyer can't make the payments, the lender can sell the car to recover some (or all) of the amount loaned.

✔ **Stockholders and earnings:** A common-stock owner may look into the amount of earnings an entity generates. One measurement of earnings is *earnings per share* (EPS). EPS is defined as the company earnings divided by average common stock shares outstanding. This ratio explains the dollar amount of earnings that a business generates for each common stock share. *Average common stock* is defined as follows:

$$\text{Average common stock} = \frac{\left(\begin{array}{l}\text{Beginning common stock balance for the period}\\ + \text{ Ending common stock balance for the period}\end{array}\right)}{2}$$

Many investors feel that EPS is an indication of a common stock's value.

✔ **Regulatory requirements:** Regulators require many financial institutions to maintain a certain amount of *equity,* which is defined as assets less liabilities. To a regulator, equity represents funds available for investors. If a financial institution violates a rule or regulation, the business can repay investors using its equity.

Considering What a CPA Does

A big advantage of the CPA credential is that it increases the variety of tasks an accountant can perform. Like many professionals, a CPA may specialize in a field or branch out into other areas of the profession.

This section explains what a CPA does and specific types of positions that are staffed by CPAs. Many of the jobs are useful in many industries. Retailers and manufacturers, for example, both need tax returns and financial statements prepared. Although specific industry knowledge is important, CPAs have a set of skills that are largely transferrable.

Many businesses will hire accountants without a CPA to operate in accounting positions with less responsibility. A staff accountant handling accounts receivable or accounts payable may not have a CPA designation. Other positions with more responsibility will require a CPA. The company controller and chief financial officer are typically CPAs.

Accounting work and controller positions

One big distinction between types of accounting work is accounting versus tax. Accounting is thought of as posting transactions and generating financial statements. Tax, on the other hand, refers to tax planning and filing tax returns. This section discusses accounting work.

A chief executive officer (CEO) is responsible for hiring senior management, and one of those positions is chief financial officer (CFO). The CFO has overall responsibility for all financial matters of an organization. Here are some specific tasks that a CFO must manage:

✔ **Controllership:** *Controllership* refers to maintaining control over the financial transactions of a company. The CFO needs to ensure that the accounting transactions are posted correctly. *Controllership* also refers to generating accurate and timely financial statements shortly after the end of each month and year.

✔ **Treasury:** *Treasury* refers to the cash needs of a company. Businesses use debt and equity in some combination to raise *capital,* which refers to the cash and other assets the company acquires. The decision on how much debt or equity to raise is in the hands of the CFO. The CFO plans for short-term cash needs to operate the company each month. The CFO also plans for long-term financing needs, such as planning for an expensive purchase (building, equipment, machinery, and the like).

✔ **Financial strategy:** The CFO has overall responsibility for financial strategy. This includes analyzing company profit by department or product line. A CFO is expected to recommend how each department can make changes to improve profit. Because nearly every company has a limited amount of capital, the CFO needs to analyze how that capital should be used to maximize earnings. That may mean buying a new piece of equipment for Department A and closing the operations of Department B. A CFO works closely with the company's operations managers to make processes more efficient.

The CFO is both an accountant and a manager. Here are some of the positions the CFO will hire and manage:

✔ **Controller and treasurer:** The CFO hires a controller to manage the accounting transactions and financial-statement process. He or she also hires a treasurer to manage the treasury activities.

✔ **Accounting manager:** A CFO, using input from the controller, may hire one or more accounting managers. These managers are responsible for certain areas of the controllership process. One manager, for example, may handle the company's accounts receivable process. That manager processes sales, receivables, and bad-debt transactions. The position also includes reporting financial results to the controller and CFO.

✔ **Staff accountant:** Accounting managers, in turn, hire staff accountants. This type of position is responsible for the day-to-day transactions of a company. If the staff accountant works with accounts receivable, he or she reviews incoming customer payments and reduces accounts receivable. That same person analyzes credit sales and posts accounts receivable. A staff accountant position may be the first position you work in as a CPA.

Not all companies have all the accounting positions I explain here. A small company may have a CFO, controller, and a few staff accountants; no accounting managers are needed to manage the company's accounting work.

Auditing, reviews, and compilations

CPAs fill the role of a third-party auditor. An *auditor* is a CPA who is independent of the company under audit. *Independence* means that the only relationship that the CPA has with the business is the fee paid for the audit. An *audit* occurs when an auditor performs procedures on the company's financial statements. The auditor uses the procedures to gather evidence about the financial statements. After completing an audit, the CPA provides a written opinion on whether the financial statements are free of material misstatement.

Reviewing jobs in the field

CPA firms perform audits. These organizations are typically partnerships formed by CPAs. Here are some of the positions you find in a CPA firm:

✔ **Partner:** A partner has an investment in the partnership. The partner is responsible for the management of a particular group of audit clients. Like a CFO, the partner selects an audit staff and manages the audit. Audits involve layers of review. The audit partner is responsible for the final review of the audit work.

- **Manager:** A manager works for the partner. Each manager may be responsible for several audits that are in process at the same time. The manager reviews the work of the audit staff below him or her. A manager is the client contact for most of the audit client's managers. When a question or concern needs to be discussed with the auditors, the company manager usually goes to the audit manager first.

- **Senior:** A senior has day-to-day responsibility for the audit work performed. This individual is present at the client's offices during the audit's fieldwork. *Fieldwork* refers to when the auditors gather evidence at the client's offices. The auditor and the client agree on when and how long fieldwork will take place.

- **Staff accountant:** Staff accountants perform the bulk of the audit procedures. This may include testing accounting transactions using company documents or interviewing the client's staff. If you join a CPA firm's audit department, you'll probably start as a staff auditor.

Going over the audit process

When planning an audit, the CPA firm creates an audit program. An *audit program* documents the procedures that will be performed for each area of the audit. An audit of cash, for example, will include a review of the client's bank account reconciliations. The auditor will use the bank statement and the client's cash activity to review the reconciliation of each bank account.

Everyone involved with the CPA firm's audit will follow the steps in the audit program. After the staff accountant or senior completes a step on the audit program, the manager and the audit partner will review the work. The senior reviews the work of each staff accountant. The multiple layers of review ensure that each step in the audit program is performed and that sufficient audit evidence has been gathered.

After the audit evidence is gathered during fieldwork, the senior and manager work on the audited financial statements. Each number in the financial statements is audited to some extent. The auditors compare their audit results with the company's financials. If differences exist, the auditor may propose an adjustment.

An *adjustment* is a proposed accounting entry to correct the financial statements. That correction may be to fix an error or to clarify an accounting issue. Adjustments are also posted based on judgments and estimates. A bank, for example, estimates the dollar amount of loans that won't be repaid. The bank then posts an entry to account for bad debt expense. An auditor may propose that the bad debt expense be increased or decreased.

The client can accept the adjustment and post the accounting entry. A client may also reject posting the adjustment. If the client rejects the proposed adjustment, that decision may impact the auditor's decision on the audit opinion. For example, an auditor may feel that the dollar amount of the adjustment requires disclosure to the financial-statement reader. The auditor may add language to the audit opinion about this area of concern.

CPA firms perform other projects that aren't considered audits, such as reviews and compilations. In these instances, the auditor isn't giving an opinion as to whether the financial statements are presented fairly. Instead, the CPA reviews the financials for proper formatting and reasonableness. If you work for a CPA firm, you'll probably work on several types of engagements.

Preparing tax returns

Besides auditing, the other large area of business for a CPA firm is tax preparation. You'll find that larger CPA firms provide both audit and tax services. Smaller firms may provide only tax services. Given the complexity of the tax code, many CPAs who specialize in tax issues work in the field year-round.

Depending on the size of the firm, you may see the same partner, manager, senior, and staff structure that I discuss in the earlier section "Reviewing jobs in the field." If you're interested in pursuing a CPA career by opening your own small business, preparing tax returns may be a way to start.

When you consider a career in either audit or tax, keep these thoughts in mind:

- **Seasonality of tax:** Working in tax requires a tremendous number of hours between January 1 and April 15. That's because corporate and other business tax returns as well as personal tax returns are due in the March and April timeframe. To succeed as a tax preparer, you need the ability to maintain a focus on detail while working long hours.

  Audit work includes heavy hours during the same timeframe. Most companies have a December 31 year-end, so the first quarter of the following year is a busy time. However, auditors can plan work and perform some procedures before December 31. In addition, some companies have fiscal year-ends that are at different points during the year. As a result, the work of an auditor can be more spread out during the year than tax work.

- **Less interaction:** Generally, tax preparers spend more time in the office working on technical issues. Audit, on the other hand, requires time at the client location. Fieldwork represents time at the client's offices performing work and talking to client personnel. If you're more outgoing and prefer more human interaction, audit may be a better choice than a career in tax.

- **Travel:** Auditors need to travel to client locations. Sometimes that travel may be difficult to plan and predict. If fieldwork takes longer than expected, an auditor may need to stay out of town longer. Generally, auditors try to work heavy hours while out of town. This approach allows them to finish the fieldwork as soon as possible. Tax accountants, on the other hand, generally travel much less.

Both audit and tax work require you to spend time on continuing education. As you see later in this chapter, some continuing education is required by the CPA industry. You'll need to spend even more time learning about your field. If you're an auditor, you'll learn about the industries of the clients you audit. Tax specialists need to stay on top of changes in the tax code.

Larger CPA firms have auditors specialize in particular industries. They might, for example, develop an expertise in financial service audits. Most of the audits you work on will be in that area. As you learn more, you'll be able to complete audit procedures more quickly. You'll also be better prepared to ask the client intelligent questions.

Audit clients want the CPA firm to staff the audit with accountants who know their industry. That knowledge means that the auditor can minimize the time that they need with client personnel. The audit process goes faster, and the CPA firm can spend less time on fieldwork.

Branching out into other careers

CPAs often become successful leaders in a variety of fields. One reason is that accountants work with a company's entire operation. CPAs see how each department operates and how it contributes to company profit. It naturally follows that a CPA can move into company management, because he or she knows how everything works.

Given this concept, many people obtain their CPA credential with the intention of moving into a non-accounting career. Here are just a few examples of careers that are staffed by CPAs:

- **Company management:** Broad knowledge of a company's business allows a CPA to move into management positions. The controller of the furniture manufacturing division, for example, may be a candidate for the vice president of operations. The controller must understand operations to handle the division's accounting properly.

- **Financial analyst:** Financial analysts perform work for company senior management. Analysts also work for investment companies that recommend stocks and bonds of other businesses as investments for their clients. Many of the skills you learn and use as a CPA are transferrable to this career.

- **Bankers and other lenders:** Bankers and other lenders make decisions about a company's ability to generate sufficient earnings to make loan payments. Lenders analyze the balance sheet to determine whether a business has sufficient assets to serve as collateral for a loan. This work requires many of the skills used by CPAs.

Comparing a CPA to Other Credentials

Two credentials are similar to the CPA designation: chartered financial analyst (CFA) and certified valuation analyst (CVA). As you move forward in your career, you may consider getting one of these other credentials, along with your CPA designation. Many people who work in these two fields have experience as CPAs.

Checking out the chartered financial analyst (CFA) credential

A *chartered financial analyst* (CFA) uses several skill sets to perform analysis on both companies and investment opportunities. You can find out details about the designation at www.cfainstitute.org. To obtain this credential, an individual must pass three exams, which are referred to as levels 1, 2, and 3. Here are some of the topics tested on the CFA exams:

- **Quantitative methods:** Many of these concepts are taught in statistics classes, which you've likely taken if you've completed an undergraduate business or accounting degree. Quantitative methods include time value of money, probability, and other types of analysis.

- **Economics:** This area includes the study of supply and demand, business cycles, inflation, and foreign currency exchange rates.

- **Corporate finance:** Corporate finance goes over the decision-making process of raising capital and investing capital in a business.

> ✔ **Portfolio management:** This area covers the concept of portfolio management and wealth planning. These areas refer to decisions about the types of investments a money manager selects. CFA exams cover many types of investments, including derivatives.

If you're more interested in analysis than generating financial statements, you may prefer working as a CFA.

Mulling over the certified valuation analyst (CVA) credential

A *valuation* places a dollar value on assets that may be difficult to value. A good example is an intangible asset, such as a patent, customer list, or trademark. A CVA takes a set of financial statements and performs additional work to compute company valuations.

A business may need to obtain a valuation in several circumstances. When a buyer and seller are negotiating the sale of a company, the parties may hire a CVA to compute the company's value. The price paid for the business may be very different from the *book value* of the assets, which is defined as assets less liabilities.

Most industries have valuation benchmarks that drive the price paid for companies in that industry. Say, for example, that clothing manufacturers typically have a sale price based on three times the annual sales in dollars. In that case, the buyer and seller will compute three times sales and include that amount in their negotiation of a price for the company. CVAs explain and provide this type of analysis.

CVAs may also be involved when the value of a company must be determined in a legal matter. If two partners are in a legal dispute over their share of the company's value, a CVA may be retained to determine the value of the partnership.

You can find out more on the CVA designation at www.nacva.com.

Understanding the CPA Licensing Requirements

The Uniform CPA Examination is developed and graded by the American Institute of CPAs, or AICPA, which is the world's largest member association for the accounting profession. The AICPA exists to set accounting standards and to support and expand the accounting profession. You can find lots of great information at their website (www.aicpa.org).

The purpose of the CPA exam is to fulfill one of several requirements for a license to practice public accounting. Passing the exam qualifies you to be certified by a state. Although the exam is the same in every state, you obtain a license to practice from a State Board of Accountancy.

Knowing what you need for a license to practice public accounting

A *certified public accountant* is someone who has earned a license in his or her state. Check out www.thiswaytocpa.com to find out the requirements for your state. Each state has requirements that address three specific areas: education, experience, and ethics.

Going over education requirements

Most states require a bachelor's degree to meet the education requirement. However, a growing number of states require 150 semester hours of college credit.

Many states are adding to the education requirement because they feel that a bachelor's degree doesn't cover all the skills sets needed for the CPA profession. The accounting industry adds rules and regulations each year. These added requirements mean that the CPA candidate needs a larger body of knowledge. As technology becomes more complex, the CPA must learn more to use technology effectively.

Meeting the experience requirement

Most states require at least two years of experience in the accounting profession. The type of experience required also varies by state. In some cases, the work must be with a public accounting firm. Many firms will hire accountants who are not yet CPAs. These accountants work lower level accounting positions until they pass the CPA exam. At that point, they may be promoted into positions with more responsibility.

Some companies will help an employee pay for the CPA exam and a review course. Ask potential employers whether they offer this type of benefit.

Addressing ethics

State Boards view ethics as very important because CPAs have a great deal of responsibility. CPAs fill most of the senior accounting positions at companies. One primary responsibility is to generate financial statements. If an unethical CPA produces financial statements that are intentionally incorrect, the impact can be enormous.

Because the CPA's potential impact on stakeholders is so great, nearly all State Boards of Accountancy require an ethics exam, known as Rules of Professional Conduct. Many also require continuing education for CPAs in the field of ethics.

Walking through CPA exam topics

To pass the CPA exam, you must pass each of these four exams:

- ✔ **Auditing and attestation (AUD):** This test covers the process of planning and implementing an audit. The test requires you to know a great deal of the language that's used to write audit opinions. Reviews, compilations, and other engagements are on the AUD test.

- ✔ **Financial accounting and reporting (FAR):** The FAR test covers the nuts and bolts of working as an accountant. You need to know how to account for a variety of accounting transactions, including accrual entries. This test also covers financial-statement presentation.

- ✔ **Business environment and concepts (BEC):** This test addresses subjects that are closer to those covered in a broad business school curriculum. The BEC test covers many decision-making tools. BEC also covers some economic topics.

- ✔ **Regulation (REG):** REG covers many issues you may see in a business law class, including agency and sales law concepts. A large portion of the REG test addresses taxation of businesses, trusts, and estates as well as individual taxation.

Chapter 2

Getting Acquainted with the CPA Exam

In This Chapter

▶ Understanding what the CPA exam tests

▶ Going over how the exam is administered

▶ Walking through the specific skills outline

▶ Looking at scoring

After you decide to get the CPA credential, you need to become familiar with the CPA exam. In this chapter, you do just that. You find out about the four tests that make up the exam. From there, you move on to understanding the exam format. The format section goes over the different ways the exam tests your knowledge and skills. Some questions require problem-solving skills, and others focus on written communication. Finally, you gain an understanding of how the exam is graded.

Knowing What's on the Exam

The CPA exam consists of four separate tests, which mirror the types of tasks a CPA may have to perform. For example, some accountants perform audits and other third-party reviews of financial statements, and those tasks are tested in the auditing and attestation (AUD) test. The following sections provide an overview of each of the four tests.

The AICPA's document "Content and Skill Specifications for the Uniform CPA Examination" explains the tests in detail, listing the percentage of test questions for each particular topic. For example, the document explains that "engagement acceptance and understanding the assignment" questions make up 12 to 16 percent of the AUD test. Knowing which areas have the most questions can help you study effectively. You can schedule each test individually, and you can take the tests in any order. To search for and download the document, visit the AICPA website, www.aicpa.org.

You register for each test individually, and you can decide the order in which to take the tests. Each test takes 3 or 4 hours, so you don't take all four tests in the same day.

Financial accounting and reporting

One test covers financial accounting and reporting (FAR). Accountants have guidelines on how to record accounting transactions and present financial statements. The process of creating financial statements is called *financial reporting*. For example, suppose you have a bank loan. The loan requires you to repay a part of the $10,000 of the principal amount (the original amount borrowed) each year. Financial reporting requires you to separate the amount due within a year (a current liability) from the remaining loan balance (a long-term liability). Now the financial-statement reader can make a more informed decision about the company's debt position. If a large amount of the principal is due within a year, that might put a strain on the company's available cash.

The FAR part of the exam frequently tests your ability to

- ✔ Prepare and review source documents and post activity in the accounting records (*source documents* are the original records that support an accounting transaction, such as an invoice from a client or a shipping document)
- ✔ Identify which financial accounting and reporting methods are appropriate for a given situation
- ✔ Perform financial analysis, including variance and trend analysis
- ✔ Produce financial reports to meet regulatory requirements

Auditing and attestation

The auditing and attestation (AUD) test involves concepts that are related to auditing financial statements and other engagements. An *engagement* is the work that a client hires an accountant to perform. An *audit* takes place when a CPA firm performs procedures on a company's financial statements. Based on those procedures, the auditing firm provides an audit opinion.

Here are some of the frequently tested areas in the AUD part of the exam:

- ✔ Accepting the audit or attestation engagement
- ✔ Understanding the entity and the entity's controls over accounting procedures
- ✔ Performing audit procedures and assessing audit evidence
- ✔ Evaluating audit findings and writing the audit report

Regulation

The regulation (REG) test covers the ethics and professional responsibilities of a CPA. It also addresses business law and federal taxation.

Here, the exam describes business situations and asks whether the accountant's behavior is ethical, based on professional standards. For example, suppose a CPA who is performing an audit of Acme Company also owns a business that sells raw materials to Acme. Professional standards require that a CPA performing an audit be independent of the client. *Independence* means that the CPA's only business relationship with the company is the audit work being performed. Because the CPA has an additional business relationship with Acme Company, the CPA is not independent. The accountant should resign from the audit.

The REG test also addresses the behavior of clients. Say that Timberrr Lumber has a policy that sales revenue is posted to the accounting records when goods are shipped to a customer. Timberrr is having a poor sales month and wants to post as many sales in the last few days of the month as possible. On the 29th day of the month, the lumber company receives a $5,000 order from a customer and posts that amount as sales revenue. Because that transaction isn't consistent with Timberrr's revenue recognition policy (the $5,000 order hasn't been shipped yet), a CPA performing an audit on Timberrr should insist that the $5,000 sales revenue be removed from the accounting records.

Financial statements are the responsibility of company management. A company accountant or outside CPA firm can recommend changes to the accounting records. However, management is ultimately responsible for generating financial statements that fairly present the company's financial position.

Completing the tax portion of the REG test is similar to the process of preparing tax returns. The candidate needs to know many of the rules for both individual and corporate taxation. The exam provides details about a tax client, and you have to calculate the tax impact of those details.

Finally, the REG test covers your basic knowledge of business law. It includes topics such as contracts, the relationship between agents and principals, and the Uniform Commercial Code (UCC).

Business environment and concepts

The business environment and concepts (BEC) test focuses on general topics that a college business major learns in undergraduate coursework. This section is less about specific accounting and more about the skills needed to manage a business.

One area tested is corporate governance, which deals with the duties and responsibilities of company executives. This includes corporate officers, such as the chief financial officer, as well as company employees (those workers who are not in management). Corporate governance also covers the responsibilities of the board of directors. For example, a majority of the firm's board of directors should be independent. In this case, *independence* means that the board member's only relationship with the company is the fee he or she receives as a board member. The individual isn't a company employee or supplier.

The BEC test also tests economic concepts and analysis. You may see questions on the impact of globalization, including the risk of converting from one type of currency to another. You're also tested on the concept of business cycles as well as interest risk.

Another area of emphasis is financial decision-making. For example, companies often have to consider whether to lease a piece of machinery or buy it. To make an intelligent decision, potential purchasers consider the cash required to buy the machine — and they consider the source of that cash.

If the firm borrows funds for the purchase, the borrowers need to consider the interest expense on the loan. When a company issues stock, they need to consider how much ownership is being sold to outside investors. Those investors will now have a say in major company decisions. To succeed on this part of the exam, you need to understand the financial tools needed to make business decisions.

Understanding the Exam Format

Many people have more success on an exam if they can visualize what will happen after they walk into the room to take the test. In this section, you find out about the technology aspects of the CPA exam and the types of questions you encounter.

Navigating the online tests

You take the CPA exam by computer. Here are some important features of the exam software:

- ✔ **Toolbar:** The toolbar displays the test and the testlet you're currently taking. A *testlet* is a section of a test; the regulation test, for example, contains three testlets of multiple-choice questions.

  The toolbar also displays the amount of time remaining to complete the exam and provides a calculator and exit button. For more-complex portions of the exam, the toolbar gives you access to a spreadsheet tool. The spreadsheet allows you to perform some simple calculations (add, multiply, and so on), just like an Excel document. For more-complex formulas, you'll need to use your calculator. Because the CPA exam requires you to know many formulas, you won't find those formulas in the spreadsheet tool.

- ✔ **Tabs:** Some exam questions, called *simulations,* provide extra information that you use to solve the question. You can access this info using tabs at the top left portion of the screen.

- ✔ **Navigation between questions:** The question numbers for your current testlet are listed at the bottom of the screen, and the question you're currently working on is inside a red box. At a glance, you can see which question you're on and how many questions remain in the testlet. The computer presents the questions in numbered order. You have the ability to skip a question as well as the ability to go back to any question to review or change an answer.

- ✔ **Testlet directions:** Each of the four tests (FAR, BEC, and so on) is divided into testlets. When you begin each testlet, you see directions for completing questions in that section of the test. The directions are displayed at the far left at the bottom of the screen, to the left of the numbered questions.

- ✔ **Multiple-choice questions:** To answer a multiple-choice question, click on the radio button next to the single best answer. If you want to change your answer, click on the radio button for your new answer choice.

- ✔ **Task-based simulation questions:** Task-based simulations provide extra resources to complete a question. After working on the question, you input your answer on the computer screen. In some cases, you choose an answer from a drop-down menu. For a journal entry, you may type in the accounts and dollar amounts to post the entry. Finally, you may be asked to type in paragraphs of text to answer in an essay format. The test provides spellcheck and some other features you may use with other word processing programs, such as Microsoft Word.

For more help, you can watch a great tutorial on the AICPA website (www.aicpa.org).

Encountering different types of questions

You can divide the CPA exam questions into three broad categories:

- ✔ **Knowledge and understanding:** The exam uses multiple-choice questions to test your knowledge and understanding of facts and figures. This is the you-know-it-or-you-don't part of the exam.

- ✔ **Application of a body of knowledge:** Task-based simulations test your ability to apply knowledge to an accounting situation. The exam provides you with resources, such as a page of authoritative literature or a spreadsheet, and you have to figure out what to do with them.

Creating the tests

All the questions you see on the exam have been reviewed extensively to ensure that they're technically correct and to verify that there's one best (or correct) answer for each question. The AICPA refers to this process as *subject matter review*. If a question involves judgment, it needs to have one answer choice that's better than the others listed. A question testing a calculation or a fact needs one correct answer.

The CPA exam includes pretest questions so that the test-makers can see whether the questions are suitable for a future CPA exam. Part of that evaluation is how well (or poorly) students answer a pretest question on an actual exam.

The subject matter review also ensures that each exam question tests the content in the AICPA's document "Content and Skills Specifications for the Uniform CPA Examination."

✔ **Written communication:** Like many other professionals, CPAs often use written communication (memos, instructions, and so on), so the exam requires candidates to write.

The later section "Going Over the Skills You Need to Succeed on the Exam" outlines the skills you need to pass the CPA exam and relates those skills to each type of test question.

Looking at the structure of the tests

Table 2-1 shows the number and kinds of questions you find on each test. All four tests on the CPA exam include multiple-choice questions. Three tests also use task-based *simulations,* which are case studies; the other test includes written communication exercises instead.

Each test contains both operational and pretest questions. *Operational* questions are scored and included in your grade. Pretest questions aren't graded (see the nearby sidebar "Creating the tests" for details).

Table 2-1	Test Formats and Time Limits on the CPA Exam		
Test Name	**Multiple-Choice Questions**	**Simulations or Writing Exercises**	**Total Time Limit**
Financial accounting and reporting	90 multiple-choice questions (including 15 pretest items)	7 simulations (including 1 pretest item)	4 hours
Auditing and attestation	90 multiple-choice questions (including 15 pretest items)	7 simulations (including 1 pretest item)	4 hours
Regulation	72 multiple-choice questions (including 12 pretest questions)	6 simulations (including 1 pretest item)	4 hours
Business environment and concepts (BEC)	72 multiple-choice questions (including 12 pretest items)	3 written communication questions (including 1 pretest item)	3 hours

The multiple-choice questions within each test are divided into three groups called *testlets*. Each exam question is assigned a medium or difficult rating, which is taken into account when your exam is scored (see the later section "How Did You Do? Knowing How the Exam Is Graded").

Most exam candidates take only one test on a single day. As you see in Chapter 3, you should plan your study over a period of months. It isn't necessary to take more than one test on one day.

Going Over the Skills You Need to Succeed on the Exam

One challenge for you as a CPA exam candidate is that you must switch gears as you move through the tests. With multiple-choice questions, you need to have a plan to eliminate incorrect answer choices. Writing a memo or a set of directions, on the other hand, requires you to put your thoughts in a logical order.

You may shift gears more smoothly if you know the skills you need to succeed on the exam. In the following sections, you take a look at two question types — simulations and written communication — in detail; then you assess the skills needed to answer each type of question. For a strategy for answering multiple-choice questions, see Chapter 4.

Applying a body of knowledge

Some questions move beyond asking you to define a concept. *Simulations* require you to apply a body of knowledge to an accounting issue. You're given a variety of tools, which may include a calculator, a spreadsheet, or some authoritative literature, and you have to figure out how to use those resources to complete a task.

Every CPA must apply knowledge to a particular type of business or industry. This skill is used by a CPA firm auditing a client and by the CPA who works for a particular corporation. The exam tests your ability to assess a company's business environment. That assessment may include the following skills:

- ✔ **Evaluation of a business process:** In this case, *evaluation* means the ability to use information to understand a business process. For example, a CPA working in a manufacturing firm needs to understand the flow of manufacturing costs as a product moves through production. This skill also includes the ability to identify and suggest changes to improve a particular process. The evaluation process may require you to review and understand a company's strategic objectives. That may include understanding a firm's products and services as well as competitive factors in the business.

- ✔ **Research:** All CPAs must perform research from time to time. You may be asked to identify an appropriate research question to address an accounting topic. The exam may also ask you to select a key search term to pull important information from a database.

  This skill requires you to assess information from several different sources and reach a conclusion on an accounting issue as well as identify the correct authoritative literature to address a topic. If you're researching an appropriate depreciation expense method for equipment, for example, you need to search the firm's database for the current depreciation method — and you need to locate the correct literature to decide on the right method.

✔ **Application of technology:** Today's CPAs work with a great deal of technology. The exam requires you to perform calculations and analysis using electronic spreadsheets like Microsoft Excel. You need to apply technology to your accounting process. In addition, you're asked how to use hardware and software to manage data. For example, the exam may ask how to integrate the company's inventory software into your inventory audit process if you need to perform an inventory count.

✔ **Analysis:** Accountants must be able to both create financial statements and analyze them. The exam may ask you to identify trends and patterns. You may also be asked to point out a variance. In accounting, a *variance* is a difference between budgeted and actual amounts.

Analysis also requires you to forecast financial results based on historical financial data. An accountant may analyze why a 10 percent increase in sales is generating a 30 percent increase in accounts receivable. In that case, the CPA may find that new customers are paying for sales at a slower rate than existing customers. Maybe the company has eased credit standards, which allows customers who don't pay as quickly to buy products.

✔ **Complex problem-solving and judgment:** This question type first requires some generic problem-solving skills. You're asked to identify a problem and then gather information to determine the best course of action. Accounting, however, requires you to apply *professional skepticism,* which means critically assessing any information gathered. In other words, you take a hard look at the data and then come up with a solution.

You'll assess a variety of solutions based on their relative strengths and weaknesses. The solution you select must fit within the regulatory and ethical framework required of a CPA. All banks, for example, are required to set aside funds to pay for potential losses from loans that default. Funding this "reserve account" requires judgment and critical analysis.

✔ **Decision-making:** This skill relates to problem-solving, but it includes some different factors. For example, you must consider the company's goals as well as constraints that limit the firm's choices, such as financial constraints or regulatory limitations. You consider alternatives and risks, and then you select the best course of action.

Say a company is considering a new supplier for a raw material. The goal is to reduce raw material costs. To make an informed decision, you'd consider whether a potential supplier could meet your demand for product, the product's price, and the quality of the material supplied.

✔ **Organization, efficiency, and effectiveness:** This is the skill of performing a task well, without wasting time or using too much of your available resources. The term *organization* refers to storing information so that data can be easily located. The faster you can locate information, the more efficient you become.

You need to organize tasks, deciding on an order for performing tasks and assigning each task to a particular person. You also need to prioritize tasks based on their relative importance. Any company that operates efficiently probably has an *operations manual.* This document, which explains how all work is performed, is a how-to manual — and it's something that a CPA needs to create and maintain for his or her business.

Written communication

CPAs, like other business professionals, must be effective in written communication. The exam assesses your writing skills by having you write. The communication questions evaluate basic skills, such as grammar and punctuation, that are required of any effective writer. You also need to be able to organize your thoughts, so consider whether the reader can follow your argument as he or she moves through your work.

Before you start writing, jot down an outline. Consider the points you want to make and put them in a logical order. Your outline will ensure that your essay has a logical flow.

Business writing also requires some additional skills:

- **Providing context for your audience:** You may need to explain accounting terminology to readers who aren't accountants. On the other hand, you may need to explain jargon used by coworkers in other fields, like engineering or human resources. Your goal is to write a document that anyone within the organization can understand.

- **Describing data and processes:** You may need to explain documents, reports, and charts. Or you may need to explain work performed by other professionals, such as outside auditors.

- **Recommending solutions:** Accountants often write memos to explain an issue, present alternatives, and recommend a course of action. In this role, the CPA must be able to persuade the reader that the recommended solution is the best one.

Understanding How the Tests Are Weighted

In the section "Going Over Skills Needed to Succeed on the Exam," you're introduced to three broad skills that are assessed on the CPA exam. Each skill is assigned a percentage range. This range represents the percentage of questions that test a particular skill category. In other words, each skill is weighted within the exam.

Three of the four tests within the exam have the same percentage ranges. The financial accounting and reporting, regulation, and auditing and attestation tests each have the same skill percentages (with the actual percentages adding to 100 percent):

- Knowledge and understanding 50% to 60%
- Application of a body of knowledge 40% to 50%

Business environment and concepts, on the other hand, has a unique weighting of skill questions, with the total actual percentage equal to 100 percent:

- Knowledge and understanding 80% to 90%
- Written communication 10% to 20%

How Did You Do? Knowing How The Exam Is Graded

To pass the CPA exam, you need a *reported score* of 75 or higher on each of the four tests that make up the exam. Your reported score isn't simply a percentage of answers that are correct; 60 out of 75 questions, for example, doesn't give you a score of 80 (percent). Instead, the reported score takes into account the difficulty of the questions. If a testlet contains many questions that are rated as difficult, for example, your test score will be adjusted based on the difficulty level of that testlet. A testlet with more questions judged as difficult will provide an bigger adjustment (add more points) to your score than a testlet with fewer difficult questions.

Your test score is also weighted based on the types of questions on each test:

- ✔ **Financial accounting and reporting (FAR), auditing and attestation (AUD), and regulation (REG) tests:** These tests have the same weightings: 60 percent of your score comes from the multiple-choice questions, and 40 percent comes from task-based simulations.

- ✔ **Business environment and concepts (BEC) test:** For the BEC, 85 percent of your score comes from the multiple-choice questions, and 15 percent comes from written communications questions.

For each test, consider the types of questions and the skills tested. Say, for example, that you've just taken the AUD test and you're starting to prepare for BEC. BEC is the only test that includes written communication questions, so when you start BEC, work on those writing skills.

For more information on scoring, look for the document "How Is the CPA Exam Scored?" on the AICPA website (www.aicpa.org).

Chapter 3

Preparing to Take the Exam

In This Chapter
▶ Meeting the requirements to take your test
▶ Scheduling your test date, time, and location
▶ Sitting at the test center and taking your test

CPA exam candidates must meet certain education and experience requirements. This chapter goes over the prerequisites you need in order to take the CPA exam. From there, you find out how to apply for the exam and how to select your exam date and location.

The chapter wraps up with an overview of your exam day. You find out ways to prepare and discover an effective test-taking strategy.

Making Sure You've Met the Prerequisites

The Uniform CPA Examination is developed and graded by the American Institute of CPAs, or AICPA (www.aicpa.org). The purpose of the CPA exam is to fulfill one of several requirements for a license to practice public accounting — to become a *certified public accountant*. Passing the exam helps qualify you to obtain a license to practice from your State Board of Accountancy. Check out www.thiswaytocpa.com to find out the requirements for your state.

This section explains the prerequisites you need in order to take the CPA exam.

Considering your amount of education

Most states require a bachelor's degree to meet the education requirement. However, many states require 150 hours of college credit, which amounts to a bachelor's degree requiring 120 to 130 hours plus additional hours toward a master's degree. States have additional requirements for the number and type of accounting courses that must be completed.

To meet this state requirement, most universities now offer a combination bachelor's and master's degree. Although the bachelor's degree may be in another area of business, such as finance, the master's degree is specifically in some area of accounting.

Keep in mind that you may be required to take an ethics exam as well as ongoing continuing education courses on ethics.

Adding in your experience

Most states require at least two years of experience in the accounting profession. The type of experience required also varies by state. In some cases, the work must be with a public accounting firm. Generally, a public accounting firm is staffed with CPAs who provide accounting, tax, and audit services for clients. Other states define experience as working as an accountant for any type of company.

Reviewing the licensing requirements

After you pass the CPA exam, you must meet the requirements of your State Board. The National Association of State Boards of Accountancy, or NASBA, helps CPA candidates with licensing requirements. NASBA (http://nasba.org) helps both U.S. citizens and international students obtain certification.

Each State Board lists its requirements on the www.thiswaytocpa.com website. Note that most states don't have a residency requirement for exam candidates who are U.S. citizens.

There's a growing demand from foreign nationals who want to obtain U.S. CPA licensure. To meet the demand, the NASBA created the International CPA Examination program. A foreign national can establish his or her eligibility through a participating State Board. You can find the details at http://nasba.org/international/international-exam.

Here's how a foreign national can apply to take the exam:

- ✔ Use the website to locate a State Board that accepts candidates from your county.
- ✔ Request application materials from the State Board. Complete and return the application along with any required fees.
- ✔ After your application is accepted, you'll receive a Notice to Schedule. Check out the section "Scheduling the Exam" later in this chapter for details on scheduling.

Foreign nationals should note that the exam is offered only in English, in the same computerized format that U.S. candidates take. You may be able to take the exam at a test center overseas, without having to travel to the U.S. Check with a State Board for more information.

Applying to Take the Exam

The CPA exam consists of four individual tests. Whenever you apply to take a test, you must submit an application to your State Board. The application may include supporting documents and may require you to pay fees. Remember that each State Board has different requirements.

Generally, exam candidates pay two types of fees. You pay an application fee when you apply and an examination fee for each test that you take. Chapter 2 explains the four tests that make up the exam.

After your State Board accepts your application and receives your fees, it notifies NASBA. The State Board verifies which tests you can take, and NASBA sends you a Notice to Schedule (NTS).

When you receive a Notice to Schedule, the next step is to schedule your test. A helpful resource for this process is the CPA Candidate Bulletin, which you can search for at www.aicpa.org.

The name listed on your NTS must match the name on the picture ID you'll bring to the test center. Your middle initial can be substituted for your middle name. If your NTS lists "T" as your middle initial and your picture identification displays your middle name as "Thomas," that's okay. Before your exam date, check both documents to make sure they match.

Applying for special accommodations

Candidates with specific needs can apply for testing accommodations. An accommodation may mean extended testing time or assistance due to a disability. Candidates who may require an accommodation should keep these points in mind:

- ✔ Candidates should apply for testing accommodations through their State Board.

- ✔ After the accommodation is approved, an explanation will be added to the Notice to Schedule (NTS) that the candidate receives.

- ✔ To schedule a test with an accommodation, call Prometric to register by phone. Candidates needing accommodations should call at least 10 days before the desired test date. Not all test locations can meet the accommodations. During the registration phone call, Prometric will check whether a location can meet the test accommodation.

Scheduling the Exam

Your Notice to Schedule (NTS) allows you to choose when and where you'll take your test. You use your NTS to contact Prometric, a firm that runs computer-based testing centers for many professional exams, including the CPA exam.

You can call the firm's Candidate Services Call Center at 800-580-9648 to schedule an appointment. The AICPA suggests, however, that scheduling your exam online (www.prometric.com) may be more efficient. When you sign up online, you see a Program Identifier Screen. Enter your examination section identification number from your NTS. That number is the also the launch code (password) you'll use to log in to your computer at the test center.

After you finish setting up your test, Prometric will provide a confirmation number by e-mail. If you call Prometric to schedule a test, the firm will still e-mail the confirmation number so you have it in writing. Keep that number for your reference and bring it to the test center.

Where to take the test

Candidates can take the tests at any Prometric facility that administers the CPA exam. Foreign nationals may be able to take the exam overseas at a Prometric location.

To find a location, head to www.prometric.com. When you go online to make an appointment, keep these factors in mind:

✔ Prometric will ask you to indicate your first, second, and third choices for a given test. Your choice includes your desired test time, date, and location. For example, your first choice may be 9 a.m. EST, February 20 in Indianapolis, Indiana.

✔ The test centers don't allow walk-ins. Everyone must schedule an exam in advance.

✔ You must set up your test at least five days prior to the desired test date. If you need special accommodations (for physical or other reasons), you must set up your test at least ten days prior to your desired test date. See the earlier section "Applying for special accommodations" for details.

When to take it

The CPA exam offers *testing windows* — time periods during a calendar year when the exam is offered to candidates. You can take the exam during the first two months of each calendar quarter:

✔ January 1 to February 28 (or 29, in a leap year)

✔ April 1 to May 31

✔ July 1 to August 31

✔ October 1 to November 30

You can take any or all four tests during the same two-month period. However, exam candidates can't take the same test more than once during the same two-month period. Chapter 4 addresses retaking a test.

To have the best chance of getting the date, time, and location you want for your test, schedule at least 45 days prior to your desired test date.

Your State Board sets a time limit for each Notice to Schedule (NTS). Your NTS allows you to take the approved test before the deadline stated on the form. If you don't, you must reapply and pay additional fees. You'll lose the fees you paid for the test that expired. Check the deadline on each NTS you receive from your State Board. You must take the test and receive a score — or let the NTS expire — before applying to take the same test again.

Canceling and rescheduling your test date

If you need to cancel and reschedule your test, you can do it by using the Prometric website (www.prometric.com) or calling the Candidate Services Call Center at 800-580-9648. Candidates needing testing accommodations need to reschedule by phone. If you choose to cancel a test — or cancel and reschedule — keep these points in mind:

✔ You may not be able to recover the fees that you paid for the original test date. In addition, you'll have to pay a fee to schedule the new test date.

✔ If you don't cancel and simply don't show up at the test site, the National Association of State Boards of Accountancy (NASBA) considers it no-show attendance. The NASBA needs three to five business days to process the no-show and allow you to reschedule your test.

> ✔ A no-show attendance may mean that you can't reschedule your exam in the same test window. You may have to wait a month or longer to reschedule your test, which will obviously affect your plan of study. Carefully consider the potential impact of a no-show attendance. To avoid this issue, contact Prometric and reschedule. No cancellations are allowed less than 24 hours from your appointment time. If less than 24 hours remain before your appointment, you are treated in the same way as a no-show.

Considerations before the Exam

The sheer amount of information on the four tests can be overwhelming. It's important to have a plan that allows you to enter each test with confidence. This section goes over how to set up a study plan that is right for you. You'll consider the amount of time needed to study for each test as well as different types of study tools. This section also explains why you should have confidence that you'll pass your tests if you've studied sufficiently.

Before each test, you're asked to attest to the fact that you've reviewed the tutorials and sample tests on the AICPA website (www.aicpa.org). A CPA candidate must also attest to having reviewed the Candidate Bulletin. Make sure you review these items in addition to your other exam preparation.

Having a study plan

Knowing how you study can help you enter the exam with confidence. For starters, consider whether you're a disciplined self-starter or you need a more structured study environment. A self-starter can set a schedule and study on his or her own. A structured review program requires you to attend study sessions, either live or online.

After you decide on the structure of your study plan, think about the tools you can use to study. Chapter 4 covers the nuts and bolts of exam study. Since everyone's study habits are different, these study tools are listed in no particular order in terms of effectiveness. Sally may prefer to read a textbook, for example, while Kathy gets more use out of reviewing flashcards. For now, consider this list of study tools:

✔ Video lectures, either live lectures or prerecorded

✔ Textbooks

✔ Study planners, either in hard copy or online

✔ Flashcards

✔ Interaction with an instructor or tutor via e-mail

Next, plan for the total amount of study time you need to pass a particular test. Test-preparation companies generally recommend a total of 400-plus hours to study for the entire CPA exam. That breaks down to about 100 hours for each of the four tests. (Head over to Chapter 2 for details on each test.) According to most test-prep companies, the financial accounting and reporting (FAR) test requires the most study time, and business environment and concepts (BEC) requires the least.

Psyching yourself up

If you've put in the time to study for the exam, you know more than you think you do. When students put in the study time, they accumulate a lot of information that may not be "top of mind." Quite a bit of information is rolling around in your head, but it's in your subconscious. You may be frustrated that you can't immediately access it, but it's there.

You may have had the experience of information coming to mind just when you need it. Students who have studied for the exam may have that same experience. That idea should give you confidence going into the exam.

Arriving at the Test Center

Here are some details about arriving at the test center. I've taken them from a sample Notice to Schedule, which you can find in the CPA Candidate Bulletin at www.aicpa.org. Review these details before you get to the testing center:

- ✔ Arrive at the test site at least 30 minutes early to ensure that you'll be allowed to take your test at the time you scheduled. Candidates who are late run the risk of losing their fees and not being able to take the test.

- ✔ You'll have to put any personal belongings in a storage locker (you'll receive a key to the locker). The test center lockers are small, so bring as few items as possible. You can't have paper, books, food, drink, purses, or personal electronic devices available during your exam. The CPA Candidate Bulletin has a complete list of prohibited items. Also, don't use any of the prohibited items during any breaks.

- ✔ Candidates receive a *Confirmation of Attendance* form at the test site. As the name implies, this form verifies that you've attended the exam. Keep this form after the exam. The document has important contact information, such as the test site phone number. You may need the contact information after the exam.

- ✔ Your photo will be taken when you arrive, and your photo identification will be scanned. You need two forms of ID. Your primary identification must include your picture. This document may be your driver's license or a passport. A secondary ID doesn't require a picture. To meet this requirement, you can bring a credit or debit card. The secondary ID must include your signature.

- ✔ The test center will use biometrics (a computer application) to capture a fingerprint.

If you've put in the hours of study, enter your test center with confidence!

Sitting at the Exam

Prometric e-mails you an appointment confirmation after you schedule your test. That confirmation will add an extra 30 minutes to your test time. If you're taking a 4-hour test, for example, your confirmation will list 4 hours and 30 minutes. That extra time is allocated for you to log in and read the test instructions, which are explained in this section.

You'll receive your Confirmation of Attendance when you enter the test site. Before you sit down at your computer, make sure you put the confirmation somewhere secure. You may be anxious as you settle into your seat — file that confirmation somewhere safe before you focus on the test.

When you sit down at a computer to start your test, keep these points in mind:

- The NTS form includes a section identification number for the test you're approved to take. That number is also the launch code (password) you use to log in to your computer session.

- You're supplied with headphones for the audio portion of the exam.

- Paper and pencil are no longer used for note-taking. Instead, candidates use *noteboards,* which are laminated, colored sheets that you use to take notes with a fine-point marker. If you need more noteboards, the test center can supply them.

- You have a limited amount of time to read and respond to the introduction section of the exam. If you take too long, you'll be logged out of the exam. Please check your time as you start to go through the introduction.

- Each test you take is divided into smaller sections called testlets, and you're allowed to take a break after you finish a testlet. Keep in mind, however, that the clock keeps running during your break. You'll be fingerprinted when you leave for a break and when you return. When you return from a break, you need to re-enter your launch code.

Following the rules

If the Board of Accountancy detects misconduct or cheating, the exam candidate may be subject to the following penalties:

- Having his or her examination grades invalidated
- Being disqualified from all future examinations
- Facing civil and criminal penalties
- Having a CPA license rescinded if the misconduct or cheating is discovered after the candidate has passed the exam and is holding a CPA license

During the exam, you may receive a warning from the test center's staff for these types of actions:

- Communicating with anyone else in the test center, whether or not that person is another exam candidate
- Copying another candidate's work or allowing another test taker to look at your own work
- Reading aloud
- Any other type of behavior that the test center's staff considers disruptive to other students

If a candidate continues improper behavior after being warned, those actions may be considered grounds for dismissal from the exam — or grounds for the Board to cancel the candidate's exam scores.

If you suspect cheating by other candidates, you can contact the NASBA after taking your test. You can call toll free at 855-228-7778 or e-mail examsecurity@nasba.org.

Your test center forwards your completed exam to the AICPA for grading. After grading is complete, the AICPA sends your exam to NASBA. That organization then forwards the exam to the proper State Board. Your Board will send you your grades. Check out Chapter 2 for details on exam grading.

Helping to improve the exam for others

If, at the end of a particular test, you feel that a question was poorly worded or didn't provide a correct answer choice, you can follow up with the AICPA Examination Team. The CPA Candidate Bulletin lists the fax and address you can use to inform the AIPCA about your concern. Although your inquiry won't impact your grade, your comment will help improve the quality of the exam questions for other candidates.

Chapter 4

Implementing a Study Program

In This Chapter
▶ Creating a strategy to answer questions
▶ Scheduling time to study
▶ Managing your time as you study

Preparing for the CPA exam is a huge investment of time. Test preparation experts suggest that you invest at least 400 hours of study time to succeed on the exam.

This chapter provides a plan to study for the exam. You'll consider how to attack questions to answer them correctly. That process includes understanding how a question writer approaches multiple-choice questions, simulations, and written communication (essay) questions. The chapter also explains how to schedule study time, given the other demands on your time (work, family time, and so on).

Putting Together a Strategy for Multiple-Choice Questions

A certain percentage of each test on the CPA exam consists of multiple-choice questions (see Chapter 2 for the breakdown). This section provides a strategy for answering multiple-choice questions effectively. You start with an overview of how the questions are structured and then move on to an approach to answer each question.

Going over the structure of a question

Multiple-choice questions are written according to a specific structure. Test writers refer to a question as an *item*. Each item has these components:

- ✔ **Stem:** The question stem contains the details you need to answer the question (such as numbers and facts) and the question itself. Each stem also includes information that isn't needed. You need to sift through the information to determine what's needed and what isn't.

- ✔ **Distractors:** Each question contains distractors, which are incorrect answer choices.

- ✔ **Correct answer choice:** A question must contain one correct answer choice. Keep in mind the correct answer choice may have more than one correct statement in that answer choice. These questions usually provide letters and roman numerals, which allow you to choose multiple statements in your answer choice. For example "A. I and II" would mean that I and II are both correct statements for answer choice A.

Mulling over traits of a well-written question

The AICPA provides test-item writers with a set of guidelines for writing effective questions. Take a look at this list of guidelines. Understanding how test questions are created can help you answer them correctly:

- **Everything needed to answer the question should be provided in the stem.** A test taker should be able to answer the question correctly without referring to the answer choices. You may experience this on the exam. You read a question and come up with the answer before reading the answer choices. Do read all the answer choices — that's a way of confirming that the answer that came to you is correct.

- **The item should provide an answer choice that is clearly the best answer.** In other words, the test taker should be able to choose an answer that is better than all the others. That distinction should be clear to the test taker who knows the content of the question.

- **Each item needs to have a standard that is used to determine the correct answer.** Although the standard may not be stated in the question, all test items must be supported by a specific source. Generally accepted accounting principles (GAAP) is a common standard used to support a correct answer choice.

- **Answer choices should avoid absolute modifiers, such as *always, never, only, none, and every*.** Most standards have exceptions, so test-item writers should avoid using absolute modifiers in answer choices.

- **The test-item writer should avoid giving away the correct answer based on how answer choices are written.** Each answer choice should be of the same approximate length. Also, each distractor (incorrect choice) should be plausible.

- **The language used to write the question stem and all answer choices should be at a sixth-grade reading level.** The test-item writer should write in a way that is clear and concise.

Answering a multiple-choice question

Here's a thought process you can use to answer multiple-choice questions (to see how it works, try answering some of the multiple-choice questions later in this book):

1. **Read the last sentence of the question stem first.**

   A typical stem lists facts, figures, and other information and then asks the question. You may find two to three sentences of information before you get to the question. Read the last sentence first so you know what data to look for in the stem — that way, you can decide what kind of information is important. If, for example, the question is "How much interest did the investor earn on the bond?" then in the stem, you need to find the interest rate and the principal amount invested. The other information may not be important.

2. **Write the answer choice letters (or roman numerals) on a noteboard.**

   For each multiple-choice question, write the letters "A, B, C, D" on your noteboard. If the answer choice uses roman numerals, jot those down. That way, as you work through the question, you can cross out incorrect choices.

3. **Read the rest of the stem and write down the data you need to answer the question.**

   Jotting down the required data separates information you need from the unneeded data in the stem, adding clarity to your work. When you review your answer choices, you can quickly refer to the data you wrote on your noteboard to verify your answer. If you were computing a financial ratio using sales and net income, write down only those facts; the other information in the stem isn't needed.

4. Use the needed data to work out the answer to the question.

Do the calculation on your noteboard.

5. Review and eliminate incorrect answer choices.

Now that you have your answer, you can start to eliminate incorrect answer choices. Cross out the letter or number of the incorrect choice on the noteboard (see Step 2). Crossing out incorrect answers reduces your likelihood of making a mental error.

When you have the correct answer, click on the answer on your computer screen. When you review your answers, you can look at the noteboard for a reminder of how you eliminated answer choices.

Test-item writers try to avoid using absolute modifiers, such as "always" and "never," in the answer choices. However, sometimes those words do slip into test items. If you see the use of those words, pay close attention. It may be a red flag that the answer choice is incorrect.

An alternative strategy for answering multiple-choice questions involves looking at answer choices to get to the correct answer quickly. After you perform the first three steps but before you do the calculations to answer the question, you look at the answer choices. Some of the information in the answer choice may jog your memory, which may help you solve the question faster than if you'd tried to come up with the information on your own. Say you know the answer has to do with accounts receivable, but you can't recall the name of the report a CPA would need. You read the choices and see that one choice mentions an aging of receivables report. That was the type of report you needed to remember — see whether that choice might be your correct answer.

Read the answer choices only after you've read the last sentence of the question stem and then read the entire stem to pull out important information. Some test-takers read the answer choices first, before doing anything else. Because only one of the answer choices is correct, reading answer choices without knowing what's being asked can confuse you. Read the stem first.

Considering Task-Based Simulations

CPA candidates need to have a plan of attack for task-based simulation questions. Simulations ask you to apply a body of knowledge to an accounting situation. This section provides two simulation examples: one for the auditing and attestation (AUD) test, and another for the financial accounting and reporting (FAR) test. Keep in mind that there are two other tests that make up the CPA exam: business environment and concepts, along with regulation. The number of simulation questions differs between the four tests. You'll see more on this point later in this chapter.

Keep in mind that all the topics for a particular test are fair game for a simulation question. That can create anxiety, because you don't know the specific topic until it pops up on your test screen. If you've created a plan to study all the material for a particular test, you'll be prepared for the simulation topic.

Even if you know the topic, you may have some concerns about how to approach the simulation. To address that concern, this section walks through techniques for answering two types of simulations. You can find details on test topics for each of the four tests later in this book.

Audit and attestation (AUD) simulation

The AUD test covers the process of auditing financial statements and audit reports. This test also addresses other engagements that a CPA may perform, such as a review or a compilation. An AUD test will often ask a simulation question about a particular auditing procedure.

Suppose a simulation addresses an audit of accounts receivable. You're presented with a *workpaper,* which is an internal document created by an auditor. The form documents what was done to audit a particular account balance in the financial statements. The simulation asks whether the work performed was appropriate for an audit of accounts receivable. The question also asks whether any accounting adjustments need to be made to the receivable balance.

Here's a plan of attack for this simulation:

1. **Consider the content of the question.**

   Think through what you know about auditing accounts receivable from your study. For example, auditors want to confirm that amounts listed as receivables are based on actual sales. To verify that the receivables exist, an auditor may send confirmation letters to customers. These letters ask the clients to confirm the dollar amounts they owe to the company under audit. To help answer this question, you may jot down "receivables, confirmation" on a noteboard.

2. **Look at the other resources provided.**

   This type of simulation may provide authoritative literature that you can reference. To use your time efficiently, you need to have some search terms in mind. Based on Step 1, you use search terms like "receivables" and "confirmation." Type a search term into the computer screen where indicated. The test software will search the literature for that particular term and show you the results.

3. **Mull over multiple-choice questions on the same topic.**

   Multiple-choice questions come before simulations. Consider whether you saw a multiple-choice question on the same topic. In this example, a question on confirming accounts receivable may help you with the simulation.

4. **After you think through these steps, you're ready to answer the question.**

Financial accounting and reporting (FAR) simulation

The financial accounting and reporting (FAR) section tests candidates on accounting transactions and how financial reports are put together.

Say a simulation question asks you a series of true/false questions about inventory. You may be provided with a database of authoritative literature that you can search. The key, however, is to know enough about the topic to come up with some effective key words.

FIFO (first-in, first-out) and LIFO (last-in, first-out) are two methods used to value inventory. If the true/false questions simply refer to "LIFO" and "FIFO," you need to know that those terms represent inventory methods. If you study the recommended topics for FAR, you'll know these terms. If you want to search the database effectively, you could use "FIFO inventory valuation rules" as a search term.

FAR is the test on the exam that contains the most number-crunching. Another inventory simulation may ask you to calculate the value of inventory, given a series of inventory purchases and sales. For this type of question, you may use the spreadsheet function. Using a spreadsheet allows you to quickly calculate answers and lets you review your work. In this case, you may need to multiply four or five different costs per unit by the number of units either bought or sold. If you input the data into a spreadsheet, the data will be easier to review and correct, if needed.

Include a label with each number you write on a noteboard or in a spreadsheet. You need to know whether a number represents a dollar amount or the number of units bought or sold. Labeling amounts helps you to avoid making mistakes and makes your review process easier.

Chapter 2 explains where to find all the extra resources on the simulation screen. During your study, work simulation questions. Nearly all study methods for the CPA exam (books, online resources, and review courses) include simulations study tips. Make sure you time yourself during your simulation study. You need to get into the habit of checking the time remaining as you work through a question.

Looking at Written Communication Questions

Essay questions, which assess your written communication skills, appear only in the business environment and concepts (BEC) test. The BEC test includes three essay questions, one of which is a pretest question that doesn't count toward your grade. You don't know which question is a pretest question, so do your best work on everything.

As a starting point, read the essay question and jot down some notes about your knowledge on the topic. Once you've written down some thoughts, you can start to organize your thoughts into an outline. After the outline is complete, you'll write the essay.

These questions assess your basic writing skills, such as grammar and punctuation, as well as your ability to put your thoughts in a logical order. Here are some ways in which the essay grader will judge your response:

- ✓ **Accuracy:** The information you provide must be technically correct.

- ✓ **Relevance:** Your response must be relevant to the reader of the memo.

- ✓ **Organization:** The grader will also judge how well you organize your thoughts. For example, a memo should make a statement, provide information to support that statement, and then move on to another idea.

A written communication question may ask you to suppose that you're the chief financial officer of a company. The company president asks you to write a memo explaining the advantages and disadvantages of issuing common stock to the public for the first time — an event often referred to as "going public," or an *initial public offering* (IPO).

Many essay questions ask the candidate to give advice on a financial decision. For example, maybe a company needs to decide whether to make a product component or to buy it from an outside company. A firm may need to decide whether to lease a new building or buy it. Your job is to use your knowledge of BEC topics to write a clear document that supports your decision.

Setting an Overall Study Schedule

After you've considered a strategy for each type of exam question, you can plan your study time. Your total study time may take 400 hours or more. Based on a web search of CPA exam test-prep providers, here are some guidelines for your study time for each test:

- ✔ **Auditing and attestation (AUD):** 100 to 130 hours
- ✔ **Financial accounting and reporting (FAR):** 150 to 180 hours
- ✔ **Regulation (REG):** 110 to 140 hours
- ✔ **Business environment and concepts (BEC):** 80 to 110 hours

After you have a general idea of how much time you'll need to study for each test, take into account personal factors that may affect your study schedule.

Scheduling factors to consider

You need to create a plan of study that's realistic. The plan needs to take into account your personal situation. Exam candidates who don't take these factors into account tend to get frustrated. If they can't implement their study plan, they feel like they're failing. To avoid frustration, consider the following factors.

Noting how much time you have before your tests

Tests are offered in four testing windows during the year (see Chapter 3 for the time periods). When scheduling your test, consider how much time you have left until the test date and how much you need to study.

Suppose that you're planning to take the FAR test, and you plan to put in 160 hours of study time. If you schedule the test in 8 weeks, you'll need to put in 20 hours of study time per week. Decide whether that amount of weekly study time is realistic. If not, consider scheduling the exam later than originally planned.

Looking at recent accounting classes

If you've taken accounting classes recently, preparing for the exam will be easier. When you come across accounting topics, they won't be foreign to you.

Some candidates take the exam long after they've had an accounting course. If those candidates are working in accounting, some CPA exam topics will be familiar. However, a working accountant's body of knowledge may be limited by their industry or job description. If you work in manufacturing, you may not remember much about accounting for a retailer. If you work as a staff accountant, you may not work on creating financial statements; that may be the chief financial officer's job. If you're working as an accountant, consider these factors.

In the most challenging situation, you don't work in the industry and you've been out of school for some time. The accounting concepts on the exam may be very unfamiliar. In that case, you'll need to invest more study time.

Regardless of your background or education, you need to create a study plan for all four tests. Although certain areas of the exam may come easier to you, you need a plan to sufficiently cover all the exam topics.

Taking job and travel issues into account

If you're working while studying for the exam, carefully consider the demands of your career. If your work schedule is consistent (maybe 8 a.m. to 5 p.m. Monday through Friday), you can plan study time before or after work. Other candidates work in careers with uncertain hours. If you work part time, for example, your number of hours may change from week to week. In that case, you can study more during lighter workweeks, which will make up for less study time during busy workweeks. Many exam candidates plan extensive study time over the weekend.

Jobs that require travel may complicate your study planning. If your career requires hours in the car, you may consider listening to exam-prep lectures on CD or over the web. Exam candidates who fly may be able to study on planes and at the airport. Some people, however, have difficulty reading and focusing while traveling. You need to decide how much study you can realistically complete while you travel.

Including personal and family issues

Parents of young children should consider whether studying at home makes sense. For some, the noise of children may be too much of a distraction. A parent may need to head to a coffee shop or library to study effectively. Many parents want to study at home, however, so they can help with their children's needs. If you or your spouse is expecting a child, that event may change your study plan. Think through these issues.

Deciding on your best time of day

You may study differently depending on the time of day. If you can focus well early in the morning, you may change your schedule and study before work. Other people have trouble getting started in the morning. Those exam candidates may benefit from studying after work.

Some types of study require more focus than others. You may decide to flip through flashcards late in the evening, when you're tired and have less focus. If you find simulation questions to be more challenging than multiple-choice, you may want to work on simulations when you're more rested and focused. Adjust your study plans based on the time of day that is most effective for you.

Using a study planner

After you address the factors that may limit your study time, you can create a written plan of study for your test. You can use a hardcopy planner or an electronic version. Some candidates use a Word or Excel document they create themselves. As long as you create a plan and input your results, you'll be on the right track.

Say you plan to take the FAR test in 8 weeks. You plan to study for a total of 160 hours, or 20 hours per week. Monday through Thursday, you plan to study two hours each night after work. That leaves 12 hours of study over the weekend — 6 hours Saturday and Sunday.

Now that you've planned the hours, map out what you'll do with your study time. First, maybe you'll read through all the material provided by your test-preparation course. You decide to create your own flashcards as you read each topic. Next, you'll watch video lectures that explain the exam content. You'll then work on practice problems for each type of test question (see Chapter 2 for info on the type of questions on the exam). You'll keep notes on areas of weakness so you can review. Finally, you'll take timed practice tests and note your scores.

To stay on track, you'll document your actual study time and the topics you study each day. You'll also write down areas of weakness and exam results, all in your study planner. You can use this information to create a comprehensive review of all the material right before your test. You can spend more time on areas of weakness so you can go into the test with confidence.

Creating a Study Plan For Each Test

Each test on the CPA exam has its own combination of questions (multiple-choice, simulation, and written communication). Each test also has unique topics that are particularly challenging.

The purpose of this section is to provide an overview of each test so you can create an effective study plan. I also address some of the most difficult topics for each test.

Auditing and attestation study plan

You have 4 hours to complete the AUD test, which consists of 90 multiple-choice questions and 7 simulation questions. Keep in mind that 15 of the multiple choice and 1 of the simulation questions are pretest items, which don't count toward your grade. As mentioned in Chapter 2, you're not told which questions are pretest items.

Test-preparation companies recommend that you spend 100 to 130 hours studying for this test. Here are some factors to consider in your study plan.

Dealing with auditing language

The auditing test may have the most challenging language on the CPA exam. You'll notice that some of the material is similar to what you see in a business law textbook. This has implications for your study plan. You may find that this material requires more focused reading than the other tests you'll encounter. If you read more slowly than most people, you may need to invest more time to get through the audit material.

One area that requires very focused reading is audit reporting. An *audit* takes place when a CPA firm performs procedures on a company's financial statements. Based on those procedures, the auditing firm provides a written audit opinion. Here are several challenges to understanding audit opinions:

- ✔ An audit opinion can be qualified or unqualified. *Unqualified* means that the auditor didn't find any material (relevant) misstatements in the financials that need to be corrected before the financial reports are issued to the public. *Qualified* indicates that more disclosure is needed in the audit report. The audit report may say, for example, that one of the financial statements can't be audited due to insufficient data provided by the client. The differences in language between all these reports can be hard to distinguish.

- ✔ CPAs can issue reports that aren't audits. An audit report provides an opinion as to whether the financial statements are fairly stated (free of material error). CPAs refer to auditing as "opining" on the financial statements. Compilations and reviews are reports on financial statements, but they aren't audit reports, because the CPA isn't providing an opinion on the financial statements.

Preparing for report questions

Most test-preparation resources provide the language used for audit reports, compilations, reviews, and other CPA engagements. Here are several study tips you can use to work with report language:

✔ **Print each example.** You may find it effective to print each report example. The typical report that a CPA provides with the financial statements is one to two pages. The purpose of printing the reports is so you can see how the reports are similar and where they differ.

✔ **Memorize the unqualified report language.** You'll almost certainly see questions about the exact language in an unqualified audit opinion. That opinion is about one page in length. Memorize the report well enough that you can write out the entire text. At that point, you'll be able to answer the unqualified report questions. You'll also be able to understand how the qualified audit report language differs from the language in unqualified reports.

✔ **Lay out the unqualified and qualified reports side-by-side.** Use a highlighter and note how the reports differ from each other. Take it one paragraph at a time. Some reports have the same paragraph language; others differ. For example, a qualified report may use the language "except for" in a paragraph. That section of the report explains the issue that causes the CPA to issue a qualified opinion. Catching that distinction as you read test questions is important. Your goal is to keep these report differences in your mind's eye as you work through the AUD test.

✔ **Memorizing other language.** As you work through questions, you may find the need to memorize portions of other reports but not the entire report. For example, you may need to memorize only some of the language for a compilation report.

✔ **Use flashcards to test yourself on reporting paragraphs that you need to memorize.** Some test-prep companies offer pre-printed flashcards on these topics. In other cases, you may need to create them yourself.

Separating definitions of risk

The AUD exam tests several definitions of risk. The definitions are similar, which can cause confusion. To keep the concepts straight, take a look at this comparison:

✔ **Audit risk:** Audit risk is the risk that an auditor will perform work and *not* discover a material misstatement (error) in the financial statements. *Material,* in this case, means an amount that is large enough to be relevant.

✔ **Internal control risk:** This is the risk that the company's internal controls aren't sufficient to produce financial statements that are free of misstatement. The "Segregating duties" section later in the chapter explains more on internal controls.

✔ **Sample risk:** Auditors often take a sample of transactions and test them. The test work is designed to see whether the accounting transactions were posted properly. The auditor calculates the percentage of sample items that were handled correctly. Based on that percentage, the auditor uses statistics to estimate the percentage of transactions that were handled correctly for the entire population (all the transactions of a given type). For example, an auditor may take a sample of invoices and verify that each invoice can be agreed to a product shipment. This work validates that the invoices sent to clients are for legitimate sales. *Sample risk* is the risk that the error found in the sample is different from the actual error rate for all of the transactions.

Financial accounting and reporting study plan

The financial accounting and reporting (FAR) test has the same format as the auditing test. You have 4 hours to answer 90 multiple-choice questions and 7 simulation questions. Fifteen of the multiple-choice questions and one of the simulation questions are pretest items, which don't count toward your grade.

Test-preparation companies recommend that you spend 150 to 180 hours studying for the FAR test. This test requires the most hours of study. This section discusses some factors to consider in your study plan.

Understanding source documents

The FAR test includes questions on your ability to post accounting transactions. CPAs post transactions using source documents. *Source documents* are the original records that support an accounting transaction.

If you haven't worked as an accountant, talk to someone working in the industry about source documents. People who work in accounting use source documents to post transactions all the time. Run down the types of transactions that your test-prep material mentions (Chapter 2 provides a link where you can search for the AICPA's Content document, which details the exam content). Ask your friend about the source documents he or she uses for each type of transaction.

Here are some common transactions and the source documents used to post the transactions:

- **Posting revenue (sales):** Source documents include a copy of the invoice that was sent to the client. If the company sells a physical product, accountants typically require a shipping document. This document verifies that the product was shipped to the client. A CPA may also review a contract with the client or some sort of customer order form.

- **Writing a check for an expense:** An accountant would need several documents before a check goes out to a vendor. Most firms use a purchase order form (P.O.). A *P.O.* is a formal request from an employee for a product or service. If you manufacture blue jeans, your factory manager may complete a P.O. for denim, a raw material used in production.

  After the purchase order is approved, an order is placed with the vendor. When the denim is received, the vendor includes a copy of the invoice and a packing slip. The *packing slip* lists what was actually shipped. An accountant agrees the information (price, number of items, and so on) among the purchase order, the order sent to vendor, the invoice, and the shipping document.

  If all the information agrees, a company official reviews the documents and writes the check for payment. Cash is reduced (credited) and an expense is posted (debited). In some cases, an expense is posted and an accounts payable balance is set up when the goods are received. When the company pays for the goods, accounts payable is debited (reduced), and cash is credited (reduced).

- **Increases and decreases to inventory:** Purchases increase inventory. An order is placed with a vendor, and goods are received into inventory. Inventory is debited (increased) and crediting sets up an accounts payable balance. When a check is written for inventory, cash is reduced (credited) and accounts payable is reduced with a debit. Inventory, keep in mind, is an asset account. The inventory item doesn't become an expense until it's sold. When a sale is made, revenue or sales is increased. At the same time, inventory is reduced and cost of sales (an expense account) is increased.

TIP

Calculating answers correctly

The FAR test involves the most mathematical calculations. As you start to work practice questions, keep these tips in mind:

- ✔ **Write down each step.** If you need to perform a calculation that requires several steps, write down those steps on your noteboard. Suppose you need to use the breakeven formula: Sales – Variable costs – Fixed costs = $0 profit. On your noteboard, write out the formula and fill in each amount. Label each number as dollars (use a dollar sign) or other appropriate units.

- ✔ **Organize your work.** As you jot down notes to answer a question, write slowly enough so that you can read your handwriting. Label each calculation on your noteboard. If you use the breakeven formula in Question 30, write "30" next to your calculation and circle it.

- ✔ **Use algebra to fill in the blank.** Often, a test question provides you with all the amounts in a formula except for one. You have to use algebra to solve for the missing amount. This type of question tests whether you know the required formula. For example, the formula for calculating ending inventory is

    Beginning inventory + Purchases – Cost of goods sold = Ending inventory

    If you were given all the amounts except cost of goods sold, you'd put the three known amounts in the formula and then use algebra to calculate cost of goods sold.

- ✔ **Review your calculations.** Use any remaining test time to review as many of your answers as possible. That includes reviewing calculations. If you number the work on your noteboard and write your amounts clearly, you'll be able to review your calculations quickly. As you work practice questions, you may find that you know the formula for a calculation but made a math error. You can catch those math errors during your review.

Comparing cash and accrual basis accounting

To understand cash and accrual basis, you first need to know about the *matching principle*. This principle dictates that revenue should be recognized (posted to the financial statements) when it's earned. Typically, a company recognizes revenue when it provides a product or service to a customer and presents the customer an invoice. The matching principle states the revenue should be recognized when it's earned, regardless of when the client payment is received.

Revenue should also be matched with the expenses incurred to produce the revenue. If you buy inventory in January to produce a good that is sold in March, the sale of January inventory is a cost of good sold (expense) balance that relates to the March revenue. If the inventory item had a January cost of $50, that amount should be posted as cost of goods sold in March. In that way, the March financial statements recognize the revenue (sale) and the $50 cost of goods sold expense.

Accrual basis accounting applies the matching principle to accounting transactions. When you have a sale but no cash has been received, you post revenue and accounts receivable. The revenue isn't related to the cash payment from the customer. If you prepay six months of your company's insurance premiums, you decrease (credit) cash and recognize (debit) prepaid insurance as an asset. No expense is recognized until the month of insurance coverage is over. At that point, prepaid insurance is reduced and insurance expense is recognized. In this case, expense recognition occurs after the cash is paid. Nearly all companies operate using accrual basis accounting.

Cash basis accounting recognizes revenues and expenses based on your checkbook (cash) activity. When a customer pays you, you recognize revenue. When you write a check, you post an expense. Cash basis accounting doesn't apply the matching principle. Using the cash basis doesn't match revenue with expenses, so it should be avoided to comply with generally accepted accounting principles (GAAP).

Regulation study plan

The format of the regulation (REG) test is the same format as the FAR and AUD tests. Regulation, however, is only a 3-hour exam. The test contains 72 multiple-choice questions (with 12 pretest items) and 6 simulations (with 1 pretest item). You can find more on test format in Chapter 2.

Test-preparation companies recommend that you spend 110 to 140 hours studying for the REG test.

Getting an overview of taxation

One challenge on the REG test is the technical difficulty of taxation questions. This part of the test requires you to memorize many statistics. For example, you need to know the standard deduction an individual can take on his or her personal tax return. Head over to www. irs.gov for this type of information.

Taxation is challenging because visualizing how the different facts and figures are connected is difficult. To help with this issue, take a look at the tax forms that contain these calculations.

Individuals file federal taxes using Form 1040. You can quickly download and print the 1040 form from the IRS website. Take a look at page 1 of Form 1040. The form starts with filing status and exemptions and then moves down to income. The REG test requires you to know facts about each section of the 1040.

As you study the tax concepts, find out where that topic is located on Form 1040. Connecting topics to the form will help you pull together the concepts. When you come across standard deductions, you'll see that information is posted on page 2 of Form 1040.

You can use the same study process for other taxes. If you're studying corporate tax topics, take a look at Form 1120, the corporate tax return form. Although you don't necessarily need to memorize the tax form, it's a great tool for understanding how tax topics relate.

Evaluating business entities

You need to understand the differences among types of business entities. The three in the following list are the most tested entities. Typically, a candidate needs to know how each of the entities is taxed. Also, the REG test may ask you about the legal liability that the business owners may encounter.

> ✔ **Sole proprietorship:** This business has a single owner. Sole proprietorships are considered *pass-through entities,* which means that the business profit or loss flows to the owner's individual tax return. So if the business earns $5,000 for the year, that $5,000 profit will be posted in income on the owner's personal tax return (Form 1040). The owner has unlimited personal liability for all business-related litigation.

✓ **Partnership:** A partnership is defined as an entity with two or more partners. The business profit or loss flows to each partner's individual tax return. The amount of profit and loss assigned to a partner is determined in the partnership agreement. If the partnership earns $20,000 for the year and the partnership agreement states that Bill earns 30 percent of the profit, $6,000 (30 percent of $20,000) will be posted to Bill's personal tax return as income. Each general partner has unlimited personal liability for all business-related litigation of the partnership. A limited partner's liability is limited to the dollar amount she has invested in the partnership. The actions of one partner can cause legal liability for all of the partners.

✓ **Corporation:** A *corporation* is defined as a tax and legal entity that's separate from its owners. The corporation has two levels of taxation. First, profit and loss are calculated on a corporate tax return. The company pays tax on that profit. *Shareholders* own common stock in the corporation. After paying taxes, the corporation may pay a dividend to shareholders. A *dividend* represents company earnings that are paid to shareholders. The dividend is then taxed on the shareholder's personal tax return. The shareholder's legal liability is limited to his common stock investment in the corporation.

Adding in business ethics

Ethics questions appear on the REG test. Reflecting a growing emphasis on ethics in the accounting field, most State Boards require annual continuing education with an ethics component. Federal and state governments as well as the media have increased their focus on ethics for business professionals.

In terms of auditing, *independence* means that a CPA's only business relationship with the company is the fee for the audit work performed. The REG test may have other questions on independence. A question may ask whether a CPA has to be independent to perform a variety of other services, including compilations, reviews, agree-upon procedures, and tax return preparation.

The test emphasizes the importance of Board members who are independent. For a Board member to be independent, the only relationship with the company is the fee he or she receives to serve on the Board. Employees and company managers may serve as Board members in most cases. However, the test points out that independent Board members are more likely to provide unbiased opinions on company activities. Unbiased advice is highly valued.

Business environment and concepts study plan

The business environment and concepts (BEC) test has a different structure from the other three tests. For the 3-hour BEC test, you find 72 multiple-choice questions (with 12 pretest items). The remainder of the test consists of three written communication questions, including one pretest item. Eighty to 90 percent of this test requires knowledge and understanding of BEC concepts. The remaining 10 to 20 percent of the exam is written communication. (Check out the earlier section "Looking at Written Communications Questions" earlier in this chapter.)

BEC topics are similar to what a business major would see in undergraduate coursework. This test includes economics and financial-analysis topics. This section covers some important topics you'll face on the BEC test.

Test-preparation companies recommend that you spend 80 to 110 hours studying for the BEC test.

Working with currency risk

Currency risk may be the most difficult subject on the entire CPA exam. *Currency risk* is the risk that a firm will incur a loss when it exchanges one type of currency for another. Companies that operate in more than one country have exposure to currency risk.

For example, suppose that Reliable Blue Jeans is a U.S.-based company that manufactures blue jeans in England and imports them to the U.S. for sale. Reliable generates financials based on U.S. dollars. To fund its manufacturing in England, Reliable converts dollars to British pounds and sends them to England.

Reliable's accountants determine that the English manufacturing plant needs $1,000,000 to operate each month. Say that, as of March 1, Reliable can convert 1 dollar into 2 pounds. When Reliable converts to pounds and sends the funds on March 1, the English plant receives 2,000,000 pounds.

On April 1, Reliable prepares to send another $1,000,000 to England. The conversion rate, however, between dollars and pounds has changed. Now, 1 dollar buys only 1.5 pounds. When Reliable converts $1,000,000, the English plant receives only 1,500,000 pounds. The dollar's buying power has *weakened* — the dollar buys fewer pounds. If you manage the English plant, you now have 500,000 fewer pounds to run the factory in April.

May 1 rolls around, and Reliable needs to send another $1,000,000 to England. The conversion rate had changed again. Now, 1 dollar buys 3 pounds. When Reliable converts $1,000,000, the English plant receives 3,000,000 pounds. The dollar's buying power has *strengthened* — the dollar buys more pounds. If you manage the English plant, you now have more pounds to run the factory in May.

To prevent these big swings in currency conversions, companies hedge currency conversion rates. A *hedge* is set up when a company pays a fee to lock in a specific currency conversion rate for a specific period of time. Reliable might pay a fee to ensure the 1 dollar converts into 2 pounds and that the conversion rate remains in place for three months. By using a hedge, Reliable knows how many pounds that English plant will receive when it converts $1,000,000.

Handling financial ratios and formulas

The BEC test covers financial ratios and formulas. Typically, you can use flashcards to write down the information covered on the test and memorize them. One way to study financial ratios and formulas is to make sure you understand some key terms.

Liquidity refers to a company's ability to generate enough cash flow to meet its short-term (current) obligations. The balance sheet separates assets and liabilities into short-term and long-term classifications. For the CPA exam, "current" means 12 months or less. You can use that definition for *current,* unless a test question tells you otherwise.

Current assets are those assets that are in cash or that will be converted to cash within 12 months. Current assets include accounts receivable. Companies expect receivables to be paid in cash within 12 months. If not, the receivable should be written off as uncollectable. In the same way, inventory is a current asset. A business expects inventory to be sold (and converted into cash) within a year. If not, the inventory is obsolete and should be written off as an expense.

Current liabilities are those debts that a firm expects to pay within a year. This category includes accounts payable and wages payable. The current portion of long-term liabilities is also a current liability. If you have to repay $100,000 in principal on a loan within a year, that $100,000 is categorized as a current liability.

Solvency is a firm's ability to generate enough cash to operate over the long term. For the CPA exam, *long-term* is considered more than a year. A long-term debt, for example, is a liability that is due in more than year.

A good starting point for understanding financial ratios and formulas is to define liquidity and solvency. Now consider some of the more frequently tested items:

- **Working capital:** Working capital is defined as current assets less current liabilities. To maintain liquidity, a company wants to have at least 1 dollar of current assets for every dollar of current liabilities. In other words, a firm wants current assets to be greater than current liabilities.

- **Current ratio:** This ratio is current assets divided by current liabilities. The ratio expresses the working-capital amounts as a ratio. A company wants a ratio greater than 1. The amount in the numerator of the fraction (current assets) should be equal to or greater than the denominator amount (current liabilities). A ratio of at least 1 means the current assets are greater than current liabilities.

- **Inventory conversion period (or inventory turnover):** Several ratios on the BEC test address how quickly companies collect cash. The faster a company can collect cash, the less cash it needs to operate each month. The inventory conversion period ratio explains the average time it takes for a firm to sell its inventory. If a company can sell inventory quickly, it can collect cash on the sales faster. This ratio is average inventory divided by sales per day. If a business has $100,000 in inventory, on average, and sells $2,000 of inventory per day, the inventory conversion period is $100,000 divided by $2,000, or 50 days. Average inventory is calculated as follows:

$$\text{Average inventory} = \frac{\left(\begin{array}{c}\text{Beginning inventory}\\\text{for the period}\end{array}\right) + \left(\begin{array}{c}\text{Ending inventory}\\\text{for the period}\end{array}\right)}{2}$$

- **Receivables conversion period (or receivable turnover):** This ratio defines how long it takes to collect accounts receivable. The ratio is average receivables divided by credit sales per day. Credit sales aren't paid in cash, so they're posted to accounts receivable. Suppose a business has $200,000 in receivables, on average, and sells $10,000 of goods on credit per day. This receivable conversion period is $200,000 divided by $10,000, or 20 days. Average receivables is calculated as follows:

$$\text{Average receivables} = \frac{\left(\begin{array}{c}\text{Beginning receivables}\\\text{for the period}\end{array}\right) + \left(\begin{array}{c}\text{Ending receivables}\\\text{for the period}\end{array}\right)}{2}$$

Segregating duties

The BEC test includes questions about internal controls. *Internal controls* are policies and procedures created by company management. The controls exist to protect company assets and other resources from theft. Internal controls also ensure that the business complies with regulatory requirements. These controls also help the company generate financial statements that are free of misstatement. This topic is also tested on the auditing (AUD) test.

One frequently tested internal control is *segregation of duties*. This concept states that if management spreads out certain duties among different employees, the risk of asset theft is lower.

Where possible, management should assign the following duties to three different employees:

- ✔ **Custody of assets:** Physical custody over assets includes keeping the company checkbook or having keys to the company equipment building.

- ✔ **Authority over assets:** A manager with the ability to sign checks has authority to move cash. Writing a check moves cash from the company to the payee on the check. The individual with physical custody of the checkbook shouldn't also have the ability to sign checks.

- ✔ **Recordkeeping for assets:** Accountants are record keepers. An accountant shouldn't have physical custody of any company assets or the authority to sign a check. When it comes to cash, the accountant should be responsible for reconciling the bank account and posting accounting transactions.

Obviously, keeping the duties segregated is tougher in a small business with fewer employees.

Following Up after Your Tests

When you pass the exam, celebrate! It's a huge accomplishment. Add that credential to your resume and any other type of social media that might be appropriate. If you're working, let your employer know. If you're interviewing, include your new designation in any cover letters, in job applications, and in your interview discussions.

Unfortunately, not every candidate passes each test on the first try. The CPA exam is a difficult exam. If you take a test and don't pass it, don't despair. Consider these steps to get back on your horse and pass the test on your next try.

First, take a break. When you hear about a test that you didn't pass, consider taking some time off before you start studying again. A break from study will allow you to look at your test results objectively, with a clear head. If you can review your test score details without getting too emotionally involved in the poor outcome, you'll be able to create a better study plan.

Considering your results

The AICPA's website (www.aicpa.org) provides a document that you can download: "How Is the CPA Exam Scored?" That document explains the feedback you receive with your exam scores.

The Board will send a Candidate Performance Report with your test scores. The report compares your performance with "just passed" candidates (those candidates who passed with a score between 75 and 80 percent). You'll see data separated by content area and by question type (multiple-choice, simulation, or written communication).

The report will provide a *category of performance*. This category is a "general indicator" of your performance, in comparison with the other candidates who took the test when you did. The comparisons provided are *weaker, comparable,* and *stronger.* A stronger score in economics concepts and analysis (a BEC content area) means that your performance on those topics was better, on average, than that of other candidates who took the test.

The Candidate Performance Report can help you identify areas of weakness so you can create a study plan to retake the test. If you missed several multiple-choice questions on bond accounting, for example, you can spend time on that content area before you retake the test. You can also improve your ability to understand and respond to multiple-choice questions.

After reviewing your scores, pull out the study plan you originally used for the test you didn't pass. Bear in mind that you've already put in quite a few hours when you studied the first time. As you study to retake the exam, you'll need to make a judgment on how much time you need to spend on each content area. Take a look at the percentage of practice questions you're answering correctly as you review. If you're getting scores of 80 percent correct or higher, you're probably ready for that portion of your test.

If you don't pass your test, your grades will come with instructions on how to retake the test. You'll have to schedule a time to retake the test in a new testing window. For info on testing windows, head to Chapter 3.

Appealing your score

Candidates can appeal a test result with a failing score. Keep in mind, however, that the appeals process requires an application and a fee. You should consider an appeal only if there are specific answers choices you want to challenge as incorrect. The exam questions go through an extensive quality control process to ensure accuracy. As a result, the number of questions with incorrect answers is very small.

When you receive notice that you failed a test, contact your Board quickly to appeal. The appeal process is available only for a short time after your exam is graded. Check with your State Board to find out how much time you have to appeal.

During your appeal, a Board representative (or their designated agent) sits with you in a secure location. You'll be able to review your multiple-choice and simulation questions and have the opportunity to challenge a correct answer choice as incorrect. Written communication questions aren't included in an appeal.

Part II
Business Environment and Concepts

	Service Departments	
	Maintenance	*Utilities*
Overhead costs incurred	$18,700	$9,000
Service provided to:		
Maintenance department	—	10%
Utilities department	20%	—
Producing department A	40%	30%
Producing department B	40%	60%
Total	100%	100%

Variance questions are nearly always on the BEC test, and you'll use variances frequently in your work as a CPA. Check out a free article on variances at www.dummies.com/extras/cpaexam.

In this part . . .

- ✔ Discover the most tested topics on the BEC test so you can tailor your study plan accordingly.

- ✔ Try your hand at 30 practice questions and then check your work with the answers and detailed explanations provided.

Chapter 5

Taking a Closer Look at the Business Environment and Concepts Test

• •

In This Chapter

▶ Understanding management oversight of a business

▶ Using analysis to make informed business decisions

▶ Working with IT systems to generate accounting data

• •

The business environment and concepts (BEC) test's content is similar to what you see in an undergraduate business school curriculum. It covers things like how companies are managed, how risks are controlled, economic analysis tools, IT systems, and elements of strategic planning.

This chapter gives you a refresher on the types of topics and questions you're likely to see on the BEC test. Keep in mind that the BEC test is the only test on the exam that uses essay questions. (Chapter 4 provides a strategy for answering essay questions.) As you read this chapter, consider how you might answer an essay question on these topics.

Governing a Company's Business Activities

The highest level of responsibility over a business is assigned to the board of directors. A business's *control environment* — management's view of the importance of controls — is also important. You may see this concept referred to as "the tone at the top." Control environment includes the policies put in place to ensure that financial reporting is accurate and that assets are used properly.

This section starts with a discussion of a company's board and wraps up with segregation of duties, which may be the most important set of controls that a business implements.

Considering the board of directors

Nearly all businesses have a *board of directors,* whose purpose is to represent the stakeholders in company matters. In a not-for-profit entity, board members may be appointed to represent the donors. In a for-profit company, the shareholders elect board members. Every public company is required to elect a board of directors. (See Chapter 8 for info on the regulation of public companies.)

The board establishes management policies for running the business. If the company has a CPA firm perform an audit, the audit report is addressed to the board. Most public companies have an audit committee made up of board members. The group is a direct line of communication from the audit firm to the board. (Check out Chapter 11 for more on audits.)

The board also handles major decisions related to the business. Here are a few examples:

- ✔ Hiring and firing senior executives, including the chief executive officer
- ✔ Deciding whether to declare a dividend
- ✔ Determining the amount and type of executive compensation for senior management

Board members must adhere to the *duty of loyalty* principle, which means that if a board member is presented with an opportunity that would help the company, he or she has an obligation to present that opportunity to the company first. In other words, the board member can't put his or her own business interests ahead of the company's interests.

Suppose a board member finds out that a warehouse is being offered for sale. The board member owns a business that could use more warehouse space. The duty of loyalty principle states that the board member should present the warehouse sale to the company first, before considering his own business interests.

Judging the firm's control environment

The auditing and attestation (AUD) test (Chapter 11) covers the area of internal controls. However, internal controls also relate to corporate governance, which the BEC test covers.

Internal controls are policies put in place to help a company achieve these objectives:

- ✔ **Operations:** Controls help a company produce a product or service efficiently. Effective internal controls ensure that company resources (raw materials, labor hours) aren't wasted during production.
- ✔ **Financial reporting:** Properly structured internal controls help a business generate reliable financial statements.
- ✔ **Regulatory compliance:** An internal control system allows a company to comply with industry laws and regulations.

In addition to the controls themselves, management needs a system to communicate internal control policies to the entire organization. Management should also follow up to ensure that employees are implementing the controls.

The BEC test includes internal control concepts that are promoted by the *Committee of Sponsoring Organizations* (COSO). COSO provides internal control guidance to corporations and promotes ideas on risk management and fraud detection. COSO's website (www.coso.org) explains that the entity is a joint initiative of five private sector groups, including the AICPA (see Chapter 3).

COSO separates internal controls into five components:

- ✔ **Control environment:** This describes management's view of the importance of internal controls. It addresses management's ethics, values, and philosophy.

- ✔ **Risk assessment:** Risk assessment is the process of evaluating risks that may prevent the company from achieving the objectives of internal controls. Risks may be internal, such as the risk that employees aren't trained on controls effectively. There are also external controls, which relate to a company's industry.

- ✔ **Control activities:** Control activities are policies put in place to ensure that the control objectives are carried out. Policies may include written approval of purchases, which ensures that resources are used responsibly. Another policy, reconciliation of bank accounts, protects company cash from theft.

- ✔ **Information and communication:** Internal controls must be in writing and communicated to everyone in the organization. All employees should be clear on their responsibilities related to internal controls. Updates need to be communicated company-wide.

- ✔ **Monitoring:** Monitoring internal controls procedures helps management assess whether the procedures are effective. Suppose, for example, that every shipping document for a product sale needs to be matched with a copy of the client invoice. Management's review indicates that 20 percent of the month's shipping documents aren't matched with an invoice. The company may conclude that the control isn't effective. To improve the control, employees need proper training.

Segregating duties to reduce risk

Segregation of duties is the process of separating critical duties among multiple employees to reduce the risk of theft. This process is a vital internal control. Although other controls — like written approvals and reconciling bank accounts — are important, how you allocate work to employees is critical. If duties aren't carefully segregated, dishonest workers can override all your other internal controls.

Here are three responsibilities that should be assigned to different staff members:

- ✔ **Custody of assets:** Employee A has access to assets, such as the company checkbook.

- ✔ **Authorization to move assets:** Employee B has authority to sign checks, which allows cash to be moved (paid). Employee B also approves purchases of large dollar amount items.

- ✔ **Recordkeeping:** Employee C is typically an accountant. Employee C reviews the records that document a transaction and then posts the activity into the accounting records. Employee C reconciles the checkbook. Employee B signs checks, and Employee A keeps the physical checkbook.

Here's a segregation of duties scenario. Suppose that a restaurant manager, Rob, has the authority to authorize payment as well as the ability to sign checks. Rob decides to generate a *disbursement voucher*. A voucher is a document that authorizes payment to an outside vendor. In this case, the voucher is for $1,000 for a payment to Northern Meat Supply. The restaurant buys meat, chicken, and fish from vendors. Using the voucher as documentation, Bob generates a check payable to Northern Meat Supply.

Sue, the restaurant's accountant, reconciles the bank account. She notices payments each month to Northern Meat Supply. She doesn't think of the payments as unusual, because the restaurant pays vendors for meat, chicken, and fish. Several months later, Rob leaves to work at another restaurant.

At year-end, the auditors perform procedures to audit accounts payable. As part of their procedures, an auditor agrees (compares) a sample of vendor payments to incoming shipments of product. The auditors find that no product was received from Northern Meat Supply. After further investigation, the company determines that Northern Meat was a *fictitious payee*. The firm was simply a bank account that Rob controlled. Because Rob had two duties that should've been segregated (authority to purchase goods and to sign checks), he was able to steal assets from the company. This scenario is common on the BEC test. Segregation of duties is also on the auditing and attestation (AUD) test.

Using Economic Analysis

To properly operate a business, managers need to understand some key economic measures. That's what you'll find in this section. Managers, for example, consider the company's industry and competitors. This analysis helps them assess their own financial strengths and weaknesses and make changes to improve profit. Marginal utility measures customer demand for a product, which also impacts profit. Finally, company profit can be affected by currency values. This chapter considers the impact of currency values on imports and exports.

Reviewing your competition

A business owner needs to understand the competitors in his or her industry. Managers also need to understand how much of a particular market is controlled by one company or a group of companies. A competitor with a large market share may be able to negotiate lower costs paid to vendors because it buys more volume. By cutting costs for materials, the company with a large market share can reduce their sale price. A competitor's lower price may force the manager's firm to cut prices, too, which reduces profit.

Company management can compare their business to the competition by performing scanning. Economists define *scanning* as collecting data from each segment of a business. Scanning allows a company to assess every aspect of a firm's business environment.

Suppose that Mountain Range Meats supplies meat and fish to restaurants. Because of the volume of sales, Mountain Range can negotiate lower beef prices with ranchers (its vendors). Mountain Range can then lower its sale prices and maintain the same profit margin (net income divided by sales).

If you manage another meat and fish supplier, the Mountain Range price-cuts put pressure on you to cut your prices. If you don't, restaurants may move their business to Mountain Range. You see the importance of understanding your competition.

Here are two terms that relate to competition. These terms refer to competitors who may have a great deal of control over the marketplace. That control may allow them to cut prices substantially, which may force competitors out of the marketplace due to lack of profit:

- **Monopoly:** A monopoly is a company that has exclusive control over a particular market. That firm is the only supplier of a specific product or service.

- **Oligopoly:** An oligopoly exists when the market for a particular product is controlled by a small group of firms. In an oligopoly, the actions of one company will greatly impact the prices and sales of the other businesses in the oligopoly.

An oligopoly is formed by horizontal merger. A *merger* occurs when companies combine their operations into one venture. A *horizontal merger* takes place when the firms that merge are in the same line of business. Suppose your town has 20 dry cleaners. Two dry cleaning firms implement horizontal mergers, each with 9 of the other existing dry cleaners. After the mergers, two large firms control all the town's dry cleaning business. The dry cleaning business is now an oligopoly in your town.

Would you like another? Forecasting sales using marginal utility

Part of any firm's analysis is forecasting sales. That forecast includes researching how much of a product or service one customer will likely buy. Research on buying habits includes the concept of marginal utility. *Marginal utility* is the amount of additional satisfaction a customer gains from consuming (buying) one more unit of a product. For example, after a customer buys one pair of jeans, would she feel enough additional satisfaction from another pair to buy a second one?

The *law of diminishing marginal utility* states that marginal utility declines with each additional unit received. As the customer uses more units of a product, she gets less satisfaction from each additional item. The customer who buys tickets to three baseball games may not go to a fourth game, because she decides that the additional satisfaction doesn't justify the cost of a fourth ticket.

Marginal utility is an important factor in forecasting sales, because a company needs to estimate the number of units an individual customer will buy.

Relating currency to imports and exports

Currency risk is the risk that a firm will incur a loss when it exchanges one type of currency for another. The BEC test may include questions about currency risk and how that risk impacts imports and exports.

Suppose that 1 U.S. dollar can be exchanged for 0.60 British pounds. Sterling Shops imports blue jeans from the U.S. At the current exchange rate, Sterling must pay 30 pounds to purchase one $50 pair of blue jeans. Now suppose that the exchange rate changes so that 1 U.S. dollar is exchanged for 0.50 British pounds. Sterling's cost to buy one $50 pair of blue jeans is now 25 pounds. Here are some terms that explain this change in currency rates:

- **Weaker dollar:** The value of the dollar is weakened in comparison with the pound. By *weaker,* economists mean that it takes fewer pounds to buy 1 U.S. dollar.

- **Stronger pound:** The pound's value is stronger, because 1 pound can buy more U.S. dollars. Instead of needing 0.6 pounds to buy 1 dollar, you now need only 0.5 pounds.

- **U.S. exports, British imports:** Because the pound buys more dollars, it's now cheaper for Britain to buy goods from the U.S. Economists state that demand for U.S. goods in Britain will increase. U.S. exports will increase, and British imports of U.S. goods will increase.

Your test may cover the relationship among exchange rates, imports, and exports.

Managing and Business Decisions

The BEC test covers several areas that deal with business decisions. In this section, you consider the financial impact of extending credit to customers, go over the decision criteria for a special order, and see a series of formulas that help a manager decide on long-term capital spending and investment.

A key concept that each manager must understand is his firm's *business cycle*. A business cycle starts when a company spends money to make a product or deliver a service. The product or service is delivered to the customer, and the customer pays the company. When the firm receives customer payments, the cycle starts over again.

A competent manager needs to know how long it takes for the cycle to be completed. Here are two reasons why:

- **Planning production:** If you know how long it takes to manufacture and sell a product, you have some idea of when your inventory will run out. You can use that knowledge to plan more production to replenish your inventory levels. After all, you can't sell more product if your shelves are empty.

- **Cash flow management:** Understanding the cycle of spending, production, sales, and cash collections allows a manager to maintain a sufficient cash balance. The key here is that a business needs enough cash available to operate while waiting for other sales to be paid. If a business requires $30,000 a month to operate, management must plan for that cash need, based on the firm's business cycle.

Say you manage Close Cut Lawn Mowers, a manufacturer of mowers. You sell mowers to home improvement stores and hardware stores. Since your clients need mowers for their customers in the spring, you forecast sales of 50,000 mowers in February and March. Your customers typically pay in 30 days. That means that the February and March sales are paid in March and April, respectively.

As a manager, you need to plan for heavy spending on materials and labor in December and January to produce mowers for February and March. You also need to plan the cash needed to meet the heavy production schedule. That's how a manager uses the business cycle to plan production, sales, and cash management.

Deciding whether to extend credit

As an owner, you need to decide whether you'll extend credit to your customers. If you extend credit, you post accounts receivable for some sales. You need to estimate how quickly you can collect on receivables. After all, you need to recover cash so you can pay for needed cash outflows (inventory purchases, payroll, and so on).

One tool to measure how quickly you'll collect on receivables is to use *days sales in accounts receivable* (DSO). This formula tells you how many business days it will take to fully recover your receivable balance. The lower the number of days, the faster you can collect your receivables.

You can use DSO in several ways. One way is to put your client payments into groups. For example, suppose you own a lumber company. You estimate that 20 percent of your clients will take advantage of a discount you offer, which means that they pay in 10 days. The remaining 80 percent of your clients pay in 30 days. Here is the number of days sales in accounts receivable:

$$(20\% \times 10 \text{ days}) + (80\% \times 30 \text{ days}) = 2 + 24 = 26 \text{ days}$$

Your lumber company will receive all your accounts receivable in 26 days.

Another version of DSO uses this formula:

$$\text{DSO} = \frac{\text{Accounts receivable}}{\text{Credit sales}} \times \text{Number of days in period}$$

Whereas the first version simply uses days, this formula also uses dollar amounts. *Credit sales* are sales that aren't immediately paid in cash. The period used is typically a month or a year. *Accounts receivable* is the average balance for the period. You can compute the average by adding the beginning and ending accounts receivable balance for the period and dividing by 2.

Suppose that average accounts receivable for the month is $30,000. Credit sales total $200,000. Using a 30-day month (which you can assume for the BEC test, unless you're told otherwise), here is the DSO calculation:

$$\frac{\$30,000}{\$200,000} \times 30 \text{ days} = 4.5 \text{ days}$$

You will collect your receivables in 4.5 days. Consider that the rate of daily sales is ($200,000 ÷ 30 days = $6,667). If you multiply $6,667 daily sales by 4.5 days, you get the $30,000 receivable balance, with rounding.

The BEC text may ask you about accounting terms used for granting discounts. These terms are included on invoices sent to clients. The most frequently tested term, "2/10 net 30," tells the customer that he can take a 2 percent discount if he pays the invoice within 10 days. If the customer owes $100 and pays within 10 days, he pays only $100 × 98% = $98. If the client doesn't take advantage of the discount, the full invoice amount is due within 30 days.

Based on the days sales in accounts receivable calculation, a business owner can make decisions about offering discounts and whether to continue offering purchases on credit. Offering discounts may speed up collections. If clients are paying receivables too slowly, the owner may offer sales on credit to fewer customers or end credit sales altogether.

Pricing a special order

Many businesses have to make decisions about pricing special orders. A *special order* is a customer order that is unexpected, typically an order placed at the end of an accounting period (month or year). Keep these tips in mind regarding special orders:

> ✔ **Fixed costs of production:** A special order assumes that all your fixed costs for the month have been paid for with production that has already occurred. That's why you should think of a special order as an unexpected order at the end of the month. You've already handled your "normal" or "expected" sales activity. As a result, the fixed costs from production aren't included in your decision about accepting a special order. Said another way, you exclude fixed costs when you're considering a price for your product.

> ✔ **Idle capacity:** Special orders assume that you have excess (available) capacity to process the order. Specifically, you have available labor hours or machine time to fill the special order.
>
> ✔ **Incremental revenue and incremental cost:** *Incremental revenue* is the additional revenue you get by selling one unit. The extra cost you incur by producing another unit of product is *incremental cost*.

Suppose you normally sell a shirt for $60. In the last week of the month, a supplier asks you whether you can fill an order for 2,000 shirts at a price of $42. Your fixed costs are $20 per shirt. Each shirt includes variable costs (cotton, thread, labor costs for assembly) of $30. Normally, your profit calculation is

$60 sale price – $20 fixed costs – $30 variable costs = $10 profit

For this special order, you exclude the $20 in fixed costs per shirt. If you sell the shirt at a sale price of $42, here's your profit calculation:

$42 sale price – $0 fixed costs – $30 variable costs = $12 profit

The special order actually produces a higher profit per shirt ($12 versus $10). Your incremental revenue for selling one shirt is $42, and your incremental cost (variable cost) is $30.

Opportunity cost is the income you earn by choosing an alternative use of a resource. If you select choice A, you're giving up income generated by choice B. The income you give up is a cost to you. Suppose that two vendors, Acme and Standard, each wanted 5,000 shirts produced in the last week of the month. You have capacity to fill only one of the special orders. If you fill the order for Acme, you have an opportunity cost for the income you didn't make by filling the order for Standard.

A *transfer price* is the price that one company division would charge another company division for a product or service. Suppose that the wedding planning division asks the dress shirts division for a price quote on white dress shirts. Accounting standards state that if the dress shirts division is operating at full capacity and selling all of its production, the shirts should be sold to the wedding planning division at the full retail price.

The transfer price issue relates to opportunity cost. Suppose the dress shirt division sells shirts to third-party customers at $70 per shirt. If its sells shirts to the other division at a lower price of $50, the dress shirt division gives up $20 per shirt as an opportunity cost. Because the dress shirt division is selling everything it produces, it will demand $70 per shirt from anyone — including another company division.

Mulling over outsourcing

Outsourcing is the decision to assign a task to an outside company instead of performing the task yourself. This is an important management decision, one that nearly every manager will face. As a result, it's frequently covered on the BEC test.

The decision to outsource is not simply about saving on costs. Managers need to consider the non-economic factors if they decide to move a task to an outside company. Take a look at these factors:

> ✔ **Quality:** Outsourcing can work if the outside firm provides the same level of quality. Say, for instance, you make baseball gloves. You decide to outsource the process of cutting the leather for each glove. The outside company ships the cut leather pieces to

your firm so that the gloves can be sewn. Suppose that, when you cut the leather in-house, you lose 2.5 percent of the leather to production errors. If the error rate incurred by the outside company is the same, outsourcing makes sense. If, instead, the other firm has a much higher error rate, you'll pay additional costs for more leather. The outsourcing may actually be more expensive. Check out the section "Including spoilage costs and quality costs" for more on these issues.

✔ **Timeliness:** If you outsource the leather cutting process, the outside company must be able to provide the completed product to your firm so you can continue production. If production has to stop because the leather cutting isn't complete, you'll incur unnecessary costs. Outsourcing may be more expensive.

✔ **Customer satisfaction:** Outsourcing can be successful if your clients are satisfied with your product or service. Customer satisfaction is similar to quality. It's all about whether or not the clients are happy with what they purchase. Many companies, for example, started outsourcing customer service call centers years ago. These companies found that labor was far cheaper overseas, so they trained and outsourced the call center function. In some cases, customer satisfaction declined so much that companies decided to pay higher costs to staff call centers in the U.S. Firms made the decision to cancel the outsourcing to avoid losing customers.

Each of these components has an impact on the decision to outsource.

Reviewing the use of capital

The BEC test covers business decisions about the use of capital. *Capital* represents the financial resources you have available for use. Companies raise capital to run their businesses in two ways. First, a company can issue stock. An investor receives common stock in exchange for capital (cash and other assets) the company puts into the business. A company can also raise capital by issuing debt, like a corporate bond. A creditor invests capital — normally cash in the business — in exchange for a bond. Chapter 8 discusses bonds in depth.

The combination of stock and debt issued to raise capital is referred to as the company's *capital structure*. One factor that determines capital structure is the firm's ability to generate earnings. A company with steady profits can afford to make principal and interest payments on debt each year. A lender would be more likely to lend to a company with a history of generating predictable earnings. These types of companies, such as a utility company, may issue more debt than equity to raise capital.

Other firms may not always be profitable year to year but may offer an opportunity for future growth. These firms will attract more equity investors. They issue more equity than debt. The BEC test may ask you to identify which types of firms are more likely to issue debt or equity.

Financing for the short term

In addition to the company's method of raising capital (stock or debt), businesses need to consider the timeframe for their capital needs. Working capital is a tool to assess short-term financing needs.

Working capital (see Chapter 4) is defined as current assets less current liabilities. It lets you calculate whether you have enough in assets to pay your liabilities over the next year:

✔ **Current assets:** Current assets include cash and assets that should be converted into cash within a year. *Accounts receivable,* which are payments you should receive in the next 12 months, are current assets. Inventory is also considered a current asset, because you expect to sell inventory and collect cash within a year.

✔ **Current liabilities:** Current liabilities include accounts payable and the current portion of long-term debt. The current portion represents principal and interest due on the debt within the next year.

Ideally, you want enough current assets to pay all your current liabilities. If current assets are less than current liabilities, you need to consider raising additional capital.

Using cost of capital for long-term financing

Companies also make decisions about long-term financing needs. This includes planning for major purchases of assets, such as buildings and equipment, in future years. When planning for long-term financing, a company needs to consider the *cost of capital*.

One type of cost of capital is the interest rate charged on long-term debt. Another type is the expected or required rate of return from an equity investor. A stock investor may insist on a dollar amount of return, in terms of a dividend payment. *Dividends* are payments of earnings to a shareholder.

Suppose that a company is planning to raise $100,000. Issuing long-term debt with a 7 percent interest rate will raise $50,000 in capital. The company will raise the other $50,000 by issuing common stock with a required dividend payment of 7 percent of the original dollars invested reach year.

Companies that issue debt are subject to *interest rate risk*. If banks and other financial institutions raise the interest rates paid on their debt, corporations often have to raise their interest rate to compete for investors. If the interest rate paid on long-term debt issued by similar companies goes up, your business will have to offer that new, higher interest rate — or risk not being able to sell debt to investors.

Suppose that your firm plans to issue a 5-year corporate bond at a 7 percent interest rate. Before you issue your bond, interest rates rise. Your competitors start paying 8 percent on debt with the same 5-year maturity date. If you don't increase the interest rate on your debt to 8 percent, you may not attract the investors you need.

Raising capital under these terms makes sense only if the rate of return on the invested capital is greater than the cost of capital — that is, 7 percent. Suppose that the company invests the $100,000 in a new machine that's more efficient than an old one. Based on the machine's ability to manufacture more product and the lower repair and maintenance cost, management determines that net income will increase 9 percent. In this scenario, paying a 7 percent cost of capital makes sense.

One measure of rate of return on an equity investment is *economic rate of return*. Here's the formula:

$$\text{Economic rate of return} = \frac{\text{Dividends paid} + \text{Change in stock price}}{\text{Beginning price of stock}}$$

Suppose you buy a stock at $50 per share. During the year, the stock pays $4 a share in dividends. The stock price increases from $50 to $56 dollars a share — a $6 increase per share. Here is your economic rate of return:

$$\text{Economic rate of return} = \frac{\$4 \text{ dividends paid} + \$6 \text{ stock price change}}{\$50 \text{ beginning price of stock}}$$

$$= \frac{\$10}{\$50} = 20\%$$

Your rate of return from both the dividends and price appreciation is 20 percent.

An investor may judge the value of an investment by discounting the cash flows to be received by a present-value factor for the cash flows. That calculation tells the investor what the future cash flows are worth today. Judging from the present value, the investor can decide whether the investment is attractive, compared with other investment options.

Here are two investments and their cash flows:

- An investor buys a $1,000, 10-year, 8 percent bond. A bond has two cash flows. One cash flow is the return of principal of $1,000 at the end of 10 years. The second cash flow is the annual interest payments of $1,000 × 8% = $80. Note that the return of principal is a single payment, while the interest payments are a series of cash flows. An *annuity* is a series of cash flows, each with the same dollar amount.

- An investor buys 100 shares of common stock. Each share pays $3 in dividends per year, or $300 total cash flow per year.

In either case, you can multiply a particular payment by a present-value factor. You can easily find the factor tables on the web. An investor needs to select a *discount rate* to use as the factor. That's the rate at which the payments are discounted. Here are two common methods for choosing the discount rate:

- **Expected rate of inflation:** The discount rate may be the rate of inflation expected during the period the dollars are invested. *Inflation* is defined as the overall increase in retail prices over time. As prices increase, the purchasing power of a dollar declines. Using the expected rate of inflation as the discount rate adjusts the cash flow for the impact of inflation.

- **Expected rate of return:** Suppose you don't want to invest in any investment unless it produces a 10 percent rate of return or higher. If you discount the payments at 10 percent and if the present value of the sum of the cash flows is greater than zero, the investment's rate of return is greater than 10 percent.

Here are two discounted cash flow calculations for the stock investment, using the $300 in annual cash flows in the earlier example. Suppose the stock investment is held for 5 years. The present-value factors are rounded:

- 8 percent, 5 years, present-value factor 0.6806: $300 × 0.6806 = $204.18

- 10 percent, 5 years, present-value factor 0.6209: $300 × 0.6209 = $186.27

Notice that the higher discount rate (10 percent) generates a lower cash value ($186.27 versus $208.18). Keep that relationship in mind: The higher the discount rate, the lower the present value of the cash flows. Note also that this is only dividend income. The calculation ignores an increase in the stock price and selling the stock for a gain. Because the gain in the stock price is less certain, you exclude a gain on stock sale from the cash flow analysis.

Discounting cash flows to a present value is a common way to evaluate a long-term capital investment. A company looking to raise capital may want to perform this analysis to see what a potential investor may also review.

Deflation is an overall decrease in prices over time. This situation doesn't happen very often, but it's a concept you should know for the BEC test. While inflation pushes up the costs a company incurs to make a product, deflation reduces those costs. If your sales price isn't changed, inflation will increase a company's costs and reduce profit. Deflation, on the other hand, will reduce company costs and increase profit.

One other way to consider cash flows is to compute payback period. *Payback period* tells you how quickly you'll recover your original cash investment. The annual cash flows generated by the resource in which you invest pay back your original investment over time. Payback period doesn't adjust cash flows to their present value. For that reason, this formula is considered a less precise tool for evaluating an investment. Here's the formula:

$$\text{Payback period} = \frac{\text{Initial investment}}{\text{Annual cash flows}}$$

If, for example, you bought a $50,000 machine that generated $10,000 in annual cash flows, your payback period is $50,000 ÷ $10,000/year = 5 years.

Comparing net present value (NPV) and internal rate of return (IRR)

You need to know two calculations that use the present value of cash flows. The first, *net present value* (NPV), is the sum of all a project's cash inflows and outflows, all of which are discounted to present value. If the sum of the inflows and outflows is a positive number, then NPV states that you should proceed with the project.

NPV assumes that the cash inflows generated are reinvested at the cost of capital rate. On the BEC test, you may be provided with a discount rate rather than a cost of capital rate. Both terms refer to the rate at which the cash flows should be discounted. If your cost of capital is 7 percent, NPV assumes that each year's cash inflows earn the 7 percent rate of return.

Suppose you purchase a $40,000 machine. You expect the machine to produce cash inflows of $7,000 each year for 8 years. You decide to use a discount rate of 6 percent. Here's how to calculate NPV:

✔ The $40,000 cash outflow is supposed to occur at the beginning of the first year. As a result, the $40,000 is already stated at its present value.

✔ The annual $7,000 is a cash inflow earned each year for 8 years. Assuming the cash inflow happens at the end of each year, the present-value factor of the ordinary annuity at 6 percent is 6.21 (rounded). (You can find present-value factor tables online.) $7,000 multiplied by the 6.21 present-value factor is $43,470.

✔ Because the present value of the cash inflows is greater than the cash outflow ($43,470 – $40,000 = $3,470), you should proceed with the project, using NPV analysis.

Internal rate of return is a slightly different formula for cash inflows and outflows. *Internal rate of return* (IRR) is the interest rate at which all the cash inflows and outflows add up to zero. With IRR, you're solving for an interest rate. Note that the BEC test may use *interest rate* or *discount rate* to mean the same thing.

You can find calculators on the web that allow you to input cash inflows and outflows to generate the IRR. The important point for the BEC test is that if the IRR of a project is greater than your company's required rate of return, you should proceed with the project. IRR supposes that the cash inflows are reinvested at the IRR rate of return.

Assessing Information Systems

All CPAs work closely with technology. The BEC test covers the concepts an accountant uses to assess IT needs and decide on spending. Technology may be one of the largest costs your company incurs.

In this section, I discuss technology spending and IT security. As technology becomes more complex, companies process and store an increasing amount of data. You'll consider the steps a CPA takes to protect company data from theft.

Deciding on computer technology needs

New technology — or improving existing technology — often requires additional spending. To make an informed decision on a technology need, consider the amount of additional revenue the technology will help you generate.

Suppose you own a catering business. To staff your catering jobs, you e-mail from your list of part-time employees and track the catering jobs they work in an Excel document. You determine that an automated system of staffing would save time, allowing you to grow your catering sales by 10 percent. If the cost of the automated system is less than the profit from a 10 percent increase in sales, investing in the technology makes economic sense.

The BEC test may have you assess technology spending by considering cost savings. Consider the same catering example. Suppose the owner is paying a part-time employee $10,000 a year to handle staffing. If an automated system can handle staffing, the part-time staffing employee can perform catering jobs instead. The former staffing person now works on revenue-producing catering work. If the automated system costs less than $10,000, buying the new technology makes sense.

Every firm needs a *disaster recovery plan* for their IT department. This topic is presented on nearly every BEC test. In the event of a disaster (flood, tornado, power outage), a business needs a written plan to "restart" their technology operations. Traditionally, disaster recovery meant having equipment (computers, servers, phones) at a separate location. If a disaster occurs, the IT department simply moves to the other location and operates from there.

Technology now allows companies to set up disaster recovery through *cloud computing*. Cloud computing means that all of the company's data is continually backed up on servers at another location. A firm may have an internal department provide this process, or hire an outside firm. If a disaster occurs, the IT department can access and use the company data that is backed up on the cloud.

Weighing IT security

All businesses need to set up controls to prevent sensitive computer data from being lost or stolen. Customers, regulators, and company shareholders all insist on IT security. Loss or theft of computer information can result in upset customers, loss of business, and possible legal issues.

Segregation of duties is a critical internal control used to reduce the risk of theft. (See the earlier section "Segregating duties to reduce risk.") Whenever possible, these three IT duties should be divided among different people:

- **Programming:** IT staff that is writing code and creating programs to solve business problems

- **Operating:** Workers using IT tools (hardware and software) to run the day-to-day business operations

- **Library:** The database administrator or librarian, who maintains, adds, updates, and files all the records for the company.

Suppose, for example, that you manage a trucking company. You have a dispatching department that sends trucks to their destinations and monitors shipments. The programming department wrote a software application for the dispatching process. If the programmers had access to the IT activity in the dispatching (operations) department, they could potentially manipulate the process. A programmer, for example, could send trucks to destinations that the programmer personally controls. The programmer could bypass the billing process so that shipments she controls are never billed.

When you see a BEC test question on IT security, consider the impact of a lack of segregation of duties.

Strategic Planning

Strategic planning is the critical process of gathering data to plan your company's direction. Planning involves budgeting, which you'll likely see on the BEC test. Nearly all firms plan costs, levels of production and sales, as well as prices. At the end of a month or year, companies compare budgeted amounts to actual results. This process is called *variance analysis*. Firms review variances to make changes and improve profit.

An increasing number of companies use a balanced scorecard to evaluate company performance. This tool considers both financial and nonfinancial measurements, which businesses find valuable. A company's strategy includes nonfinancial measurements, like customer satisfaction and product quality. These issues are discussed in this section.

Cause and effect: Managing with balanced scorecards

A *balanced scorecard* is a strategic planning tool that aligns business performance with a company's vision and goals. The scorecard is considered *balanced* because it includes both financial and nonfinancial measurements. Nonfinancial measurements may include the number of incoming customer calls or the average time to resolve a client complaint.

Balanced scorecards are often communicated using a *strategy map*, which displays cause-and-effect relationships in the form of a graph or chart. The elements of your strategy (causes) connect to the results your business achieves (effects).

Suppose that you manage a warehouse that supplies auto parts to repair shops in your city. You implement a strategy to lower prices on all your products by 10 percent. The lower-price strategy results in increased sales. In this example, the price cut is a cause, and the increased sales are an effect.

Plans versus results: Budgeting with variance analysis

Proper planning requires that your firm have a formal budgeting process. That means that you have a process for implementing a budget: You gather information from all company departments and put together budgets that management discusses and approves. Part of the budgeting process is to plan your costs and levels of production and sales. Finally, you review your actual results and compare them with your budget.

A *variance* is defined as a difference between budgeted and actual results. Companies review variances related to costs and those tied to sales:

✔ **Favorable variance:** A favorable variance means that actual costs are lower than planned or that actual sales are higher than planned. You see that a favorable variance increases profit, either with lower costs or higher sales.

✔ **Unfavorable variance:** An unfavorable variance means that actual costs are higher than planned or that actual sales were lower than planned. An unfavorable variance decreases profit, either with higher costs or lower sales.

The BEC test may have you calculate material and labor variances. This section provides an example of a material variance.

To generate a budget, accountants compute standards. For example, if you manufacture wooden doors, you plan your budget by computing a standard price for the wood you purchase and a standard amount of wood per door. Suppose you budget a 60-inch square piece of wood to manufacture a door, and the material has a cost of $20. Here are two possible variances from your budgeting plans:

✔ **Material price variance:** You pay more or less for the wood.

✔ **Material usage (or efficiency) variance:** You use more or less wood than you planned.

On a basic level, you have a variance because you paid more or less than planned or you used more or less than planned.

If your actual use of wood is the same as your budgeted amount, you don't have a material usage variance. Suppose, however, that your actual cost is $23 per door. You have an unfavorable price variance because you paid more than you planned.

To study this topic, memorize the formulas to compute material and labor variances; you can find them easily on the web. You'll find price and usage variances for material and price and usage variance for labor.

Operating the Business and Related Accounting Issues

The BEC test covers a variety of ratios and formulas that people use to judge company performance. This section covers the issue of incentive compensation as a tool to reward employees. It also goes over a variety of tools to measure cost and evaluate spending decisions.

Going over ratios to measure performance

Every business needs tools to analyze its performance. One type of tool is financial ratios. A manager can calculate these ratios periodically to get a sense of how the company is performing. (See the earlier section "Deciding whether to extend credit" for financial ratios related to liquidity and solvency, such as the days sales in accounts receivables ratio.)

Can you pay me back? Times interest earned ratio

One useful ratio is *times interest earned,* which indicates the amount of earnings available to make interest payments on debt:

$$\text{Times interest earned ratio} = \frac{\text{Earnings before interest expense and taxes}}{\text{Interest expense on debt}}$$

If a plumbing company has $200,000 in earnings and incurred $50,000 in interest expense, for example, the times interest earned ratio would be $200,000 ÷ $50,000 = 4 times. If you're a banker considering a loan to this company, you see that the plumbing firm earns four times the amount of money it needs to pay interest on its current debt. That ratio would be a part of your decision process for approving a new loan.

Companies with predictable sales and earnings, such as electric utility companies, are more likely to carry more debt as a part of their capitalization. See the earlier section "Reviewing the use of capital" for a discussion of the types of companies that can afford to make debt payments.

How do you raise money? Total debt to total assets ratio

The combination of stock and debt issued to raise capital is referred to as the company's *capital structure.* A useful ratio to explain capital structure is the *total debt to total assets ratio.* As the name implies, you simply divide total debt by total assets:

$$\text{Total debt to total assets ratio} = \frac{\text{Total debt}}{\text{Total assets}}$$

You can find total debt and total assets in the balance sheet. This ratio explains how a company raises money to run its business.

Suppose a utility company has $50 million in debt and $20 million on common stock outstanding. The debt to assets ratio is $50 million ÷ $20 million, or 2.5 to 1. For every dollar of common stock outstanding, the utility has 2.5 dollars of debt. Investment analysts often compare a company's ratios to those of other companies in the same industry.

How efficiently are you using your assets? Asset turnover ratio

Another ratio calculates *asset utilization,* or how efficiently you use the assets you purchase. The *asset turnover ratio* tells you how much you generate for every dollar in assets:

$$\text{Asset turnover ratio} = \frac{\text{Sales generated by the assets}}{\text{Value of the assets}}$$

The more dollars in sales you generate for every dollar in assets, the more effectively you're using your assets. If you use assets effectively, you can minimize the dollars you need to invest in assets.

Suppose a plumbing company uses a $30,000 truck that's equipped with $10,000 in equipment. The truck and its equipment are *assets,* which are defined as resources used to make money. If the truck is used to generate $120,000 in sales in a year, the assets have "turned over" 3 times ($120,000 sales ÷ $40,000 assets). For every dollar in assets, the plumbing company generated $3 in sales.

The concept of *just-in-time (JIT) inventory management* may show up on your BEC test. By implementing JIT, companies receive goods (raw materials or component parts) only when they are needed for production. This method minimizes the dollars invested in inventory, because goods are received and immediately moved into production.

JIT requires that a manager carefully plan exactly when goods are needed in production. If the production area runs out of goods, production may have to stop. The company will incur many costs (labor costs, costs to operate a factory) while waiting for goods to show up. JIT reduces costs but requires careful planning.

Aligning goals with incentives: The impact of incentive compensation

Corporate governance refers to the company systems and practices that are put in place to direct and control the company. One aspect of corporate governance is incentive compensation. *Incentive compensation* is a type of reward program based on a performance measurement, such as company-wide profits, profits of a specific division or department, expense savings, or sales growth.

From a corporate governance point of view, the goal of incentive compensation is to ensure that the performance measurement is aligned with company goals. If it is, the employee will be rewarded for helping the company achieve an objective (higher profits, cost savings, or increased sales). If the two aren't aligned, the worker's incentive won't help the company reach its goals. In fact, the employee may end up working against company objectives.

A BEC test question may give you a scenario and then ask you whether the incentive compensation is aligned with company goals. For example, suppose that a company sells truck tires. The sales staff is provided incentive compensation based on gross sales. Company profit, on the other hand, is calculated based on net sales. The business deducts sales returns, discounts, and bad debt from gross sales to arrive at net sales. If tires are returned — or if clients don't pay for sales — gross sales are reduced to arrive at net sales.

In this case, the incentive compensation isn't aligned with company goals. Salespeople are motivated to sell tires, regardless of whether a client will return the goods or won't pay for them. As a result, gross sales may be much higher than net sales. The incentive compensation should reward salespeople for net sales, not gross sales.

Measuring costs

To effectively manage your business operations, you need a system to measure your costs. *Measuring costs* is the process of collecting all the costs incurred to make a product or service. You need to know the total cost in order to price a product:

Total cost + Profit margin = Sale price

Suppose you manufacture baseball bats, and you measure your total costs as $200. You want to earn a 15 percent profit above your costs. To calculate a sale price, you multiply $200 total cost × 15% = $30. Thirty dollars is your *profit margin*. Your sale price will be

$200 total cost + $30 profit margin = $230 sale price

Measure and collect all the costs of running your business and assign them to a product or service. That includes costs that aren't directly related to the production of your product. If a company doesn't assign all costs to a product, total company profit will be less than planned. Put another way, you need to recover all the costs you incur to run the business. You recover costs by collecting cash from sales.

Going over types of costs

To capture all your costs, you need to know how costs are categorized. Understanding these categories will help you identify all the costs incurred to run your business.

As a starting point, you can take the four terms defined below and pair them up. Generally, costs are either direct or indirect. Consider those terms together. The same cost can also be classified as either a product cost or a period cost. The BEC test often provides a list of costs for you to analyze. The test asks the student to classify costs as either direct or indirect. After that classification, the student determines whether the cost is a product or period cost.

✔ **Direct costs:** Direct costs can be directly traced to the product or service. If you make shoes, for example, the raw materials (leather) and labor costs to make shoes are direct costs. You can compute the specific amount of leather material used in each shoe and the labor time required to make a shoe.

✔ **Indirect costs:** Indirect costs can't be directly traced to a product or service. Instead, these costs are allocated, based on some activity level. Suppose you incur costs to repair and maintain machines used to make shoes. You can't trace the cost of repairs to a specific pair of shoes. So instead, you assign repair costs based on the number of hours the machine is used. Indirect costs are also referred to as *overhead costs*. To find out more, check out the later section "Applying overhead costs."

✔ **Product costs:** Product costs, like direct costs, are directly related to production. Material and labor costs are product costs. These costs also change with a company's level of sales and production. Nearly all costs can be classified as either a product cost or a period cost.

✔ **Period costs:** These costs are incurred due to the passage of time. For example, interest costs on debt, rental expense, and insurance cost are period costs. Most automated accounting systems allow an accountant to set up monthly reminders to post entries. Period costs need to be posted each month, so an accounting system can include these entries in the automated reminder list. When another month goes by, an accountant posts these expenses. Period costs do not change with the level of company sales or production.

Including spoilage costs and quality costs

Spoilage costs may be less apparent than other costs you measure, but they need to be a part of your planning process. *Spoilage costs* represent waste, scrap, and other costs that can't be directly applied to your product during production.

Suppose you make men's dress shoes. Leather is a big component for each shoe. Obviously, you can't use every square inch of leather you purchase for shoe production. Some leather will be scrapped after a piece of leather is cut for a shoe. That type of cost is referred to as *normal spoilage*. Normal spoilage is unavoidable and is part of the normal production process.

Abnormal spoilage, on the other hand, is avoidable. If, for example, a poorly trained employee runs leather through a machine incorrectly and the leather can't be used, that's an abnormal spoilage cost. The leather run through the machine isn't used to produce a good that can be sold.

The spoilage concept moves you to a discussion of quality costs. To ensure that you produce a quality product, you may incur some of these costs:

✔ **Prevention costs:** These costs are incurred to avoid or minimize defective products. The cost of training employees in the production process is a prevention cost.

✔ **Appraisal (inspection) costs:** This is the cost of identifying defective products before they're shipped to a customer. Everyone buys products, such as clothing, that have a tag stating that the good was inspected.

✔ **Internal failure costs:** These costs are incurred to fix a product that's found to be defective before it's shipped to a client. Internal failure costs include *rework costs,* which is the cost to fix a defective product so that it can be sold to a customer.

✔ **External failure costs:** External failure costs are costs to fix a defective product after the product is in the customer's hands. Companies want to avoid this quality cost the most, because the customer may not want to do business again after dealing with a defective product.

Often, companies offer a warranty. A *warranty* is a period of time during which the company will fix or replace a defective product at no cost to the customer. Repair costs related to a warranty are external failure costs.

Quality costs are incurred so that a company can deliver quality products to customers.

Applying overhead costs

Indirect costs are also defined as *overhead costs*. Because overhead costs can't be directly traced to a product or service, the costs are allocated. Costs are allocated based on a level of activity, typically machine hours or labor hours. The activity should have an impact on the cost incurred. Machine hours, for example, are a reasonable activity measure to allocate machine costs.

During a budgeting (planning) meeting, a manufacturer will compute a *predetermined overhead rate*. The manager will consider an overhead cost, such as repair and maintenance on machines. That cost will be allocated based on some level of activity that relates to machine use, such as machine hours (how many hours the machine is expected to run during the year). Cost is divided by the activity level to compute an overhead rate per hour. That rate is used to allocate the overhead cost to each product.

Here's how to calculate the predetermined overhead rate:

$$\text{Predetermined overhead rate} = \frac{\text{Overhead cost}}{\text{Estimated activity level}}$$

Suppose you manufacture garden equipment. You use a machine to produce a shovel. As with any machine, you incur repair and maintenance costs. The costs can't be directly traced to each shovel you produce, so you decide to assign costs based on machine hours.

Suppose the machine is used for about 1,000 hours per year, and the annual repair cost is $2,000. It's a fixed cost, based on a contract you sign with a repair company. That means that the repair cost per hour is $2,000 ÷ 1,000 hours = $2 per hour. If making a shovel takes 15 minutes (or a quarter of an hour) of machine time, you'd assign $2.00 ÷ 4 = $0.50 = 50 cents of indirect machine costs to each shovel. The $0.50 per shovel is the predetermined overhead rate.

Note that the machine hours are an estimate. A company calculates overhead rates during the budgeting process at the beginning of the year. Part of that process involves estimating levels of production and sales for the year. Based on the production estimate, you can estimate your machine use.

Keep in mind that the overhead cost can be variable rather than fixed. The repair company could charge an hourly rate for repairing the machine rather than a fixed contract rate. In that case, you'd estimate the number of repair hours needed for the machine and then multiply the number of hours by the repair cost per hour.

Say, for example, that you estimate 60 hours of repair hours per year at a quoted repair cost of $30 per hour. Your overhead cost would be 60 hours × $30 per hour = $1,800. That overhead cost would be divided by machine hours: $1,800 ÷ 1,000 hours = $1.80 per hour.

Allocating costs between departments

Some departments in your business are *service departments*. They exist to support the activities of production departments (the departments that produce your products and services). Accounting, legal, and human resources departments are good examples of service departments. To calculate your total costs, you need to fully allocate service department costs to production departments. Then you can allocate the full costs to your product.

The BEC test may include questions on the *direct method of cost allocation* between departments. This method doesn't allocate costs between service departments. As the name implies, all costs are allocated directly to production departments.

Here's an example of the direct method. Suppose you manufacture windows. You have two major production departments: a glass department and a wood frame department. You're assigning the costs of two service departments: human resources and accounting. The accounting department estimates that their time and expenses are allocated to other departments based on these percentages:

Human resources department: 10 percent

Glass department: 45 percent

Wood frame department: 45 percent

The accounting department's total costs are $100,000. Here's the process you use to allocate the accounting department costs, using the direct method:

1. **Eliminate the percentage of time assigned to any service department.**

   Subtract the percentage from 100 percent. The allocation to the human resources department is 10 percent, and 100% – 10% = 90%. The accounting costs allocation to production departments is 90 percent of the total.

2. **Divide each of the production department percentages by the adjusted new total percentage calculated in Step 1.**

   The glass department is 45 ÷ 90 = 50%. The wood frame department is also 45 ÷ 90 = 50%.

3. **Multiply the service department cost (accounting department) to be allocated by the percentages in Step 2.**

   The glass department is $100,000 × 50% = $50,000. The wood frame department is also $100,000 × 50% = $50,000. The entire $100,000 is now allocated to the two production departments.

Working with joint costs

Joint costs are incurred when the same costs are used to produce more than one product. During joint production, the products being produced can't be distinguished from each other. When each product can be identified in production, accountants refer to that point as the *split-off point*. A product may incur costs after split-off, called *separable costs*. These costs can be assigned to production of one specific product.

Accountants use methods to allocate joint costs to individual products. One method on the BEC test is the *net realizable value* (NRV) method. The NRV method assigns costs based on the product's sales value less separable costs.

Suppose you manufacture two mountain bikes: the Rugged model and the Mountain View model. In your latest production run, you incurred $10,000 in joint costs to produce both bikes. Here are the steps to allocate the joint costs to each of the bikes:

1. **Compute the sales value of each bike.**

   This amount is the total sale proceeds you receive when each bike is sold. Suppose that Rugged sales proceeds are $40,000 and Mountain View sale proceeds are $30,000.

2. **Calculate the separable costs for each product.**

   Rugged separable costs are $28,000, and Mountain View separable costs are $15,000.

3. **Subtract separable costs from sales to compute net realizable value (NRV).**

   Rugged NRV is $40,000 sales proceeds – $28,000 separable costs = $12,000. Mountain View NRV is $30,000 – $15,000 = $15,000. Total NRV for both bikes is $12,000 + $15,000 = $27,000.

4. **Calculate each bike's percentage of total NRV.**

   Rugged's percentage is $12,000 ÷ $27,000 = 0.44 = 44%. Mountain View's percentage is $15,000 ÷ $27,000 = 0.56 = 56%. Note that the two percentages, 44 percent and 56 percent, add up to 100 percent.

5. **Multiply the NRV percentages by the $10,000 in joint costs to allocate those costs.**

   Rugged's joint cost allocation is 44% × $10,000 = $4,400. Mountain View's joint cost allocation is 56% × $10,000 = $5,600. To check your work, verify that the two allocations add up to the $10,000 total, which is true here.

Now that you've assigned the joint costs, you can add in the separable costs to calculate the total cost of each product:

Rugged total cost: $28,000 separable costs + $4,400 joint costs = $32,400

Mountain View total cost: $15,000 separable costs + $5,600 joint costs = $20,600

In some cases, joint production also generates a byproduct. A *byproduct* is simply a product that's produced during the production of another product; it isn't the primary reason the goods are produced. This product is just something extra. Using the NRV method for joint costs, any net realizable value from the sale of a byproduct is used to reduce the joint cost total.

Suppose that while producing mountain bikes, you produce some aluminum tubing that isn't used for the bike frames. If you were able to sell the aluminum tubing as a byproduct, the sales proceeds would reduce your total joint costs.

Chapter 6

Business Environment and Concepts Practice Questions

● ●

The business environment and concepts (BEC) test covers many topics that students learn in an undergraduate business curriculum. The BEC test covers economics and business decision tools. You'll also see questions on using technology and on IT security issues. As you take the BEC test, approach the questions from a business manager's point of view.

Corporate Governance

1. From a corporate governance standpoint, which of the following best describes the main goal of a form of executive compensation?

   (A) Adequately compensate executives.

   (B) Align the incentives of executives with those of the corporate shareholders.

   (C) Motivate management to engage in activities that have the prospect of maximizing corporate profits.

   (D) Keep management from shirking.

2. The COSO definition of internal control considers control activities a(n)

   (A) Component of internal control.

   (B) Control objective.

   (C) Element of the control environment.

   (D) Portion of information and communication.

3. If internal control is properly designed, the same employee should **not** be permitted to

   (A) Sign checks and cancel supporting documents.

   (B) Receive merchandise and prepare a receiving report.

   (C) Prepare disbursement vouchers and sign checks.

   (D) Initiate a request to order merchandise and approve merchandise received.

4. A director of Riley Corporation is made aware of an opportunity that would be advantageous and of interest to the corporation. Which of the following represents his best course of action?

   (A) Reject the opportunity for both himself and Riley Corporation.

   (B) Accept the opportunity on behalf of himself if there is no conflict of interest.

   (C) Bring the opportunity to Riley Corporation.

   (D) Accept the opportunity on behalf of Riley Corporation.

Cost Measurement and Assignment

5. For a manufacturing company, which of the following is an example of a period cost rather than a product cost?

   (A) Depreciation on factory equipment.

   (B) Wages of salespersons.

   (C) Wages of machine operators.

   (D) Insurance on factory equipment.

6. In developing a variable factory overhead application rate for use in a process costing system, which of the following could be used in the denominator?

   (A) Estimated direct manufacturing labor hours.

   (B) Actual direct manufacturing labor hours.

   (C) Estimated factory overhead.

   (D) Actual factory overhead.

7. Hartwell Company distributes service department overhead costs directly to producing departments without allocation to the other service department. Information for the month of January 2014 is as follows:

	Service Departments	
	Maintenance	Utilities
Overhead costs incurred	$18,700	$9,000
Service provided to:		
Maintenance department	—	10%
Utilities department	20%	—
Producing department A	40%	30%
Producing department B	40%	60%
Total	100%	100%

   The amount of utilities department costs distributed to producing department B for January 2014 should be

   (A) $3,600

   (B) $4,500

   (C) $5,400

   (D) $6,000

8. Lane Co. produces main products Kul and Wu. The process also yields byproduct Zef. Net realizable value of byproduct Zef is subtracted from joint production cost of Kul and Wu. The following information pertains to production in July 2014 at a joint cost of $54,000:

Product	Units Produced	Market Value	Additional Cost After Split-Off
Kul	1,000	$40,000	$0
Wu	1,500	$35,000	$0
Zef	500	$7,000	$3,000

If Lane uses the net realizable value method for allocating joint cost, how much of the joint cost should be allocated to product Kul?

(A) $18,800

(B) $20,000

(C) $26,667

(D) $27,342

Economics and Strategy

9. If the U.S. dollar declines in value relative to the currencies of many of its trading partners, the likely result is that

   (A) Foreign currencies will depreciate against the dollar.

   (B) The U.S. trade deficit will worsen.

   (C) U.S. exports will tend to increase.

   (D) U.S. imports will tend to increase.

10. Which of the following activities involves collecting data about all segments of the firm's general environment to understand the effects of economic changes on the firm's industry?

    (A) Monitoring.

    (B) Assessing.

    (C) Forecasting.

    (D) Scanning.

11. The law of diminishing marginal utility states that

    (A) Marginal utility will decline as a consumer acquires additional units of a specific product.

    (B) Total utility will decline as a consumer acquires additional units of a specific product.

    (C) Declining utilities cause the demand curve to slope upward.

    (D) Consumers' wants diminish with the passage of time.

12. Which of the following types of merger is most likely to contribute to the formation of an oligopoly?

    (A) Horizontal.

    (B) Conglomerate.

    (C) Divestiture.

    (D) Vertical.

Financial Management

13. Net working capital is the difference between

    (A) Current assets and current liabilities.

    (B) Fixed assets and fixed liabilities.

    (C) Total assets and total liabilities.

    (D) Shareholders' investment and cash.

14. The theory underlying the cost of capital is primarily concerned with the cost of

    (A) Long-term funds and old funds.

    (B) Short-term funds and new funds.

    (C) Long-term funds and new funds.

    (D) Any combination of old or new, short-term or long-term funds.

15. The market value of a firm's outstanding common shares will be higher, everything else equal, if

    (A) Investors have a lower required return on equity.

    (B) Investors expect lower dividend growth.

    (C) Investors have longer expected holding periods.

    (D) Investors have shorter expected holding periods.

16. Amicable Wireless, Inc., offers credit terms of 2/10, net 30 for its customers. Sixty percent of Amicable's customers take the 2% discount and pay on day 10. The remainder of Amicable's customers pay on day 30. How many days' sales are in Amicable's accounts receivable?

    (A) 6

    (B) 12

    (C) 18

    (D) 20

Information Technology

17. Which of the following most likely represents a significant deficiency in the internal control?

    (A) The systems analyst reviews applications of data processing and maintains systems documentation.

    (B) The systems programmer designs systems for computerized applications and maintains output controls.

    (C) The control clerk establishes control over data received by the information systems departments and reconciles totals after processing.

    (D) The accounts payable clerk prepares data for computer processing and enters the data into the computer.

18. Management of a financial services company is considering a strategic decision concerning the expansion of its existing local area network (LAN) to enhance the firm's customer service function. Which of the following aspects of the expanded system is the least significant strategic issue for management?

    (A) How the expanded system can contribute to the firm's long-range business plan.

    (B) How the expanded system would support daily business operations.

    (C) How indicators can be developed to measure how well the expanded system achieves its business objectives.

    (D) How the expanded system will contribute to the reduction of operating costs.

19. The ability to add or update documentation items in data dictionaries should be restricted to

    (A) Database administrators.

    (B) System programmers.

    (C) System librarians.

    (D) Accounting managers.

Performance Measures

20. A strategy map in the balanced scorecard framework is

    (A) A statement of what the strategy must achieve and what is critical to its success.

    (B) Key action programs required to achieve strategic objectives.

    (C) Diagrams of the cause-and-effect relationships between strategic objectives.

    (D) The level of performance or rate of improvement needed in the performance measure.

21. In the cost of quality, spoilage is an example of

    (A) Prevention costs.

    (B) Appraisal costs.

    (C) Internal failure costs.

    (D) External failure costs.

22. A company reports the following account balances at year-end:

Account	Balance
Long-term debt	$200,000
Cash	$50,000
Net sales	$600,000
Fixed assets (net)	$320,000
Tax expense	$67,500
Inventory	$25,000
Common stock	$100,000

(continued)

(continued)

Account	Balance
Interest expense	$20,000
Administrative expense	$35,000
Retained earnings	$150,000
Accounts payable	$65,000
Accounts receivable	$120,000
Cost of goods sold	$400,000
Depreciation expense	$10,000

Additional Information:

1. The opening balance of common stock was $100,000.

2. The opening balance of retained earnings was $82,500.

3. The company had $10,000 common shares outstanding all year.

4. No dividends were paid during the year.

For the year just ended, the company has times interest earned of

(A) 3.375 times.

(B) 6.75 times.

(C) 7.75 times.

(D) 9.5 times.

23. An organization has total asset turnover of 3.5 times and a total debt to total assets ratio of 70%. If the organization has total debt of $1,000,000, then it has a sales level of

(A) $5,000,000.00

(B) $2,450,000.00

(C) $408,163.26

(D) $200,000.00

Planning, Control, and Analysis

24. Lincoln Company, a glove manufacturer, has enough idle capacity available to accept a special order of 20,000 pairs of gloves at $12.00 a pair. The normal selling price is $20.00 a pair. Variable manufacturing costs are $9.00 a pair, and fixed manufacturing costs are $3.00 a pair. Lincoln will not incur any selling expenses as a result of the special order. What would be the effect on operating income if the special order could be accepted without affecting normal sales?

(A) No change.

(B) $60,000 increase.

(C) $180,000 increase.

(D) $240,000 increase.

25. Light Company has 2,000 obsolete light fixtures that are carried in inventory at a manufacturing cost of $30,000. If the fixtures are reworked for $10,000, they could be sold for $18,000. Alternately, the light fixtures could be sold for $3,000 to a jobber located in a distant city. In a decision model analyzing these alternatives, the opportunity cost would be

(A) $3,000

(B) $10,000

(C) $13,000

(D) $30,000

26. A company manufactures a product that has the direct material standard cost presented below. Budgeted and actual information for the current month for the manufacture of the finished product and the purchase and use of the direct material are also presented.

Standard cost for direct material:

    1.60 lb. @ $2.50 per lb. = $4.00

	Budget	Actual
Finished goods (in units)	$30,000	$32,000
Direct material usage (in pounds)	$48,000	$51,000
Direct material purchases (in pounds)	$48,000	$50,000
Total cost of direct material purchases	$120,000	$120,000

The direct material efficiency (usage) variance for the current month is

(A) $500 favorable.

(B) $3,000 favorable.

(C) $7,500 unfavorable.

(D) $8,000 unfavorable.

27. Spring Co. had two divisions, A and B. Division A created Product X, which could be sold on the outside market for $25 and used variable costs of $15. Division B could take Product X and apply additional variable costs of $40 to create Product Y, which could be sold for $100. Division B received a special order for a large amount of Product Y. If Division A were operating at full capacity, which of the following prices should Division A charge Division B for the Product X needed to fill the special order?

(A) $15

(B) $20

(C) $25

(D) $40

Risk Management

28. Which of the following is necessary in order to calculate the payback period for a project?

   (A) Useful life.

   (B) Minimum desired rate of return.

   (C) Net present value.

   (D) Annual cash flow.

29. Net present value (NPV) and internal rate of return (IRR) differ in that

   (A) NPV assumes reinvestment of project cash flows at the cost of capital, while IRR assumes reinvestment of project cash flows at the internal rate of return.

   (B) NPV and IRR make different accept-or-reject decisions for independent projects.

   (C) IRR can be used to rank mutually exclusive investment projects, but NPV cannot.

   (D) NPV is expressed as a percentage, while IRR is expressed as a dollar amount.

30. Which of the following formulas should be used to calculate the economic rate of return on common stock?

   (A) (Dividends + change in price) divided by beginning price.

   (B) (Net income – preferred dividend) divided by common shares outstanding.

   (C) Market price per share divided by earnings per share.

   (D) Dividends per share divided by market price per share.

Chapter 7

Answers to Business Environment and Concepts Practice Questions

. . . .

As you read through these answers, put your business manager hat on. The business environment and concepts (BEC) test covers many topics that a business manager must know. Managers, for example, need to understand economics and business cycles. They must be able to manage technology to run their businesses. This material isn't just about accounting. These test topics require you to broaden your view.

Corporate Governance

1. **B.** From a corporate governance standpoint, the main goal is to align the incentives of executives with those of the owners.

2. **A.** Auditing standards divide internal control into five interrelated components as follows: (1) control environment, (2) risk assessment, (3) control activities, (4) information and communication, and (5) monitoring.

3. **C.** This answer is correct because the preparation of disbursement vouchers and signing of checks places an individual in a position in which he or she can both prepare erroneous vouchers and then pay them.

4. **C.** The duty of loyalty principle indicates that the director should first present the opportunity to Riley Corporation.

Cost Measurement and Assignment

5. **B.** Salespersons' wages are not associated with the production process and therefore aren't considered a product cost. The wages of salespersons are considered a period cost and are expensed in the period incurred.

6. **A.** An overhead application rate, which is commonly called a *predetermined overhead rate,* is computed as follows:

$$\frac{\text{Estimated variable overhead costs}}{\text{Estimated activity level}} = \text{Predetermined rate}$$

Estimated figures are used because actual figures are unknown at the beginning of a period. *Estimated direct manufacturing labor hours* is correct because this figure is a commonly used activity base.

7. **D.** This answer is correct because under the direct method, service department costs are allocated directly to the producing departments based on relative services provided, and

services to other service departments are ignored. Therefore, even though maintenance used 10 percent of the utilities department services, the 10 percent is ignored and no utilities cost is allocated to maintenance. The $9,000 of utilities cost is allocated to departments A and B based on relative service performed: 30/90 to A and 60/90 to B, where $90 = 30 + 60$. Department B would be allocated $6,000 of utilities cost:

A: $(30/90)\,(\$9,000) = \$3,000$

B: $(60/90)\,(\$9,000) = \$6,000$

8. **C.** This answer is correct because *net realizable value* (NRV) is the predicted selling price in the ordinary course of business less reasonably predictable costs of completion and disposal. The joint cost of $54,000 is reduced by the NRV of the byproduct ($7,000 − $3,000 = $4,000) to get the allocable joint cost ($50,000). Here are the computations for allocating the joint cost:

	Sale Value at Split-Off	*Weighting*	*Joint Costs Allocated*
Kul	$40,000	$\dfrac{\$40,000}{\$75,000} \times \$50,000$	$26,667
Wu	$35,000	$\dfrac{\$35,000}{\$75,000} \times \$50,000$	$23,333
Total	$75,000		$50,000

Therefore, $26,667 of the joint cost should be allocated to product Kul.

Economics and Strategy

9. **C.** A weaker dollar decreases the prices of U.S. exports, which should increase the demand for these goods.

10. **D.** *Scanning* involves a review of all segments of the general environment. *Monitoring* involves a study of environmental changes identified by scanning. *Assessing* involves changes in a firm's strategy. *Forecasting* is the process of developing probable projections.

11. **A.** Marginal utility determines how much of a product or service a customer will buy, based on his or her perception of the product's value. A customer's use of the product is referred to as the product's *utility*. *Marginal utility* measures the change in utility when a customer buys and uses one more unit of product. The *law of diminishing marginal utility* states that marginal utility declines with each additional unit the consumer receives.

12. **A.** An oligopoly is formed by the combination of firms in the same line of business, as in a horizontal merger. An *oligopoly* is a market for a good or service that is dominated by a small number of firms.

Financial Management

13. **A.** *Net working capital* is equal to current assets minus current liabilities.

14. **C.** The theory underlying cost of capital relates to existing long-term financing and new long-term financing. *Cost of capital* is defined as the cost a company incurs to raise funds to run a business. When a company issues debt, the cost of capital is interest expense on debt.

If a firm issues equity, their cost of capital is the required rate of return demanded by the shareholders. The stockholder's return is earned by receiving dividends and by selling the equity investment for a gain. Raising funds to run the business focuses on the long term (multiple years).

15. **A.** Investors value common shares more highly if they have a lower required return because then they apply a lower discount rate to the expected future dividend stream of the company.

16. **C.** The requirement is to calculate the number of days' sales in accounts receivable. Choice (C) is correct because 60 percent of the company's customers pay in 10 days and 40 percent pay in 30 days. The days' sales is equal to 18 days because $(0.60 \times 10) + (0.40 \times 30) = 18$.

Information Technology

17. **B.** The systems programmer should not maintain custody of output in a computerized system. At a minimum, the programming, operating, and library functions should be segregated in such computer systems.

18. **D.** Cutting costs, per se, is the least important issue. Payoff, or return on costs, is a more relevant strategic consideration.

19. **A.** Access must be controlled to ensure integrity of documentation, although "read" access should be provided to other parties because it's important for applications development and maintenance.

Performance Measures

20. **C.** A *strategy map* consists of diagrams of the cause-and-effect relationships between strategic objectives.

21. **C.** Spoilage is an example of producing substandard products but discovering the lack of quality prior to shipment to the customer.

22. **C.** You calculate *times interest earned* as earnings before interest and taxes divided by interest expense:

$$\frac{\text{Sales} - \text{Cost of goods sold} - \text{Administrative expense} - \text{Depreciation expense}}{\text{Interest expense}}$$

$$= \frac{\$600,000 - \$400,000 - \$35,000 - \$10,000}{\$20,000}$$

$$= \frac{\$155,000}{\$20,000}$$

$$= 7.75 \text{ times}$$

23. **A.** You calculate the level of sales for the company using both ratios as follows:

$$\text{Total assets} = \frac{\text{Total debt}}{0.70} = \frac{\$1,000,000}{0.70} = \$1,428,571.40$$

$$\text{Sales} = 3.5 \times (\text{Total assets}) = 3.5 \times (\$1,428,571.40) = \$5,000,000.00$$

Planning, Control, and Analysis

24. **B.** In analyzing a special order, the incremental revenue less the incremental costs determines the effect on operating income. The incremental revenue is the selling price of the special order gloves, $12.00 per pair. Incremental costs include only the variable costs of $9.00 per pair. Fixed costs don't change in the short run, so they aren't included. The effect on operating income is calculated as follows:

	Per Unit	*Per 20,000 Units*
Incremental revenue	$12	$240,000
Less incremental costs	($9)	($180,000)
Additional to operating income	$3	$60,000

25. **A.** *Opportunity cost* is the income obtainable from an alternative use of a resource. The opportunity cost in this problem is the $3,000 for which the obsolete fixtures could be sold (rather than reworking them).

26. **A.** This alternative correctly calculates the direct material efficiency (usage) variance as the difference between the standard pounds allowed for the actual units produced ($32,000 \times 1.60 = 51,200$) and the actual pounds used (51,000), multiplied by the standard price ($2.50):

$$(51,200 - 51,000) \times \$2.50 = 200 \times \$2.50 = \$500$$

27. **C.** The requirement is to determine the appropriate transfer price for Product X. Choice (C) is correct because if Division A is operating at full capacity, it can sell all that it can make. Therefore, it should transfer the product at its opportunity cost of $25, the price at which it could sell the product to another buyer.

Risk Management

28. **D.** The payback method evaluates investments on the basis of the length of time until the initial investment is returned. If annual cash flows are constant, the payback period is calculated as follows:

$$\frac{\text{Initial investment}}{\text{Annual cash flow}}$$

29. **A.** Net present value (NPV) assumes that cash inflows from the investment project can be reinvested at the cost of capital, whereas internal rate of return (IRR) assumes that cash flows from each project can be reinvested at the IRR for that particular project. This underlying assumption is considered to be a weakness of the IRR technique.

30. **A.** This answer is correct because return on stock is measured by the return to the investor both in appreciation and in dividends:

$$\frac{\text{Dividends} + \text{Change in price}}{\text{Beginning price}}$$

Part III
Financial Accounting and Reporting

	Accounts Receivable		
12/31/Y1	100,000	591,000	Year 2 collections from customers
Year 2 Credit sales	611,000	45,000	Year 2 AR write-off
12/31/Y2	?		

Accrual-based accounting is a big part of the CPA exam. Four or five adjustments for accrual account-ing appear on most FAR tests. To further brush up on your knowledge of accruals, check out the free article at www.dummies.com/extras/cpaexam.

In this part . . .

✔ Get up to speed on the nuts and bolts of working as a CPA so you can succeed on this number-crunching test.

✔ Test your knowledge with 30 practice questions and then see how well you did by reviewing the answers and detailed explanations.

Chapter 8

Taking a Closer Look at the Financial Accounting and Reporting Test

. . . .

In This Chapter

▶ Digging into accounting standards

▶ Understanding accounts in the financial statements

▶ Posting accounting transactions

. . . .

The *financial accounting and reporting* (FAR) test covers the nuts and bolts you need in order to work as a CPA. To pass this test, you need to be proficient in posting accounting transactions. After reading a question, you'll need to know which accounts are affected by the transaction. You'll also have to compute the proper dollar amounts to post and figure out whether each account should be debited or credited.

In this chapter, you get a handle on the rules of the road of accounting — that is, accounting standards. Accrual accounting, for example, is the required accounting basis to conform to generally accepted accounting principles (GAAP). Using accrual accounting is a standard, along with valuing assets at historical cost. The FAR test includes many accounting standards.

Starting with Standards for Financial Statements

As a CPA, your work may need to comply with the accounting standards of several regulators. In this section, you discover the entities that set accounting standards and find out how those entities relate to each other. You also get an overview of the financial reporting and disclosure standards for the accounting industry and consider which basis of accounting you should use for your transactions.

Reviewing regulators and reporting methods

The FAR exam tests you on the reporting requirements that are set by regulators in the accounting industry. Most of these regulators ask for and consider information from the general public regarding regulatory matters, and companies and individuals are often asked to provide comments about proposed regulations. Here's an overview of the regulators you should know:

✓ **Securities and Exchange Commission (SEC):** According to the SEC website (www.sec.gov), this organization exists to "protect investors, maintain fair, orderly and efficient markets, and facilitate capital formation." One way to protect investors is to ensure that companies provide sufficient financial information to the public. If investors can review adequate financial information, they can make informed decisions about investing in a company's stock or bond offering.

The SEC was created in response to the stock market crash of 1929. After the crash, legislators and securities industry officials determined that many investors had bought securities based on little or no accurate financial information. As a result, many investors were unaware of the financial risk they were taking. To address this concern, Congress passed the Securities Act of 1933, which requires that companies selling securities to the public disclose accurate financial information.

The SEC's Division of Corporate Finance oversees the financial disclosure process. Companies must disclose financial data when they issue stock to the public for the first time — at the *initial public offering*, or IPO. After the IPO, businesses must report financial information on a periodic basis. Financial reporting for a security trading in the marketplace is regulated based on the Securities Act of 1934.

- **Financial Accounting Standards Board (FASB):** This private-sector organization establishes financial reporting standards for nongovernmental entities, whether they're private (for-profit) businesses or not-for-profits. You can find a more detailed explanation of this organization at www.fasb.org. As long as FASB's standards operate in the best interests of the public, the SEC relies on FASB to create financial reporting standards.

- **Governmental Accounting Standards Board (GASB):** The GASB regulates accounting for public-sector entities: federal, state, city, and other governments. The entity's website, www.gasb.org, explains that GASB exists to ensure accountability and to help financial-statement readers make well-informed decisions.

- **International Financial Reporting Standards (IFRS) Foundation:** A CPA's work may involve companies that operate outside the U.S. The IFRS Foundation is a private-sector organization that works on international accounting issues. One of the foundation's objectives is to create a single set of international accounting standards, or International Financial Reporting Standards (IFRS). Those standards are developed by the International Accounting Standards Board (IASB).

Here are the three types of regulated entities and how they relate to their regulators:

- **For-profit (business) entities:** For-profit businesses exist to generate a profit and produce a return for the owners or shareholders (if the company issues stock). FASB has oversight over for-profit businesses. If a for-profit company issues stock to the public, the SEC has oversight when the stock is issued and for as long as the public owns stock.

- **Not-for-profit (nongovernmental) entities:** Charitable organizations are nongovernmental entities. You can think of these entities as "mission-driven businesses." The goal is not to generate a profit but to fulfill a mission (helping the poor, feeding the hungry, and so on). FASB regulates not-for-profit businesses, which must answer to contributors, such as donors and grantors. Governments as well as private foundations and individuals provide grants for not-for-profits, and the contributors need information on how their dollars are spent.

  Not-for-profits have some of the same accounting issues as for-profits. For example, both types of entities must account for employee retirement plans and other worker benefits.

- **Governmental entities:** Governmental entities (federal, state, city, and local governments) are regulated by GASB. The main source of income for these entities is tax dollars. Those taxes may include income tax, sales tax, or estate taxes. A government focuses on proper approval of spending, budgeting, and documentation of spending results. All this activity is important to taxpayers.

Understanding these entities and how they're regulated will help you keep the regulatory bodies straight in your mind.

Going over specific financial statements

The FAR test covers the basic financial statements that most entities are required to create. In this section, you find out more about those financial statements and also see additional disclosures. All this information helps a financial-statement reader get a clear picture of the company's current financial condition.

Starting with the balance sheet and income statement

The balance sheet and income statement are the first reports that a businessperson normally considers. To a non-CPA, these two financial statements are the most important.

The balance sheet information is generated as of a certain date. This report lists a company's asset, liability, and equity balances:

- **Assets:** An asset is a resource used to make money in your business. Inventory, investments, and fixed assets (trucks, equipment, buildings, and so on) are considered assets. Your accounts receivable balance is also an asset because it represents cash you'll eventually receive from clients.

- **Liabilities:** Liabilities represent debts owed to other people. If a company doesn't pay a liability, the creditor has a *claim,* or ownership right, on company assets. Liabilities include accounts payable as well as long-term debts, like loans.

- **Equity:** You can define equity in several ways:

    - Equity represents ownership in a business. If the equity section of the balance sheet has a balance of $100,000, that means that the owner's investment in the business is $100,000.

    - You can also understand equity using the *balance sheet formula,* which is

        $$\text{Equity} = \text{Assets} - \text{Liabilities}$$

        If you were to sell all your assets and pay off all your liabilities, any funds that remained would be considered your equity balance.

An *income statement* is also called a *profit and loss statement.* This report always covers a period of time (month, quarter, or year) rather than a specific date. The income statement includes these amounts:

- **Revenue:** Sales to customers are the primary source of revenue.

- **Expenses:** Expenses are the spending incurred to generate revenue.

- **Net income:** Net income, which is also called *profit* or *earnings,* is the difference between revenue and expenses. The *income statement formula* is

    $$\text{Net income} = \text{Revenue} - \text{Expenses}$$

The FAR test will make a distinction between a subsidiary ledger and general ledger. As the name implies, a *subsidiary ledger* posts transactions for a portion of the activity in an account. A good example is a company that tracks many different types of inventory items.

Suppose that Sturdy Hardware has a subsidiary ledger for tools in inventory. That ledger tracks purchases and sales of the tool portion of inventory. Sturdy has other subsidiary ledgers for inventory, such as lawn equipment and painting supplies. The inventory subsidiary ledgers are combined to generate the *general ledger* for inventory. The general ledger accounts for all of the activity that's needed to post the inventory balance to the financial statements.

Considering the statement of cash flows

After preparing the balance sheet and income statement, an accountant typically moves on to statement of cash flows. The *statement of cash flows* documents a firm's sources and uses of cash for a particular period of time, such as a month or year. The statement separates cash flows into three activities, as you see in Table 8-1.

Table 8-1	Activities on the Statement of Cash Flows		
Type of Activity	*Description*	*Example Inflow*	*Example Outflow*
Operating activities	Operating activities represent the cash inflows and outflows from your day-to-day business activities. Most of your cash transactions will be operating activities.	Cash receipts from customers	Paying for inventory and company payroll
Financing activities	Raising money to run your business — and paying it back — are considered financing activities.	Cash received from issuing stock or debt	Paying stockholders a dividend
Investing activities	Buying and selling assets are considered investing activities.	Writing a check for a new company truck	Selling a piece of equipment

The process described here is the *direct method of the statement of cash flows*. You can visualize the process of preparing the statement of cash flows by thinking about your company checkbook. You prepare the statement by grouping your deposits, checks, and debits into operating, financing, and investing activities.

When you're going through your company checkbook, pick out the transactions that relate to financing and investing activities first. There will be fewer of those transactions. After you finish that process, all the remaining cash flows relate to operations. This trick makes the process go quickly, because you're pulling out the smaller set of cash transactions first.

You finish the statement of cash flows by adding the net change in cash for each of the three activities. Say that the net change in cash for the year is a $5,000 increase. You add your beginning balance in cash to the net change, and you have your ending balance in cash for the period. If your beginning balance in cash is $30,000, your ending balance in cash should be $30,000 beginning balance + $5,000 net increase in cash = $35,000 ending cash balance.

To wrap up this process, verify that the ending balance in cash ($35,000) agrees with the ending balance in the balance sheet for the last day of the period. If you're preparing a statement of cash flows for May, the $35,000 cash balance should agree with the cash balance in the May 31 balance sheet. If the two numbers don't agree, review your statement of cash flows for errors.

Accountants typically prepare the balance sheet and income statement before the statement of cash flows, so if the two cash balances don't agree, the error is likely in the cash flow statement.

The *indirect method of cash flows* deals with cash flows for operating expenses slightly differently. This method relates to the accrual basis of accounting. The *accrual basis* posts revenue when it's earned and posts expenses when they're incurred, regardless of when cash moves. The accrual method generates entries to accounts receivable (for revenue) and accounts payable (for expenses).

With the indirect method, the cash flows for operating activities start with net income at the top. You can assume that the company uses the accrual method (unless otherwise stated). So the top line in the operating activities section is net income using the accrual method. You then reconcile from net income to cash flow from operating activities.

To reconcile from net income to cash, you remove the non-cash income statement activity. In other words, you remove the income-statement impact of using the accrual method. Here are two examples:

- ✔ The balance in prepaid insurance declines in March. The journal entry to decrease prepaid insurance is a debit (increase) to insurance expense and a credit (decrease) to prepaid insurance. In March, insurance expense is greater than *cash paid* for insurance expense. Keep in mind that the cash basis wouldn't post insurance expense unless cash was paid during the period. In this case, the insurance expense was posted due to a prepaid balance. To reconcile from net income to cash, you add the decrease in the prepaid balance to the net income.

- ✔ Depreciation expense and amortization expenses are non-cash items. These entries reduce net income but don't involve a decrease in cash. To reconcile from net income to cash flow for operations, these expenses are added back. The cash method doesn't account for either of these expenses, because nothing happens to cash. (Head to the later section "Recalling fixed assets" for more on depreciation, and see "Working with intangible assets" for info on amortization.)

Earlier in this section, I explain how to group the cash flow activities together using your checkbook. After you go through your checkbook, you'll have the net change in cash flows for operations. That amount is your check figure for the indirect cash flow method. When you finish reconciling from net income to cash, the cash total should agree to the change in cash flows for operating activities. If the reconciliation doesn't agree to the change in cash, check your work for errors.

Adding in other statements and disclosures

To be well-informed, a businessperson needs to review more than the balance sheet, income statement, and statement of cash flows. The FAR test covers information on other financial statements and disclosures, such as the statement of comprehensive income and the statement of changes in equity.

Comprehensive income differs from net income. *Net income,* or profit, is revenue less expenses. *Comprehensive income* takes net income and adds in other items that haven't been realized yet. In other words, net income includes only *realized income* (from completed transactions). For example, consider a gain or loss on an asset. To realize a gain or loss, there must be both a buy and a sale. If you buy an asset for $10,000 and sell it for $12,000, that's a $2,000 realized gain. If, instead, you buy an asset for $10,000 and it has a current market value of $13,000, you have a $3,000 unrealized gain. The gain is unrealized because no sale has occurred. Comprehensive income adds several types of unrealized gains and losses to net income. To report this information to financial statement readers, accountants generate a *statement of comprehensive income.*

The *statement of changes in equity* (also called the *statement of retained earnings*) is another report you need to know. Equity represents ownership in the business. It's defined in the balance sheet as assets less liabilities. This statement discloses changes in equity during a particular period (month or year). Here are some transactions that change equity:

- ✔ **Net profit or loss for the period:** A firm's net income (earnings) increases equity. A business can keep the earnings for company use; accountants refer to those dollars as *retained earnings*.

- ✔ **Dividends:** Companies can choose to pay a portion of earnings to shareholders through *dividends*. A dividend payment to shareholders reduces equity.

- ✔ **Gains and losses:** A gain or loss is generated when an asset is sold. A gain increases equity, and a loss reduces equity.

- ✔ **Effects of changes in accounting policy:** Every company should have written accounting policies, which are normally included with the financial statements and in an annual report. For example, management should decide on a policy of how to value inventory (see the later section "Mulling over inventory valuation"). If a firm changes its inventory valuation policy, the change will impact the cost of goods when inventory is sold and the company's net income. Accountants are required to present the impact of the change *retrospectively*, as if the new accounting policy had always been in place. The dollar amount of the impact is presented in the equity statement.

- ✔ **Effect of a correction of a prior period error:** If an accountant finds an error in the accounting records for a prior period, he or she posts the financial impact of the error to the equity statement. When a company computes net income for a given period, that amount is posted as an increase to equity. The income statement accounts (revenue and expenses) are adjusted to zero at the end of each period. Revenue and expense accounts are *temporary accounts*. The balances do not carry over from one period to the next. When you start the next period (month or year), the revenue and expense accounts all start at zero. Financial-statement readers need to know about errors made in a prior period. Because the income statement starts each new period at zero, accountants post the impact to a prior period's net income in the equity statement.

Another required disclosure is the *notes to financial statements* section, which includes a *summary of significant accounting policies*. That summary notes how the company values its assets and liabilities.

The notes also disclose any *related-party transactions*. These are transactions in which the parties already have a relationship. For example, if a business bought supplies from a company controlled by a board member, that transaction would be a related-party transaction. Because the parties already have a relationship, the terms of the exchange may be better than if they were not related. Maybe the board member's firm is able to charge a higher price. See the later section "Remembering related parties" for more info.

If you search for examples of notes to financial statements on the web, you'll find many other types of disclosures. The goal in preparing a financial statement is to reveal anything that a financial-statement reader may find important.

Reporting on a segment

A segment of a business operates with some level of autonomy. Accountants use the term *operating segment* to describe a department or division of a business. To be considered an operating segment, an area of the company must meet each of these three criteria:

✔ The entity generates revenue and expenses from its business activity.

✔ Senior management reviews the operating results of the entity. The results allow management to allocate resources and assess performance.

✔ Discrete, identifiable financial information is available.

A company is required to present separate financial information for *reportable segments*. Not all segments are large enough to be considered reportable segments. A segment is reportable if any of these criteria is true:

✔ Revenue is at least 10 percent of the total revenue of all reported operating segments. The 10 percent revenue includes intersegment revenue — revenue from sales between two segments. Note that this rule specifies *reported* operating segments, not all operating segments.

✔ Profit is at least 10 percent of the combined profit (or loss) of all reported operating segments.

✔ Assets are at least 10 percent of the combined revenue, profit (or loss), or assets of all operating segments. Note that this asset calculation may be 10 percent of any of three elements. Note also that the rule includes all operating segments, whether or not they're reportable.

A reportable segment can be a combination of segments that are similar. The segment may produce a similar product or service, or the segments may sell to the same type of customer.

Choosing an accounting basis

An accounting basis dictates how you post all your accounting entries and determines when you recognize income and expenses. You explain the basis you choose in the notes to the financial statements.

Generally accepted accounting principles (GAAP) are the set of guidelines that accountants are required to follow, with some exceptions. GAAP requires accountants to use the accrual method of accounting (head to Chapter 4 for details on this method). Accrual accounting recognizes revenue when it's earned and recognizes expenses when they're incurred. Most companies use the accrual basis of accounting, and most of the questions in the FAR test use the accrual basis of accounting.

Other methods of accounting may be used in some cases. *Cash basis* (see Chapter 4) recognizes revenue when cash is received and recognizes expenses when they're paid. The cash basis is used by very small businesses, maybe a part-time sole proprietor, for example. The cash basis is also used for some types of tax returns. *Modified cash basis* uses the accrual basis for long-term balance sheet items and uses the cash basis for current assets and liabilities (where *current* refers to 12 months or less).

Going Through the Accounts

This section walks through specific accounts that appear on the FAR test. You'll see a discussion of many of the important accounts that are most frequently tested. You'll start with asset accounts and then move to liability and equity topics. This section wraps up with a discussion of revenue recognition. After reading this section, you'll have an idea of which accounts are affected for many types of accounting transactions.

Checking out asset accounts

The balance sheet formula is Assets – Liabilities = Equity. This section details some of the important asset accounts that appear on the FAR test.

Going over prepaid assets

The term *prepaid assets* refers to an account created when a company pays in advance for a product or service. This topic is very common on the FAR test. The two most common prepaid accounts are prepaid rent and prepaid insurance.

Rent, interest expense, and insurance expenses are all incurred with the passage of time. So at the end of a given month, accountants record all three of these expenses.

Suppose that on March 1, you prepay for 6 months of insurance on a company vehicle. If you prepay $12,000, you debit (increase) prepaid insurance $12,000 and credit (reduce) cash $12,000. The $12,000 represents 6 months of coverage, or $2,000 each month. At the end of the month, your firm has incurred one month of insurance expense. So on March 31, you debit (increase) insurance expense $2,000 and credit (reduce) prepaid insurance $2,000. The prepaid insurance account now has a balance of $10,000.

Reviewing bad debt and accounts receivable

In addition to cash, accounts receivable is considered a current asset balance. *Current assets* are assets that are in cash, or that will be converted to cash, within 12 months.

The FAR test covers the two ways a company can account for bad debt expense:

- ✔ **Direct write-off method:** When a receivable is determined to be uncollectable (maybe because the customer went out of business), the company debits (increases) bad debt expense and credits (reduces) accounts receivable.

- ✔ **Allowance method:** The allowance method matches revenue with the expenses incurred to generate the revenue (see Chapter 4 for details). In this case, bad debt expense is matched with revenue from sales. Accountants prefer this method because it complies with the matching principle.

The allowance method estimates bad debt expense based on a percentage of credit sales. *Credit sales* are sales that create an accounts receivable balance. Suppose that a company has $100,000 in March credit sales. Based on the company's collection history, the firm estimates that 2 percent of receivables will never be collected. The amount posted to bad debt expense for March credit sales is $100,000 × 2% = $2,000. The journal entry is "debit bad debt expense $2,000" and "credit allowance for doubtful accounts $2,000."

Allowance for doubtful accounts is a contra-asset account. It reduces the balance of an asset account, in this case accounts receivable. The financial-statement reader may be interested in the net accounts receivable balance for March sales. That balance is $100,000 accounts receivable less $2,000 allowance for doubtful accounts, which equals $98,000. The net accounts receivable balance is what the company *expects to collect* from March sales.

Suppose that $500 of the March receivable balance is determined to be uncollectable. The company would debit (reduce) allowance for doubtful accounts $500 and credit (reduce) accounts receivable $500. If the firm knows that amount will not be collected, there's no need for an allowance estimate.

If the business recovers an amount previously written off as uncollectable, the company makes two journal entries. Say that $200 of the $500 written off is subsequently paid by the customer. First, the firm reverses $200 of the write-off entry. Accounts receivable is debited for $200, and allowance for doubtful accounts is credited $200. The company then debits cash and reduces (credits) accounts receivable for the $200 payment.

Mulling over inventory valuation

Inventory is often the largest asset account balance for a firm. How a large balance in inventory is valued has a big impact on a company's profit. The valuation method assigns a dollar amount to inventory, which is posted to cost of sales when the item is sold.

This section discusses several issues related to inventory valuation: the principle of conservatism, lower of cost or market (LCM), and the issue of obsolete inventory.

Accountants must apply the *principle of conservatism*. When making a judgment, an accountant should choose the more conservative approach:

- ✔ For income-statement issues, a conservative approach recognizes expenses immediately and delays the recognition of revenue. Those steps reduce net income, which is considered a conservative approach.

- ✔ A conservative approach to the balance sheet is to avoid overstating the value of assets, such as inventory and equipment. When in doubt, the accountant should choose a lower asset value. The balance sheet should also avoid understating liabilities.

If an accountant applies the principle of conservatism, he or she avoids presenting financial statements that are overly optimistic.

The conservative principle is applied to inventory using the *lower of cost or market* (LCM) guideline, where the term *market* refers to the current replacement cost of the inventory. Following this guideline ensures that the value of inventory isn't overstated. To illustrate the concept, suppose an accountant is assessing these inventory amounts:

- ✔ Net realizable value (NRV) is $100,000. NRV represents the expected selling price less any costs to complete and dispose of the goods.

- ✔ Net realizable value less the normal profit margin is $85,000.

- ✔ The inventory's original cost is $75,000.

- ✔ Inventory can be replaced at a cost of $60,000.

If the market value is below cost, LCM states that the market value should be used to value inventory. However, the market value is limited by a ceiling and a floor value:

- ✔ **Ceiling value:** The market value cannot be higher than the net realizable value.

- ✔ **Floor value:** The market value cannot be lower than net realizable value less the normal profit margin.

In this case, the market value cannot be lower than $85,000 (NRV less the normal profit margin). To determine LCM, compare the market value of $85,000 with the cost of $75,000. The lower of cost or market is the $75,000 cost — this is the value you use for inventory.

The FAR exam also tests your knowledge of gross profit and how that concept relates to the formula for ending inventory. Consider these two formulas:

- Gross profit = Sales – Cost of goods sold (*Note:* Gross profit can also be calculated as a percentage of the sales price.)
- Ending inventory = Beginning inventory + Purchases – Cost of goods sold

A typical CPA test question will ask you to use the gross profit formula to compute cost of goods sold. After you have cost of goods sold, you'll have to complete the ending inventory formula. Here's an example: Suppose that a company's gross profit is 25 percent of sales and that total sales equals $100,000. If your gross profit is 25 percent of sales, your cost of goods sold is 100% – 25% = 75%. In this case, cost of goods sold is $100,000 × 75% = $75,000.

If you're given these amounts for inventory, you can add in the cost of goods sold total you just computed:

$20,000 beginning inventory + $60,000 purchases – $75,000 cost of goods sold = Ending inventory

Your ending inventory is $80,000 – $75,000 = $5,000.

If inventory is *obsolete,* it can't be sold to a customer. If you can't generate revenue with an inventory item, it's no longer an asset. Obsolete inventory should be written off as an expense. That entry is "debit loss on obsolete inventory and credit inventory."

If you look at your inventory in total, you may need to expense only a portion of your inventory due to a decline in value. If inventory has a decline in value that isn't considered temporary, it should be written down to the new dollar value. If, later on, the value of the inventory increases, you can increase the value of the inventory — but only up to the original cost of the inventory.

An *interim period* is an accounting period that's less than one year. Most companies generate financial statements each month and quarter. Those reports are considered to be interim financial statements. Consider some changes in inventory values during interim periods. For example, suppose you have $10,000 in software in inventory. You determine that, due to changes in technology, the software inventory should be valued at $6,000 on March 31. You post a March 31 entry to debit loss on obsolete inventory $4,000 and credit inventory $4,000. On April 30, the software inventory is judged to be worth $8,000. Keep in mind that the value of the inventory on March 31 is $6,000. On April 30, you reverse part of the March entry by debiting (increasing) inventory $2,000 and credit (reduce) loss on obsolete inventory $2,000. Your adjusted inventory balance is $10,000 – $4,000 + $2,000 = $8,000.

Recalling fixed assets

Fixed assets are in the long-term asset category. This section discusses several concepts that frequently appear on the FAR test.

Accountants create a company policy to determine whether costs are capitalized. *Capitalization* means that the cost of the item will be posted as an asset. If the spending creates a resource that will be used over the long term to generate revenue, accountants create a new asset in the financial statements. If the company decides that the spending will *not* create an asset, the cost is expensed.

Suppose you buy some office supplies and a desktop computer. Many companies simply expense office supplies immediately. Although they may use the supplies over time, the dollar amount of the expense is comparatively small. An accountant may conclude that the cost of creating an asset — and accounting for it — is not worth the information gained from posting an asset.

Many companies create a capitalization policy based on a minimum dollar amount. Say, for example, that you have a $200 policy set. If you spent $70 on office supplies, that cost would be immediately expensed. The $400 you spend on a desktop computer is capitalized as a new asset. The asset, a desktop computer, will be depreciated over time. This capitalization policy may be included in the notes to the financial statements. (See the earlier section "Adding in other statements and disclosures" to find out more on the notes.)

Most fixed assets depreciate. *Depreciation* is an estimated amount. It's the original cost expensed over the life of the asset. The term is also defined as the decline in value of an asset due to the passage of time. The two definitions can be connected. *Assets* are defined as any resource you use to generate revenue in your business. Say you own a plumbing company. Over time, you use a plumbing truck to perform plumbing work — and generate revenue. As you drive more miles, the truck's value declines. Although you can look at depreciation due to an asset's use, depreciation is usually accounted for based on the passage of time.

Accountants assign each asset a *useful life*. The useful life is the period of time when the asset can be used to generate revenue. At the end of the useful life, the asset may or may not have further value to the company. The end of the useful life may also mean that the asset is fully depreciated.

Salvage value represents the value of an asset when it is fully depreciated. If you can sell the asset after you use it, any cash received is considered salvage value. You can relate salvage value to the trade-in value a car dealer offers you when you trade in your car and buy another one.

Depreciation of fixed assets represents an expense to a business. As the asset depreciates, the accountant debits (increases) depreciation expense and credits (increases) accumulated depreciation. *Accumulated depreciation* is a contra-asset account: It's posted to the fixed assets section of the balance sheet, but it's increased by crediting. The accumulated depreciation account reduces the fixed asset's value.

It's most effective to have a specific accumulated depreciation account for each type of asset. That allows the financial-statement reader to see both the cost and accumulated depreciation for each asset. As you see in the following example, the reader can then make a judgment on how soon the asset will need to be replaced.

For example, the plumbing company should have a plumbing-truck account and an accumulated-depreciation truck account. That format allows the financial-statement reader to quickly see the truck's *book value,* which is defined as an asset's historical cost less the accumulated depreciation for the asset. If the truck had a cost of $30,000 and accumulated depreciation of $25,000, the truck's book value would be $30,000 – $25,000 = $5,000. Someone reading the financial statements would probably conclude that the truck should be replaced soon.

Here are several depreciation methods that appear frequently on the FAR test:

- ✔ **Straight-line depreciation:** Straight-line assumes that the asset is depreciated evenly over its useful life. If a piece of equipment has a $20,000 cost and a 5-year useful life (with no salvage value), the annual depreciation is $20,000 ÷ 5 years, or $4,000. If the same asset had a $2,000 salvage value, the salvage value would be subtracted from the cost. An asset's cost less salvage value is called the *depreciable base*. The truck's depreciable base is $20,000 – $2,000 = $18,000. The new straight-line depreciation would be $18,000 ÷ 5 years, or $3,600 per year.

- ✔ **Double-declining balance (DDB) depreciation:** DDB is an accelerated depreciation method, which means it recognizes more depreciation in the early years and less in later years. To calculate DDB, compute straight-line depreciation as a percentage; then double the percentage. Assuming straight-line depreciation over 4 years, for example, the percentage is ¼ each year, or 25 percent. The 25 percent rate is doubled to 50 percent. To find depreciation for Year 1, multiply the cost of a $20,000 asset by 50 percent: $20,000 × 0.50 = $10,000. For Year 2, you calculate book value less accumulated depreciation: $20,000 – $10,000 = $10,000. You then multiply that result by 50 percent to get Year 2 depreciation: $10,000 × 0.50 = $5,000. As soon as book value less accumulated depreciation declines to your salvage value, depreciation stops. Accountants assume that when you reach salvage value, you sell the asset.

✔ **Sum of years' digits (SYD) depreciation:** The SYD process is also an accelerated depreciation method. The first step is to compute the percentage depreciation for the year. The formula for that percentage is (Remaining useful life) ÷ (Sum of the years' digits). To compute sum of years' digits, add the numbers that make up the years of depreciation. For a truck with a 5-year useful life, for example, sum of years' digits is 1 + 2 + 3 + 4 + 5 = 15. In Year 1, the percentage is 5 ÷ 15 = 33 percent. Depreciation for Year 1 is the depreciable base × 33 percent. If the depreciable base is $18,000, the depreciation is $18,000 × 0.33 = $6,000. The Year 2 sum of years' digits is 1 + 2 + 3 + 4 = 10. You multiply the new fraction by the same depreciable base of $18,000. You continue this process for all 5 years.

Note that regardless of the depreciation method you choose, the total dollars to depreciate are the same. Specifically, the total depreciation will be the depreciable base (cost less salvage value). What differs among depreciation methods is the depreciation recognized each year. An accelerated method books more depreciation in early years and less in later years. The straight-line method recognizes the same amount of depreciation each year.

Planning with future value and present value

Accountants need to plan the cash flows needed to purchase fixed assets. Depending on the cost, a business may need to set aside dollars for several years to fund the purchase of an expensive asset. To keep planning simple, company management may prefer to invest a specific amount each year to fund the purchase.

The FAR test may ask you to compute the annual deposit needed to accumulate a certain amount of dollars by a future date. The test question will provide you with a table of future-value factors. To select the right factor, you need to know the difference between these terms:

✔ **The future value of a single sum versus the future value of an annuity:** A *single sum* means that one amount is invested, whereas an *annuity* represents an amount invested each year.

✔ **Ordinary annuity versus an annuity due or annuity in advance:** An *annuity due* or *annuity in advance* assumes that the dollars are invested at the beginning for a period (month or year). The *ordinary annuity* assumes that dollars are invested at the end of each period.

Suppose that in 5 years, a company will need $200,000 to purchase a machine. The firm wants to make the same annual deposit into an account at the beginning of each year. The account will pay a 6 percent compounded annual return. With *compounding*, the interest earned on the principal amount invested will be reinvested each year.

For this example, you'd choose the annuity in advance at a rate of 6 percent for five periods. The future-value factor, which you'd pull from the table, is 5.975 (rounded). To calculate the required annual investment, you divide $200,000 by the future-value factor: $200,000 ÷ 5.975, which is approximately $33,473. You'd need to make five annual payments of $33,473 (each made at the beginning of the year) to accumulate $200,000.

Present value analysis takes amounts to be paid or received in the future and discounts the value of each payment into present-day dollars. The discounting uses some type of percentage rate. The FAR test may refer to the rate as an *interest rate, discount rate,* or *required rate of return.* Keep in mind that the rate provided in the question is the rate you use to discount the payments. (***Note:*** For a future value calculation, the FAR test may also use interest rate or required rate of return.)

Just as with future value, the present value calculation may be for a single sum (lump sum) or an annuity (series of payments). In either case, you multiply the payment amount by a present-value factor. Be careful to select the correct factor, based on whether the question involves a lump sum or an annuity.

To select the correct factors, remember that a future-value factor is always greater than 1, because the future value will be larger than the beginning value. Present value is the opposite: Present-value factors are less than 1, because the present value is less than the future amount.

Working with intangible assets

Companies may have other assets that are intangible — that is, they aren't physical assets. Accountants also define *intangible assets* as nonmonetary assets. Patents, copyrights, and trademarks are classified as intangible assets. During the time the patent is in effect, for example, the patent holder has the exclusive right to manufacture and sell an invention.

Generally, intangible assets are added to the balance sheet as assets when they're purchased. Companies may create intellectual property, such as an invention that receives a patent. The spending incurred to create that patent is immediately expensed. The business does not post those costs to an asset account.

The reason an intangible asset can't be created internally has to do the principle of conservatism. The principle states that, when in doubt, accountants should post expenses sooner than later. That's being conservative, because recognizing expenses sooner reduces net income sooner.

For example, when a drug company spends money on research and development (R and D) to develop new drugs, the company can't know which R and D dollars will result in a drug compound that will be patented. So to be conservative, the business expenses R and D spending as it's incurred. Intangible assets are purchased, not created internally by company spending.

An intangible asset typically has a useful life. For a patent, that useful life is a period of time that the patent is legally in force. The value of the patent is amortized over the patent's useful life. *Amortization* is the process of moving the cost of an intangible asset to an expense account. This process is similar to depreciation for fixed assets. (Check out the "Recalling fixed assets" section for details on depreciation.)

The estimated useful life of an intangible asset may change. A legal issue or a change in the product's industry may mean that the value of the patent is different from what it was when first estimated. Maybe new software technology makes a patented piece of software less useful. In that case, the useful life should be shortened. A shorter useful life will change the annual patent amortization.

For example, suppose that a $100,000 patent is estimated to have a 10-year useful life. The business uses the straight-line method to amortize the same dollar amount each year ($100,000 ÷ 10 years = $10,000 per year). At the end of 5 years, the company determines that the remaining useful life is only 3 years — not another 5 years. Here are the steps an accountant would take to change the annual amortization:

1. **Compute the amortization recognized to date.**

   In this case, that amount would be $10,000 × 5 years = $50,000.

2. **Compute the unamortized value of the patent.**

   That amount is $100,000 original patent value – $50,000 amortization to date = $50,000 unamortized value.

3. **Divide the unamortized value by the new estimate of remaining useful life to determine the new annual amount of amortization.**

   $50,000 unamortized value ÷ 3 years remaining useful life = $16,667 (with rounding).

The company would amortize the patent $16,667 each year for the remaining three-year life.

Leasing assets

Many companies lease assets instead of buying them. The party who owns the asset and leases it is the *lessor,* and the party who leases the assets and makes payments is the *lessee*.

The FAR test covers two types of leases. An *operating lease* is a lease that's comparable to the lease you take out on a car. The lessor records the lease payments as rental revenue, and the lessee posts the payments as rental expense. No asset is created.

The test also covers *direct financing* leases, or *capital leases*. In this case, the lessor creates an asset when the lease agreement is set up. Accountants view direct financing leases as similar to an installment agreement to purchase an asset. If any one of the following four criteria is true, then the lease should be treated as a capital lease:

- ✔ The lease transfers ownership of the asset to the lessee at the end of the lease.

- ✔ The lease contains a *bargain purchase option*. This option allows the lessee to purchase the leased item at a price that is less than the fair market value.

- ✔ The term of the lease is greater than 75 percent of the asset's useful life.

- ✔ Present value of the minimum lease payments is greater than 90 percent of the fair market value of leased asset.

Two other points must be true in order to treat the transaction as a capital lease. First, the collectability of the minimum lease payments must be predictable. In other words, the lessor expects the lessee to make the lease payments as scheduled. Also, there are no material uncertainties regarding any costs yet to be incurred by the lessee. The lessee's costs are known.

An operating lease treats lease payments as rental revenue. However, for capital leases, the lessor treats the lease payments as interest revenue. With a capital lease, just as with a home loan, you assume that each payment includes a portion for principal pay down and a certain amount of interest revenue. So with each payment, the principal amount of the lease declines. As the principal amount declines, so does the interest revenue earned on the principal amount.

Looking at nonmonetary exchanges

A *nonmonetary exchange* (NME) occurs when a business exchanges one asset for another. This transaction may take place without any cash. In other cases, although cash changes hands, the cash is only a fraction of the value of the assets exchanged. On the FAR test, you commonly see NME questions in which cash is exchanged along with assets. The cash in the exchange is referred to as *boot*.

To account for an NME, you need to determine whether the transaction has commercial substance. A transaction has *commercial substance* if a company's expected cash flows will change as a result of the transaction. For example, suppose two businesses, Acme and Standard, decide to exchange machines. A machine is an asset — a resource that a business uses to generate revenue — so an asset generates cash flow.

Commercial substance means that when Acme gives up an asset and receives a machine from Standard, the cash flow generated changes. If Acme used the old machine to generate $10,000 in cash flow a year and the new machine generates $15,000, the transaction has commercial substance. Determining commercial substance is important because the treatment of gains and losses for NEM transactions differs, depending on the existence of commercial substance.

Suppose that Acme and Standard enter into in a nonmonetary exchange that lacks commercial substance. That means that the machines exchanged generate the same amount of cash flow. Acme gives up a machine with a book value of $50,000 and pays boot (cash) of $10,000. Standard gives Acme a machine with a fair market value of $80,000. If this weren't an NME, it would look as if Acme had a gain on the exchange. The cash and the book values of the asset that Acme gave up total $60,000 (that is, $10,000 + $50,000), and Acme receives an asset with an $80,000 market value. The gain appears to be $80,000 – $60,000 = $20,000.

Accounting rules, however, state that the gain is not recognized. Instead, the machine acquired is posted to Acme's books as the cash paid, plus the book value given up ($60,000). The journal entry would be as follows:

> Debit machine $60,000
>
> Credit cash $10,000, credit machine $50,000

As you study NME questions, make sure you determine whether or not the transaction has commercial substance.

Accounting for investments

Companies include investments in the asset section of the balance sheet. Businesses hold both common stock and debt issued by other companies as investments (see the later section "Catching up on liabilities and equity" for info on long-term debt). This section explains an issue related to corporate bonds held as an investment.

The issuer of a bond pays the entire interest due to the current owner, regardless of how long the current owner has owned the bond. This creates an issue when a bond is sold from one investor to another between interest dates. That issue is called *accrued interest*. Accrued interest is the dollar amount of interest the buyer owes the seller when a bond is purchased. To calculate that interest, a test question may ask you to count the number of days in a given period.

Suppose a company owns a $10,000 IBM corporate bond that has a coupon rate of 6 percent. The *coupon rate* is the annual interest rate stated on the bond certificate. Each year, the investor earns $600 (that is, $10,000 × 6%). For the FAR test, assume that corporate bonds pay interest twice a year, or semiannually. In this case, the investor would be paid $300 twice per year.

The IBM bond pays on interest June 1 and December 1 of each year, and Bob buys the bond from Jim on September 1. Bob, the buyer, will receive the entire 6 months of interest on December 1, even though Bob will have owned the bond for only 3 months (September 1 to December 1). To keep this example simple, assume the September to December period is exactly 3 months and that June 1 to December 1 is exactly 6 months.

To ensure that interest is properly distributed, Bob (the buyer) pays 3 months of interest to Jim (the seller) when he purchases the bond on September 1. If Bob pays a price of $10,000 for the bond, he pays $10,000 + $150 to Jim on September 1. On December 1, Bob receives the entire $300 of interest for the 6-month period.

From an accounting standpoint, Bob would recognize $150 in interest income on the bond for the period from September 1 to December 1. Jim would post $150 as interest income. Jim earned interest from June 1 to August 31.

Valuing certain investments

Your FAR test may include two methods of valuing investments: the cost adjusted for fair value method and the equity method:

- **Cost adjusted for value method:** This method starts with the cost of your investment. The value of your investment increases as the market value increases. Market declines reduce the value of the investment. Each month of year, you verify the market value of the investment and then adjust the investment's value in your accounting records.

- **Equity method:** The equity method also starts with your investment's original cost. However, no adjustments are made for changes in the market value of the investment.

Suppose you buy 100 shares of IBM common stock at $40 per share. You record the new asset, Investment in IBM Stock, at $100 \times \$40 = \$4,000$. With the cost adjusted for fair value method, $4,000 is your beginning carrying amount for the investment, and the value of the investment account is adjusted for increases and decreases in the price of the IBM common stock. The equity method records Investment in IBM Stock at cost — $4,000 — but does not adjust the carrying value of the investment for changes in the market price.

A *personal financial statement* presents the assets and liabilities for an individual. You can picture a personal financial statement as your own personal balance sheet. A personal financial statement is comparable to the documents you fill out when applying for a loan at a bank. The bank needs to know what assets you have, because those assets could be sold to pay on your loan. A lender also needs to know your total liabilities, to see how much debt you already have. The banker will also look at your income. If they judge that your income isn't sufficient to pay principal and interest on all of your loans, they will not lend you more money.

If a large portion of your assets includes a business interest (ownership in a business), accounting rules state that the fair value of that interest should be identified separately in your personal financial statement. This assumes that the business is a *going concern* — that is, that the business is a viable entity that will generate sales and earnings in future years.

Investment in a partnership is included in each partner's personal financial statement. A partnership is a *pass-through entity,* an entity in which the profit and loss flows through to the owners. The partnership entity files a tax return, but the profit and loss on the partnership flows through to the personal tax returns of the partners.

The allocation of profits and losses is documented in the *partnership agreement.* For example, suppose that the partnership agreement indicates that Barbara, a partner, should receive a bonus of 20 percent of the partnership's net income after accounting for Barbara's bonus. In other words, Barbara gets 20 percent of the partnership's net income less Barbara's bonus.

If the partnership's net income was $100,000, Barbara would receive a bonus of $20\% \times (\$100,000 - x)$, where x is Barbara's bonus. Here's the solution, solving for x:

$x = 0.2(\$100,000 - x)$	Multiply 0.2 by the numbers in the brackets.
$x = \$20,000 - 0.2x$	Add $0.2x$ to both sides.
$1.2x = \$20,000$	Divide both sides by 1.2.
$x \approx \$16,666.67$	Round to the nearest cent.

Barbara's bonus is $16,666.67

Catching up on liabilities and equity

This section includes lot of information regarding long-term debt. You see a discussion of accrued liabilities and go over debt retirement and bond amortization. The section also talks about other types of liabilities, such as deferred taxes and pension liabilities. You finish up with equity test topics.

Accruing liabilities

The *accrual basis* of accounting recognizes revenue when it's earned and recognizes expenses when they're incurred. The accrual basis doesn't rely on cash deposits to recognize revenue. You aren't required to write a check to recognize an expense. The terms "earned revenue" and "incurred expenses" are not connected to cash movements in your business.

Many businesses ask customers to make a deposit before a product or service is delivered. In some cases, the product or service is created to meet specific client specifications. These types of products may not be sellable to any customer other than the individual who ordered the specific product. To cover the costs of this unique order, a company may ask for a deposit.

A customer deposit is considered *unearned revenue*. When the payment is received, the company debits (increases) cash and credits (increases) a liability account, unearned revenue. The account may also be called *customer deposits*. The revenue is not earned until the company delivers the product or service. At that point, the firm debits (reduces) unearned revenue and credits (increases) revenue.

If you issue a corporate bond, you're a creditor, and you recognize interest expense for bond interest. When you post interest expense, you *accrue* it. You accrue interest expense for any liability that's charged interest. Here are two related issues that you may see on the FAR test:

- ✔ **Interest payment date after end of period:** When you get to the end of a period (month or year), you need to post accrued interest for liabilities — even if the cash payment isn't paid until after the end of the period. Suppose that you owe $500 in interest for the month of December. You make your debt payments (principal and interest) on the fifth day of the following month. On December 31, you need to debit (increase) accrued interest expense and credit (increase) interest payable for $500. That entry posts the December expense to the correct year. When you write the check for the December interest on January 5, you debit (reduce) interest payable and credit (reduce) cash by $500.

- ✔ **Non-interest bearing bond or note:** These notes do not pay interest until the debt instrument (bond or note) matures. At maturity, the investor receives a return of principal (the face amount of the note or bond) plus all the interest earned. In this case, the issuer of the bond or note still needs to post accrued interest each month and year — even if the cash payment for interest isn't paid until the bond or note matures. The issuer should calculate the dollar amount of the annual interest. As soon as you have that number, you debit (increase) accrued interest expense and credit (increase) interest payable.

For info on how bond owners post interest income, see the earlier section "Accounting for investments."

Another type of accrual relates to compensating employees. Many companies offer paid vacation, sick days, and other personal days as an employee benefit. Normally, the firm's benefits manual or website will explain how many days a worker earns as a benefit each year.

At the end of the year, companies record a liability for the days that have been earned by workers but not yet taken as a benefit. This assumes that the days carry over as a benefit into future years. Suppose that Sally is paid $1,000 a week as a salary. She earns two weeks of vacation as a benefit each year. Sally is able to carry over unused vacation into future years.

The company's accounting staff needs to post an accrual entry at year-end for the two weeks of vacation Sally has earned but has not taken. The firm debits (increases) accrued vacation expense $2,000 and credits (increases) accrued vacation payable $2,000. That amount represents two weeks of Sally's salary.

The account titles may vary slightly. The important point is that the business needs to post an expense and a payable for the vacation days Sally has earned. This first entry gets the expense posted to the year that Sally earned the vacation days. When she takes those earned days as vacation in a future year, the firm debits (reduces) accrued vacation payable and credits cash. Cash is paid to Sally during her vacation.

Dealing with long-term debt

Retirement of debt means that the owner of the debt is repaid and that the debt is removed from the issuer's financial statements.

The most common debt instrument on the FAR test questions is a bond. Bonds are normally issued at the debt's *face amount,* the amount stated on the bond certificate. Face amount is also what is repaid to the investor at maturity. When a bond is retired, the issuer debits (reduces) bond payable and credits (reduces) cash.

The FAR may test a few other situations related to debt retirement. For example, a bond may be issued at more or less than the face amount. Also, some bonds allow the issuer to repay principal over time rather than at maturity. In that case, the issuer isn't repaying the entire principal balance at maturity; some principal has already been repaid.

When calculating a gain or loss on debt retirement, compare the dollar amount of the liability removed with the cash (or other assets) given up. If those two amounts differ, you have a gain or loss. If you need a debit entry to balance debits and credits, you have a loss. For example, say you give up a piece of equipment with a book value of $600,000 to retire a $500,000 face-amount bond issue. The entry is to debit (reduce) bond payable $500,000 and credit (reduce) equipment $600,000. To balance debits and credits, you need a $100,000 debit. That debit is posted to loss on debt retirement.

If you retire a $500,000 bond payable in exchange for equipment with a $450,000 book value, you debit $500,000 bond payable and credit equipment $450,000. To balance debits and credits, you need a $50,000 credit. That credit is a gain on bond retirement.

Amortizing bonds

A bond is normally issued at its face amount, or *par amount,* which is the principal amount stated on the face of the bond certificate. In some circumstances, however, bonds are issued at a discount or premium.

With a discount, the coupon rate on the bond is less than the coupon rate for similar bonds that are being issued. A *discount* is a price that is less than the face amount. The coupon rate is the interest rate stated on the bond certificate.

Say a firm wants to issue a $100,000 face-amount, 10-year, 6 percent coupon bond. Other 10-year bonds of similar quality are being issued at 7 percent. To entice an investor to buy the 6 percent bond, the company would need to issue the bond at a discount. If the business issued the $100,000 face amount bond for $98,000 in cash, this is the journal entry they would post:

Debit cash $98,000, debit discount on bond payable $2,000

Credit bond payable $100,000

Keep in mind that the issuer always pays the face amount to the investor at maturity. It follows that the liability created, or bond payable, is always for the face amount of the bond.

To make debits balance with credits, the company posts a $2,000 debit to "discount on bond payable." The discount represents an additional expense to the issuer. Although the bond was issued at $98,000 to entice a buyer, the issuer still has to pay $100,000 at maturity. In essence, the issuer held a sale. The discount is the lower sale price for the bond.

A bond discount is *amortized;* the balance in the discount account is moved into expense over the life of the bond. Bond amortization and fixed-asset depreciation are both methods used to post expenses. Say that the $2,000 discount is amortized on a straight-line basis over the 10-year life of the bond. The annual amortization would be $2,000 ÷ 10 years = $200. Here's the journal entry:

Debit $200 amortization expense, credit $200 discount on bond payable

Bonds may also be issued at a *premium,* or at an issue price that is more than par. If the coupon rate on the bond is more than the current market rate for bond of similar quality, the bond is issued at a premium.

Suppose a $100,000, 10-year, 6 percent bond is issued at a price of $104,000. Ten-year bonds of similar quality are being issued with 4 percent coupons, so the 6 percent bond is more attractive. Here's the journal entry when the bond is issued:

Debit cash $104,000

Credit bond payable $100,000, credit premium on bond payable $4,000

Note that the bond payable is credited for $100,000. That's the same credit to bond payable that was posted for the bond issued at a discount.

The premium, which represents additional income to the issuer, is amortized into bond income over the life of the bond. If the $4,000 premium is amortized on a straight-line basis over the 10-year life of the bond, the annual amortization would be $4,000 ÷ 10 years = $400. Here's the journal entry:

Debit $400 premium on bond payable, credit $400 bond income

Throwing in other long-term debts

Two other types of liabilities are frequently tested on the FAR test. Both liabilities may be current liabilities (due within a year) or long-term liabilities (payable in a year or longer), but they're more commonly tested as long-term debts.

A *deferred tax liability* is a tax payment that is due in a future period. These liabilities occur because of a difference in accounting treatment between a company's accounting records and the tax return. Accountants also refer to this as a *book versus tax difference.*

Depreciation is a frequently tested topic with deferred taxes. It's common to have a depreciation method for the accounting records that's different from the tax return (see the earlier section "Recalling fixed assets" for info on depreciation methods). Consider the financial impact of using an accelerated depreciation method for taxes and a straight-line method for the accounting records (book):

- An accelerated method (like double-declining balance) generates more depreciation expense in the early years than the straight-line method.
- Higher depreciation expense in early years lowers net income in the early years.
- Lower net income in the early years results in a lower tax liability.

Total depreciation over the asset's useful life is the same, regardless of the depreciation method chosen. If accelerated depreciation generates lower net income and a lower tax bill in the early years, the business will post more net income and more tax liability in *later years*. That's because accelerated depreciation methods post less depreciation in later years.

Say, for instance, that the sum of years' digits (SYD) method (an accelerated method) generates $100 of depreciation in the first year of an asset's useful life. Straight-line depreciation posts $50 of depreciation. So in Year 1, SYD generates $50 more expense, which would mean that net income is lower by $50. If the tax rate is 40 percent, SYD generates a tax liability that is $20 lower ($50 × 0.40).

For deferred taxes, keep in mind that any difference between accounting records and the tax return that results in a different level of net income may create a deferred tax liability. That situation may also create a *deferred tax asset*. With a tax asset, net income is lower in future years, which creates less tax liability.

Another long-term liability that shows up on the FAR test is pension liabilities. A *pension* is a series of payments from an investment fund to a retired former employee. Here are two types of plans:

- **Defined benefit:** Defined benefit plans require a company to pay specific dollar amounts to retired employees. It's the company's responsibility to invest enough dollars to pay the required pension amounts.

- **Defined contribution:** A defined contribution plan requires the business to invest specific dollar amounts in the retirement plan. The pension payout is based on the investment performance of the retirement plan. The company isn't obligated to pay a specific pension amount.

Businesses need to consider two calculations for pensions. The *projected benefit obligation* (PBO) defines the dollar amount that the company must pay at a future point in time. *Plan assets,* on the other hand, represent the value of the dollars currently invested to meet the PBO. If the PBO exceeds the fair market value of the plan assets, the company needs to recognize a liability for that obligation in the balance sheet.

Finishing with equity

Normally, when companies pay dividends to shareholders, they do so in cash. However, businesses can use other assets as *property dividends*. Whether cash is paid or some other asset is distributed, the transaction reduces the equity section of the balance sheet.

For example, suppose a company owns land at a cost of $100,000. The firm wants to pay a property dividend to a large shareholder. The company *declares* a dividend on March 27. This *declaration date* is the date on which the board of directors announces the next dividend payment. Now assume that the land has a fair market value of $150,000 on the declaration date. When the property dividend is paid, the firm makes this journal entry:

Debit property dividend $150,000

Credit gain on disposition of property $50,000, land $100,000

This entry treats the land as if it were sold at fair market value. The debit to property divi-dend reduces equity for the fair market value of the land. Land is credited for its carrying amount ($100,000). Because land doesn't depreciate, the land's carrying value (cost less accumulated depreciation) is the same as original cost (check out the earlier section "Recalling fixed assets" for details on depreciation). The difference between the carrying amount and fair value is a $50,000 gain. You know it's a gain because you need a credit entry to make total debits equal credits.

Stock appreciation rights (SARs) are a method to reward valuable employees for staying with your firm. The reward is the increase in the market price of the company's stock. A firm starts out by setting an *exercise price,* the stock price that's subtracted from the market price to determine the value of the SAR. For example, suppose that the exercise price is $20. One SAR allows the holder to receive the difference between the market price and the exercise price in cash. In this example, assume 10,000 rights are issued on December 31, Year 1.

To earn the benefit from exercising the SARs, the employee must complete a *service period.* Say the service period is 2 years. That means that the worker can exercise the SARs and receive cash starting on December 31, Year 3. Suppose that the market price of the stock on December 31, Year 2, is $40. A typical FAR test questions will ask you to calculate the com-pensation expense and the liability for the SARs plan for Year 2. Here are the steps to answer the questions:

1. **Compute the difference between the market price of the stock and the exercise price per share.**

   As of December 31, Year 2, the calculation is $40 – $20 = $20. Twenty dollars is the value of one right.

2. **Multiply the value of one right by the number of rights issued.**

   That amount is $20 × 10,000 = $200,000. The $200,000 is total *estimated compensation expense*.

3. **To compute the compensation expense, divide the total estimated compensation expense by the service period.**

   That calculation is $200,000 ÷ 2 years = $100,000 per year of service. At the end of Year 2, 1 year of the service period has passed. The company should debit compensa-tion expense $100,000 and credit liability for SARs $100,000.

When the service period ends on December 31, Year 3, an employee can exercise the SARs. Note that the market price of the stock may have changed, so the amount of compensation expense and liability may be adjusted. When the value of a right is paid to the worker, the firm debits (reduces) liability for SARs and credits cash.

Posting gains and losses from stock options

An *option* on stock is very similar to a stock appreciation right. An option is a contract in which the buyer of the option has a right to do something and the seller has an obligation. The option buyer controls the transaction.

Suppose that, on March 1, you buy an option to purchase 100 shares of IBM common stock at a price of $40 per share. You have the right to buy the shares any business day until June 1. The $40 price is called the *strike price* or *exercise price,* and June 1 is the *expiration date.* When you buy an option, you refer to the shares, strike price, and expiration date as an *option position.*

The value of your stock option has two components:

- ✔ **Time value:** The more time you have until expiration, the better the chance that the market price of the stock will move above the strike price. If the stock price, for example, increases to $50 by March 31, you can buy the stock at the strike price of $40 — and sell the stock at the market price of $50. A FAR test question will provide the dollar amount of time value.

- ✔ **Intrinsic value:** This term isn't one that you'll necessarily see on the FAR test. Option professionals use *intrinsic value* to refer to the current difference between the strike price and the exercise price. Suppose that, on March 31, the intrinsic value of the option is $45 – $40 = $5. The total value of your option is the time value plus the intrinsic value.

Here's a typical FAR question on options. Say that, on March 1, the time value of your option is $500. You're putting together the financials as of March 31, and you need to know the value of the option position on that date. The time value on March 31 is $300. The lower time value should make sense, because less time remains on the option contract before expiration. The intrinsic value of the option position is 100 shares × ($45 – $40) = 100 × $5 = $500. The total option position value is the $300 time value plus the $500 intrinsic value, or $800.

Options are accounted for using fair market value. When you purchase the option position on March 1, the fair market value is simply the time value of $500. That assumes that there's no difference between the strike price and exercise price — that is, no intrinsic value.

On March 31, the option position's fair market value is adjusted to $800. The difference of $300 increase ($800 – $500) is recorded as a gain on option position in the income statement.

Wrapping up with revenue

Under the matching principle (see Chapter 4), accountants want to match revenue with the expenses incurred to generate that revenue. Revenue is recognized when it's earned. Revenue is earned when the product or service is delivered to the client. When you ship the customer the blue jeans he bought, for example, you post revenue.

Sometimes businesses exchange products and services instead of paying each other cash. For example, if you manage a theatre, you may provide 100 tickets to a show in exchange for a carpentry company's time to build a set for the show. Consider when both parties would recognize revenue.

In order to recognize revenue, the other party would need to use the service provided. If the carpenter uses tickets for a show, the theatre company would post revenue. The carpenter has used the service he purchased. Instead of paying cash, the carpenter paid with a service.

When the tickets are used, the theatre company debits (increases) accounts receivable and credits (increases) revenue. Later, when the carpenter builds the set, the theatre company would debit (create) an asset called *theatre set* and credit (reduce) accounts receivable. The theatre now has an asset, a set that it will use to generate ticket sales.

Considering Important Transactions and Events

This section addresses corrections of errors in the financial statements. You also see an in-depth discussion of earnings per share (EPS), which is a critical measurement of company profitability. The section also covers disclosures for related party transactions and subsequent events.

Correcting errors and reviewing accounting changes

A theme throughout accounting is the need to provide relevant financial information that allows investors to make informed decisions. This section discusses several topics that require a CPA to provide added financial disclosure. You find out how to correct an error in a prior year's financial records. You also go over the process of creating consolidated financial statements. A consolidation shows a financial-statement reader what the records would look like if two companies were combined into one.

Changing the accounting records

A correction of a prior-period error is posted to equity (see the earlier section "Adding in other statements and disclosures" for details). If a correction needs to be disclosed, the amount is included in the statement of changes in equity, also called the *statement of retained earnings*.

The balance of a temporary account is adjusted to zero at the end of each accounting period — typically the end of each month. Revenue and expense accounts are temporary accounts. Every month, revenue and expenses are netted against each other to calculate net income. Net income is posted to retained earnings. A net profit increases retained earnings, and a loss decreases retained earnings.

When you find an error after the fiscal year is over, you cannot make an adjustment to net income. Net income was posted to retained earnings in the prior year, which adjusted the account to zero. To disclose the correction, you *restate* the financial statements for the prior year. That restatement includes an adjustment to retained earnings to correct the error. The correction is made *net of taxes,* which means that the impact on the federal tax return is also posted.

Most companies have a capitalization policy, which sets a dollar amount that determines whether costs should be capitalized as assets or immediately expensed. Suppose that a truck with a cost of $20,000 was immediately expensed in the prior year. Company policy dictates that costs greater than $500 should be capitalized. The company made an error in a prior period.

Consider the impact of the error on the financial statements. To finish setting up the example, suppose that the $20,000 truck should be depreciated at an annual rate of $4,000 per year. Suppose also that the $20,000 truck was purchased on January 1 of Year 1.

The correct accounting treatment for Year 1 is to post a new truck asset for $20,000 and recognize $4,000 of depreciation expense. Instead, no asset was created, and $20,000 was immediately expensed. Expenses are overstated by $16,000 (that is, $20,000 – $4,000). If expenses are too high, that means that net income for the year is too low by $16,000. If net income is too low, it follows that the tax liability is too low. Less income would result in fewer taxes paid. If, for example, the federal tax rate was 30 percent, the tax liability is understated by $16,000 × 0.30 = $4,800.

The company would restate the prior-year financial statements by reducing retained earnings for the net of tax correction of $4,800.

Dealing with consolidations and combinations

A *consolidation* is a set of financials that combines two companies. In most cases, the consolidated financials represent a what-if scenario. Those two companies still operate independently. The consolidation shows the financial-statement reader how the financials would look if the companies were combined.

One company may invest in another company's debt. Firms also invest in the equity (common stock) of other businesses. If Acme, for example, buys 20 percent of Standard's common stock, Acme would debit Investment in Standard to account for the cost of the investment.

When a company buys a large enough percentage of ownership in a business, the buyer is referred to as the *parent*. The acquired company is called the *subsidiary*. The percentage of stock purchased has several components, which you can find in any other reputable test-prep resource. The purpose of this section of to explain the concept of consolidations.

To prepare consolidated financial statements, you start by posting the parent and the subsidiary's financial results in two separate columns. You then need to eliminate intercompany activity. *Intercompany activity* represents transactions between the parent and subsidiary.

Suppose, for example, that the subsidiary sold the parent inventory for a $100 profit; the subsidiary's $100 profit would need to be eliminated in consolidation. In addition, the parent's value for that inventory would need to be reduced by that amount of the subsidiary's profit ($100). The eliminating entry — in consolidation — would be to debit (reduce) net income $100 and credit (reduce) inventory $100.

The elimination entries are posted in a column next to the parent and subsidiary financial statements. To compute the consolidated financials, you add across the columns to get a consolidated balance for each account. To find consolidated inventory, you add the parent and subsidiary's inventory balance and then subtract the intercompany $100 elimination entry.

Going over other income statement activity

In this section, I go into more detail about the income statement. You see a discussion of earnings per share, an important measure of profitability. I also cover other transactions that aren't related to day-to-day business operations, such as extraordinary items. I wrap up this section with an overview of comprehensive income.

Looking over earnings per share

One important indicator of profitability is *earnings per share (EPS)*. EPS is defined as net income available for common shareholders divided by average common stock shares outstanding. EPS tells a financial-statement reader how much a company earns for each share of stock outstanding. The more a business can earn per common stock share, the more valuable a share of stock becomes.

Average common stock shares outstanding refers to the average number of shares during the period, usually a year. The average is computed as follows:

$$\text{Avg. common shares} = \frac{\left(\begin{array}{c}\text{Beginning}\\ \text{common stock shares}\\ \text{outstanding}\end{array}\right) + \left(\begin{array}{c}\text{Ending}\\ \text{common stock shares}\\ \text{outstanding}\end{array}\right)}{2}$$

Note that the basic EPS formula is calculated using common stock outstanding. *Shares outstanding* refers to shares held by the public. The basic formula does not include preferred stock shares in the denominator. *Preferred stock* is "preferred" or "better" than common stock for two reasons:

✔ If the company generates earnings, preferred shareholders receive a dividend before any dividend payments to common shareholders.

✔ Preferred shareholders can make a claim on the assets of the company before common shareholders. If the company liquidates, creditors and owners stand in line to make a claim of ownership for the assets that remain. Preferred shareholders have a claim on assets before common shareholders.

When net income is calculated for basic EPS, any dividends paid to preferred shareholders are subtracted. Here's how the basic EPS formula looks, given any preferred dividends:

$$\text{Basic EPS} = \frac{\text{Net income} - \text{Preferred stock dividends}}{\text{Average common stock shares outstanding}}$$

Companies that use basic EPS have a simple capital structure. A *simple capital structure* means that the company hasn't issued any securities that are potentially dilutive. *Dilutive securities* are securities that can be converted into shares of common stock. Dilutive securities have the potential to increase the number of common shares outstanding.

Take a look at the basic EPS formula. Suppose that net income less preferred stock dividends is $10,000. If 5,000 common stock shares are outstanding, basic EPS is $10,000 ÷ 5,000 shares = $2 per share. If dilutive securities are converted into 5,000 additional common stock shares, EPS would be $10,000 ÷ 10,000 shares = $1 per share. The numerator ($10,000) didn't change, but the denominator (common shares outstanding) doubled. Dilutive securities can reduce EPS.

To fully inform financial-statement readers, businesses with dilutive securities also present *dilutive EPS*. The numerator for dilutive EPS is the same as in basic EPS. In each case, you use Net income – Preferred stock dividends. The denominator of the formula, however, is different. Dilutive EPS assumes that any securities that can be converted into common stock are converted. Those common stock conversions have the impact of increasing common stock shares outstanding. Here are some potentially dilutive securities that you may see on the FAR test:

✔ **Stock options:** I explain this security earlier in the section "Posting gains and losses from stock options."

✔ **Convertible bonds and convertible preferred stock:** Convertible securities give the owner a choice to convert the security into a certain number of shares of common stock at a given price. If a bond is convertible, the terms of the conversion are stated on the bond certificate. Some preferred stock shares have an option to convert to common stock shares.

✔ **Rights and warrants:** Rights and warrants are normally attached to a bond or preferred stock certificate. Rights and warrants give the owner the choice to purchase a certain number of shares of common stock at a specific price.

If any of these securities are converted to common stock, they lower earnings per share. This assumes that net income for the year is unchanged and that total common stock shares outstanding increases.

FAR test questions normally list several types of dilutive securities and ask you to convert the number of additional shares of common stock outstanding. When you know the new number of common stock shares, you can compute dilutive EPS.

Adding in extraordinary and unusual items to find net income

Operations are the day-to-day activities you perform to run your business. For example, to make blue jeans, your business may buy denim as a raw material, pay payroll, and collect payments from blue jean sales. Those are your normal business operations. However, if you issue stock or sell a building, those activities aren't directly related to selling blue jeans. In other words, those transactions are not due to normal operations.

A multi-step income statement is divided into two main parts: an operating section and a non-operating section. In some cases, a third section of the income statement lists discontinued operations and extraordinary items. Here's an explanation of a multi-step income statement:

- ✓ **Operating income:** The operating section of the income statement is presented in this format:

  Sales − Cost of sales = Gross profit

  Gross profit − Other expenses (selling, general, admin.) = Operating income

- ✓ **Non-operating income:** Several items are added or subtracted from operating income to arrive at non-operating income. Interest income and expenses are listed in this section. Also, any gains and losses on asset sales that aren't related to operations are posted here. If the blue jean company sold a building, for example, the gain or loss would be listed in this section.

- ✓ **Discontinued operations and extraordinary events:** The third section of the income statement starts with non-operating income. You then adjust non-operating income for rare, extraordinary events that occur in the business. Here are two main categories that are tested:

  - **Discontinued operations:** Discontinued operations are the costs incurred to eliminate a company division or department. They might include severance pay to workers or the cost of selling division assets at a loss.

  - **Extraordinary items:** Extraordinary items are transactions that are both unusual and infrequent. A loss due to a rare weather occurrence would be considered an extraordinary item. If a factory were damaged due to a tornado in an area of the country where tornados are rare, that event would be considered extraordinary.

    A business may have other events that are unusual but aren't considered infrequent. For example, if a manufacturing company's employees are unionized, a loss due to the costs of a worker strike may be unusual but not infrequent. Based on the industry, strikes may happen occasionally. The loss for worker strike would be posted as a separate item in the non-operating income section, not under extraordinary items.

Non-operating income is adjusted for discontinued operations and extraordinary items to arrive at net income.

Nailing down comprehensive income

Comprehensive income adjusts net income for some additional gain and loss activity. Companies that report both net income and comprehensive income must provide a schedule that reconciles the differences between those two amounts. *Other comprehensive income* is the difference between net income and comprehensive income.

Here are the two most common gains and losses that are included in comprehensive income (and excluded from net income):

- **Change in market value of securities held as available for sale.** *Available for sale* (AFS) securities are purchased with the intent of selling them in the short term. At the end of each accounting period, the value of AFS securities is adjusted to the current fair market value. The unrealized gain or loss is recorded as other comprehensive income.

- **Gains and losses from foreign currency exchange rates**. Assume your U.S.-based company owns a subsidiary that does business in Britain, using the British pound as the currency. You're required to convert the activity for all your overseas operations into U.S. dollars. When you translate the British financial results into U.S. dollars, you may have a gain or a loss, depending on the exchange rate for dollars versus pounds. That gain or loss is included in comprehensive income. (Chapter 4 explains currency risk and hedging to reduce that risk.)

FAR test questions typically provide gains and losses for one or both of these situations. The question asks you to compute net income, comprehensive income, or the difference between the two (other comprehensive income).

A question about foreign currency may bring up the concept of a functional currency. *Functional currency* is defined as the primary form of currency that a company uses to operate its business. If a U.S.-based company has most of its operations in Mexico, the Mexican peso is the firm's functional currency. Note that the U.S. company generates financials in U.S. dollars, even though the functional currency is the peso. The U.S. firm will translate pesos into dollars for the purposes of financial reporting.

Adding other required disclosures

Additional disclosures are required for two important situations. Accountants may need to explain related-party transactions. A related party has a unique connection to a company, beyond a relationship as a vendor or customer. CPAs also have to address events and transactions that occur after the financial statements have been prepared. You see a discussion of those subsequent events in this section.

Remembering related parties

A *related party* is someone who has a relationship with a company other than being a vendor or a customer. Transactions involving related parties need to be identified and disclosed to financial-statement readers. The reader can make a judgment on whether the related-party transaction was beneficial to the company issuing the financial statements.

Here are some transactions that may indicate a related-party transaction:

- Borrowing or lending on an interest-free basis or at an interest rate that's below current market rate

- Completing a real estate transaction at a price below fair market value

- Exchanging one asset for a similar asset, which is referred to as a nonmonetary exchange (NME); head over to "Looking at nonmonetary exchanges" for more on NMEs

- A loan agreement that doesn't document when and how borrowed funds will be repaid

An auditor will perform procedures to locate related-party transactions and to ask company management about all related-party situations. Those procedures can include reviewing company regulatory filings as well as reading minutes from board of directors meetings.

An *audit* takes place when a CPA firm performs procedures on a company's financial statements. Based on those procedures, the auditing firm provides a written audit opinion. The audit opinion states whether the financial statements were prepared in accordance with generally accepted accounting principles (GAAP).

The auditor will ask management whether the related-party transaction has the same terms as an arm's-length transaction. An *arm's-length transaction* is one between two parties that have no relationship other than as vendor and customer. Note these two outcomes:

✔ If management can substantiate that the transaction was done on the same terms as an arm's-length agreement, the related-party transaction is simply disclosed.

✔ If management cannot substantiate that the transaction was done on the same terms as an arm's-length agreement, the transaction does not meet GAAP requirements. The auditor should express a qualified or adverse opinion on the financial statements. See more on audit opinions in Chapter 4 and in Chapter 11, which provides detail on the auditing and attestation (AUD) test.

Disclosing subsequent events

A *subsequent event* is an event or transaction that occurs after the balance sheet date but before the financial statements are issued. The balance sheet date is the date used on the balance sheet report — December 31, for example. Not surprisingly, gathering documentation and creating the financial reports takes time. As a result, the financial statements are issued sometime after the balance sheet date.

The FAR test asks questions about two types of subsequent events:

✔ **Type 1 subsequent event:** This event or transaction existed on or before the balance sheet date. Suppose that date is December 31. If a Type 1 event comes to the attention of an auditor, he or she requests that management make an adjusting entry to reflect the Type 1 event. The adjusting entry will change the financial statements as of December 31. If management doesn't post an adjusting entry, the auditor should issue a qualified audit opinion.

You have a Type 1 event, for example, if ongoing litigation that existed before the balance sheet date is resolved before the financial statements are issued. Company management should make an adjustment to recognize any legal expense or losses as of December 31.

✔ **Type 2 subsequent event:** This event or transaction didn't exist on or before the balance sheet date. This event happens after the balance sheet date but before the financial statements are issued. If a Type 2 event comes to the attention of an auditor, he or she requests that management disclose the event in the notes to the financial statements. If management doesn't disclose the subsequent event, the auditor should issue a qualified audit opinion. (See the earlier section "Adding in other statements and disclosures" for info on notes to the financial statements.)

A Type 2 event occurs, for example, when a business finds out that a customer has gone bankrupt after the balance sheet date but before the financial statements are issued. If management didn't know about the bankruptcy before December 31, there's no need to post an adjustment for any receivables owed by the customer. Instead, management should disclose the bankruptcy in the notes to the financial statements.

Type 1 and Type 2 subsequent events are assumed to be material events or transactions. *Material,* in this case, means that the event or transaction is large enough to be relevant and meaningful to the financial-statement reader. If the item isn't material, an auditor won't insist that management take action regarding an adjustment or disclosure. I discuss materiality in detail in Chapter 11.

Dealing with contingent liabilities

A *contingent liability* is a liability that may be incurred, depending on the outcome of a future event. Contingent liabilities are posted in the balance sheet when the liability is both probable and the amount can be reasonably estimated.

If both of the conditions are not met, an accountant may explain the contingent liability in a footnote that addresses the likelihood that the event will occur. The language used may be *probable, reasonably possible,* or *remote.* A footnote also explains how accurately the company can predict the dollar amount of the liability. The likelihood may be *known, reasonably estimated,* or *not reasonably estimated.*

The policy for dealing with contingent liabilities is consistent with the principle of conservatism, which I discuss in the earlier section "Mulling over inventory valuation." When in doubt, accountants should choose to disclose liabilities that may occur.

Accounting for Government Entities

The FAR test gauges your understanding of government accounting transactions. The general fund normally accounts for the most transactions in a government entity. You also need to know how purchases for goods and services are approved and implemented.

Government accounting uses the modified accrual basis of accounting. *Modified accrual* states that revenue should be recognized when it's available and measurable. For this basis, revenue is available when it's collectable within the current period or soon thereafter.

Checking out financial reports for a general fund

The most common FAR government test questions involve the *general fund.* Governments (federal, state, and local) account for spending in funds. A government entity uses funds just as a for-profit company uses divisions or departments. The general fund accounts for all the activity not accounted for in any other fund.

The general fund is comparable with income or cash flow from operations in a for-profit business (see the earlier section "Considering the statement of cash flows"). The general fund accounts for much of the day-by-day, generic operations of a government entity. Here's what you can find in the general fund:

✔ **Real accounts:** The general fund uses three accounts that are related to the balance sheet. These accounts are referred to as *real* because they post the actual (not budgeted) balance sheet–type activity of the government entity. Real accounts include current assets, current liabilities, and fund balance. *Fund balance* is the equity component of the general account balance sheet.

✔ **Budgetary accounts:** Government entities also use *budgetary accounts,* a set of accounts specifically to account for budgeted amounts:

- Governments use accounts for estimated revenue (possible tax revenue) and for other estimated financing sources (such as user fees for city facilities). These two accounts are the inflows.

- The outflow accounts are appropriations, encumbrances, and other financing uses. I cover appropriations and encumbrances in the next section.

Any remaining revenue balance after subtracting budgeted spending is posted to the budgetary fund balance. You see that both the real accounts and the budgetary accounts use a fund balance account.

✔ **Nominal accounts:** These accounts are used for the income-statement component of the government's actual spending. Whereas real accounts handle actual balance sheet activity, nominal accounts address income statement activity. Nominal accounts include revenue and other financing sources, such as proceeds from a bond issue or from a sale of assets. Expenditures, a nominal account, are part of the spending process I explain next.

Presenting appropriations, encumbrances, and expenditures

Government accounting has a unique process for approving spending. After a legislator suggests a purchase, the funds are first *appropriated,* which means that government officials approve the spending. Many governments (federal, state, and local) have appropriation committees that facilitate this process. Once appropriated, the funds are put in a government's budget. When the spending is budgeted, you book an entry for an *encumbrance*.

Suppose a legislator suggests a purchase of $3,000 in lifeguard stands for your city's municipal pool, and the $3,000 is appropriated. An encumbrance means that $3,000 is set aside specifically for the purchase of the lifeguard stands. Here's the journal entry:

Debit encumbrance $3,000, credit reserve for encumbrance $3,000

The reserve account allows the government entity to segregate the $3,000 encumbrance for future spending.

When the lifeguard stands are received, the city posts this entry:

Debit reserve for encumbrance $3,000, credit encumbrance $3,000

Debit expenditures $3,000, credit vouchers payable $3,000

The *expenditure account* is an expense account for government accounting. The voucher payable account is a liability account, similar to an accounts payable. This process is a frequently tested area on the FAR test.

Keeping Up with Not-for-Profits

One tested area of not-for-profits on the FAR exam is financial statements. You may be tested on similarities and differences between not-for-profit (NFP) and for-profit financial statements. Here's an overview of the basic financial statements:

Starting with the statement of financial position

The *statement of financial position* is similar to the balance sheet for a for-profit entity. The statement lists balances for assets and liabilities for a not-for-profit. Note, however, that NFPs don't have equity as an account, because shareholders do not own the NFP. An NFP exists to fulfill a mission, not for the benefit of shareholders. Instead of equity, NFPs use an account called *net assets*. The accounting equation for an NFP is

Assets – Liabilities = Net assets

The net asset section may include assets that have restrictions on their use. Net assets are assigned to one of three categories:

- **Unrestricted net assets:** This category is for assets donated to the NFP without any specific designation for the asset's use. Management can designate these assets for any use that fits the NFP's mission.

- **Temporarily restricted net assets:** If a donor places a restriction on the use of assets, the dollars are assigned to this category. Suppose net assets are donated to an NFP that encourages hiking and biking. A donor contributes funds for a ride-your-bike-to-work program. When the assets are used, the NFP must document that the funds were spent in compliance with the donor's restriction.

- **Permanently restricted net assets:** The NFP must keep permanently restricted assets "in perpetuity" (forever). Typically, the NFP benefits when the assets are invested. The donor most often gives the NFP permission to use interest and dividend income earned on the assets for some specific purpose. For example, many donors to schools donate permanently restricted assets but allow the earnings on the invested assets to be used for scholarships.

Assets can be reclassified from one net asset category to another, as long as the NFP gets approval from the donor.

Moving on to the statement of activities

The *statement of activities* is similar to an income statement for a for-profit entity. The document presents the results of the non-for-profit's fulfilling its mission. The NFP takes donations and spends them on activities. As a result, the statement of activities lists revenue (donations) and expenses (spending on activities).

A statement of activities groups revenue and expenses by net asset category. You see categories for revenue and expenses on the left-hand column and asset categories (unrestricted, temporarily restricted, and so on) across the top of the report.

Revenue can be broken down into several categories. They include contributions, dues, grants, and investment income on assets donations to the NFP. Expenses are normally segregated between program expenses and supporting services. *Program* refers to direct expenses for a specific activity, such as education or an event. *Supporting services* are the other expenses incurred that aren't directly related to the NFP activity, such as administrative costs and fundraising.

NFPs use the accrual method of accounting. When a donor commits to make a donation of some sort, the revenue from the donation is considered earned. The documentation for a donation is typically a signed letter or e-mail. Expenses are recognized when incurred. In this case, expenses are posted when the NFP spends on an activity.

Here is the formula for the statement of activities:

Revenue – Expenses = Change in net assets

Net assets are also included in the statement of financial position, so the statement of activities makes a connection to the financial position report. If revenue is greater than spending (expenses) for a project, the net asset balance will increase. If, for example, fees for an educational program (an activity) are $1,000 but expenses are only $800, net assets would increase by $200. That increase in net assets will be reflected in the statement of financial position. Keep in mind that the $200 must be spent on activities that fulfill the NFP's mission.

Adding in the statement of cash flows and notes

The financial statements of a not-for-profit also include a statement of cash flows and note to the financial statements. These NFP reports are very similar to what you find in a for-profit's set of financial statements. See the earlier sections "Considering the statement of cash flows" and "Adding in other statements and disclosures."

Chapter 9

Financial Accounting and Reporting Practice Questions

• •

The financial accounting and reporting (FAR) test covers the nuts and bolts of working as an accountant. One focus of this test is the typical transactions that an accountant posts each month and year. The FAR test also goes over accounting principles.

Business Combinations and Consolidations

1. Sun Co. is a wholly owned subsidiary of Star Co. Both companies have separate general ledgers and prepare separate financial statements. Sun requires standalone financial statements. Which of the following statements is correct?

   (A) Consolidated financial statements should be prepared for both Star and Sun.

   (B) Consolidated financial statements should be prepared only by Star and **not** by Sun.

   (C) After consolidation, the accounts of both Star and Sun should be changed to reflect the consolidated totals for future ease in reporting.

   (D) After consolidation, the accounts of both Star and Sun should be combined into one general-ledger accounting system for future ease in reporting.

Basic Concepts

2. UVW Broadcast Co. entered into a contract to exchange unsold advertising time for travel and lodging services with Hotel Co. As of June 30, advertising commercials of $10,000 were used. However, travel and lodging services were **not** provided. How should UVW account for advertising in its June 30 financial statements?

   (A) Revenue and expense is recognized when the agreement is complete.

   (B) An asset and revenue for $10,000 is recognized.

   (C) Both the revenue and expense of $10,000 are recognized.

   (D) **Not** reported.

3. When a company estimates its bad debt expense using the percent of net credit sales method, which of the following statements is true?

   (A) Matching is being followed.

   (B) Matching is **not** being followed.

   (C) Bad debt expense is **not** being matched with revenue.

   (D) Going concern is **not** being followed.

4. The premium on a 3-year insurance policy expiring on December 31, Year 3, was paid in total on January 1, Year 1. Assuming that the original payment was initially debited to an expense account and that appropriate adjusting entries have been recorded on December 31, Year 1 and Year 2, the balance in the prepaid asset account on December 31, Year 2, would be

(A) Zero.

(B) Lower than the balance on December 31, Year 3.

(C) The same as the original payment.

(D) The same as it would have been if the original payment had been initially debited to a prepaid asset account.

Error Correction

5. On January 2, Year 4, Raft Corp. discovered that it had incorrectly expensed a $210,000 machine purchased on January 2, Year 1. Raft estimated the machine's original useful life to be 10 years and its salvage value to be $10,000. Raft uses the straight-line method of depreciation and is subject to a 30% tax rate. In its December 31, Year 4, financial statements, what amount should Raft report as a prior period adjustment?

(A) $102,900

(B) $105,000

(C) $165,900

(D) $168,000

Accounting Changes

6. Evergreen Company purchased a patent on January 1, Year 1, for $178,500. The patent was being amortized over its remaining legal life of 15 years, expiring on January 1, Year 16. During Year 4, Evergreen determined that the economic benefits of the patent would **not** last longer than 10 years from the date of acquisition. What amount should be charged to patent amortization expense for the year ended December 31, Year 4?

(A) $10,500

(B) $17,850

(C) $20,400

(D) $35,700

7. Ball Corporation had the following infrequent gains during Year 1:

A $240,000 gain on sale of a plant facility; Ball continues similar operations at another location.

A $90,000 gain on repayment of a long-term note denominated in a foreign currency.

A $190,000 gain on reacquisition and retirement of bonds.

In its Year 1 income statement, how much should Ball report as total infrequent gains, which are **not** considered extraordinary?

(A) $520,000

(B) $430,000

(C) $330,000

(D) $190,000

8. A company reports the following information as of December 31:

Sales revenue	$800,000
Cost of goods sold	$600,000
Operating expenses	$90,000
Unrealized holding gain on available-for-sale securities, net of tax	$30,000

What amount should the company report as comprehensive income as of December 31?

(A) $30,000

(B) $110,000

(C) $140,000

(D) $200,000

Inventory

9. Loft Co. reviewed its inventory values for proper pricing at year-end. The following summarizes two inventory items examined for the lower of cost or market:

	Inventory item #1	Inventory item #2
Original cost	$210,000	$400,000
Replacement cost	$150,000	$370,000
Net realizable value	$240,000	$410,000
Net realizable value less profit margin	$208,000	$405,000

What amount should Loft include in inventory at year-end if it uses the total of the inventory to apply the lower of cost or market?

(A) $520,000

(B) $610,000

(C) $613,000

(D) $650,000

10. Lin Co. sells its merchandise at a gross profit of 30%. The following figures are among those pertaining to Lin's operations for the 6 months ended June 30, Year 2:

Sales	$200,000
Beginning inventory	$50,000
Purchases	$130,000

On June 30, Year 2, all of Lin's inventory was destroyed by fire. The estimated cost of this destroyed inventory was

(A) $120,000

(B) $70,000

(C) $40,000

(D) $20,000

Fixed Assets

11. Madden Company owns a tract of land, which it purchased in Year 1 for $100,000. The land is held as a future plant site and has a fair market value of $140,000 on July 1, Year 4. Hall Company also owns a tract of land held as a future plant site. Hall paid $180,000 for the land in Year 3, and the land has a fair market value of $200,000 on July 1, Year 4. On this date, Madden exchanged its land and paid $50,000 cash for the land owned by Hall. It is expected that the cash flows from the two tracts of land will **not** be significantly different. At what amount should Madden record the land acquired in the exchange?

(A) $150,000

(B) $160,000

(C) $190,000

(D) $200,000

12. A machine with a 4-year estimated useful life and an estimated 15% salvage value was acquired on January 1. Would depreciation expense using the sum-of-the-years' digits method of depreciation be higher or lower than depreciation expense using the double-declining balance method of depreciation in the first and second years?

	First year	*Second year*
(A)	Higher	Higher
(B)	Higher	Lower
(C)	Lower	Higher
(D)	Lower	Lower

Monetary Current Assets and Liabilities

13. In its December 31, Year 1, balance sheet, Fleet Co. reported accounts receivable of $100,000 before allowance for uncollectable accounts of $10,000. Credit sales during Year 2 were $611,000, and collections from customers, excluding recoveries, totaled $591,000. During Year 2, accounts receivable of $45,000 were written off and $17,000 was recovered. Fleet estimated that $15,000 of the accounts receivable at December 31, Year 2, was uncollectable. In its December 31, Year 2, balance sheet, what amount should Fleet report as accounts receivable before allowance for uncollectable accounts?

    (A) $58,000

    (B) $67,000

    (C) $75,000

    (D) $82,000

14. On September 1, Year 1, a company borrowed cash and signed a 2-year interest-bearing note on which both the principal and interest are payable on September 1, Year 3. The company did **not** elect the fair value option for reporting this note. On December 31, Year 2, the liability for accrued interest should be

    (A) Zero.

    (B) For 4 months of interest.

    (C) For 12 months of interest.

    (D) For 16 months of interest.

Present Value Fundamentals

15. On January 1, Year 1, Beal Corporation adopted a plan to accumulate funds for a new plant building to be erected beginning July 1, Year 6, at an estimated cost of $1,200,000. Beal intends to make five equal annual deposits in a fund that will earn interest at 8% compounded annually. The first deposit is made on July 1, Year 1. Present value and future amount factors are as follows:

Present value of 1 at 8% for 5 periods	0.68
Present value of 1 at 8% for 6 periods	0.63
Future amount of ordinary annuity of 1 at 8% for 5 periods	5.87
Future amount of annuity in advance of 1 at 8% for 5 periods	6.34

    Beal should make five annual deposits (rounded) of

    (A) $151,200

    (B) $163,200

    (C) $189,300

    (D) $204,400

Present Value Bonds

16. On March 1, Year 1, Harbour Corporation issued 10% debentures dated January 1, Year 1, in the face amount of $1,000,000, with interest payable on January 1 and July 1. The debentures were sold at par and accrued interest. How much should Harbour debit to cash on March 1, Year 1?

(A) $ 966,667

(B) $ 983,333

(C) $1,016,667

(D) $1,033,333

17. How would the amortization of discount on bonds payable affect each of the following?

	Carrying value of bond	*Net income*
(A)	Increase	Decrease
(B)	Increase	Increase
(C)	Decrease	Decrease
(D)	Decrease	Increase

Present Value Debt Restructure

18. E & S Partnership purchased land for $500,000 on May 1, Year 1, paying $100,000 cash and giving a $400,000 note payable to Big State Bank. E & S made three annual payments on the note totaling $179,000, which included interest of $89,000. E & S then defaulted on the note. Title to the land was transferred by E & S to Big State, which cancelled the note, releasing the partnership from further liability. At the time of the default, the fair value of the land approximated the note balance. In E & S's Year 4 income statement, the amount of the loss should be

(A) $279,000

(B) $221,000

(C) $190,000

(D) $100,000

Present Value Pension

19. A necessary condition for the recording of a pension liability is present when

(A) Projected benefit obligation exceeds accumulated benefit obligation.

(B) The market-related asset value exceeds accumulated benefit obligation.

(C) Accumulated benefit obligation exceeds the fair value of plan assets.

(D) Projected benefit obligation exceeds pension plan assets.

Present Value Leases

20. On January 1, Year 1, JCK Co. signed a contract for an 8-year lease of its equipment with a 10-year life. The present value of the 16 equal semiannual payments in advance equaled 85% of the equipment's fair value. The contract had no provision for JCK, the lessor, to give up legal ownership of the equipment. Should JCK recognize rent or interest revenue in Year 2, and should the revenue recognized in Year 2 be the same or smaller than the revenue recognized in Year 1?

	Year 2 revenues recognized	Year 2 amount recognized compared to Year 1
(A)	Rent	The same
(B)	Rent	Smaller
(C)	Interest	The same
(D)	Interest	Smaller

Deferred Taxes

21. Purl Company began operations on January 1, Year 1. It recognizes income from construction-type contracts under the percentage-of-completion method for financial reporting. However, on its income tax returns, Purl appropriately reports revenues under the completed-contract method. Information concerning income recognition under each method is as follows:

Year	Percentage-of-Completion	Completed-Contract
Year 1	$450,000	$0
Year 2	$675,000	$425,000
Year 3	$825,000	$925,000

For all affected years, assume the income tax rate is 30% and there are no other temporary differences. For Year 3, Purl should record an increase (decrease) in the deferred tax liability account of

(A) $165,000

(B) $70,000

(C) ($30,000)

(D) ($100,000)

Stockholders' Equity

22. Tyson Corp. purchased trading securities in March 1, Year 1, for $200,000. Tyson uses a December 31 year-end. The following information pertains to a property dividend of the trading securities purchased in March.

	Fair Value
Declaration date: December 20, Year 1	$300,000
Record date: January 10, Year 2	$310,000
Distribution date: January 28, Year 2	$305,000

How much gain should Tyson recognize in Year 1 as a result of this property dividend?

(A) $0

(B) $100,000

(C) $105,000

(D) $110,000

23. Wolf Co.'s grant of 30,000 stock appreciation rights enables key employees to receive cash equal to the difference between $20 and the market price of the stock on the date each right is exercised. The service period is Year 1 through Year 3, and the rights are exercisable in Year 4 and Year 5. The market prices of the stock were $25 and $28 at December 31, Year 1 and Year 2, respectively. What amount should Wolf report as the liability under the stock appreciation rights plan in its December 31, Year 2, balance sheet?

(A) $0

(B) $130,000

(C) $160,000

(D) $240,000

Investments

24. The market price of the common stock of an investee company increased during the year. How will the investor's investment account be affected by the increase in market price of that common stock under each of the following accounting methods? Assume the fair value option is **not** elected.

	Cost adjusted for fair value method	*Equity method*
(A)	No effect	No effect
(B)	No effect	Increase
(C)	Increase	No effect
(D)	Increase	Increase

Statement of Cash Flows

25. In a statement of cash flows (operating activities shown using the indirect approach), a decrease in prepaid expenses should be

    (A) Reported as an inflow and outflow of cash.

    (B) Reported as an outflow of cash.

    (C) Deducted from net income.

    (D) Added to net income.

26. On December 1 of the current year, Bann Co. entered into an option contract to purchase 2,000 shares of Norta Co. stock for $40 per share (the same as the current market price) by the end of the next two months. The time value of the option contract is $600. At the end of December, Norta's stock was selling for $43, and the time value of the option is now $400. If Bann does **not** exercise its option until January of the subsequent year, which of the following changes would reflect the proper accounting treatment for this transaction on Bann's December 31 year-end financial statements?

    (A) The option value will be disclosed in the footnotes only.

    (B) Other comprehensive income will increase by $6,000.

    (C) Net income will increase by $5,800.

    (D) Current assets will decrease by $200.

Personal Financial Statements

27. A business interest that constitutes a large part of an individual's total assets should be presented in a personal statement of financial condition as

    (A) A single amount equal to the proprietorship equity.

    (B) A single amount equal to the estimated current value of the business interest.

    (C) A separate listing of the individual assets and liabilities, at cost.

    (D) Separate line items of both total assets and total liabilities, at cost.

Interim Reporting

28. An inventory loss from a market price decline occurred in the first quarter. The loss was **not** expected to be restored in the fiscal year. However, in the third quarter, the inventory had a market price recovery that exceeded the market decline that occurred in the first quarter. For interim financial reporting, the dollar amount of net inventory should

    (A) Decrease in the first quarter by the amount of the market price decline and increase in the third quarter by the amount of the market price recovery.

    (B) Decrease in the first quarter by the amount of the market price decline and increase in the third quarter by the amount of decrease in the first quarter.

    (C) **Not** be affected in the first quarter and increase in the third quarter by the amount of the market price recovery that exceeded the amount of the market price decline.

    (D) **Not** be affected in either the first quarter or the third quarter.

Segment Reporting

29. The following information pertains to Klein Corp. and its operating segments for the year ended December 31, Year 1:

Combined profit of segments reporting profit	$600,000
Combined loss of segments reporting loss	($400,000)
Combined profit and loss of all segments	$200,000

Klein has a reportable segment if that segment's operating profit or loss is

(A) $25,000 profit.

(B) $60,000 profit.

(C) $55,000 loss.

(D) $55,000 profit.

Partnership Accounting

30. Beck, the active partner in Beck & Cris, receives an annual bonus of 25% of partnership net income after deducting the bonus. For the year ended December 31, Year 1, partnership net income before the bonus amounted to $300,000. Beck's Year 1 bonus should be

(A) $56,250

(B) $60,000

(C) $62,500

(D) $75,000

Answers and Explanations to Financial Accounting and Reporting Practice Questions

●●●

*T*he financial accounting and reporting (FAR) questions require more math calculations than any of the other tests. FAR also requires the student to understand and use many types of formulas. Some of these questions require multiple steps to compute an answer. For these reasons, it's important for you to review your FAR answer calculations.

Business Combinations and Consolidations

1. **B.** Star owns Sun; therefore, consolidated financial statements should be prepared for Star but not Sun.

Basic Concepts

2. **B.** Choice (B) is correct because UVW has provided $10,000 in advertising services and has a receivable for the travel and lodging services.

3. **A.** When bad debt expense is estimated based on a percentage of credit sales, the *matching principle* is being followed. The entity is attempting to estimate what part of this year's sales will not be collected, thereby matching this year's expense with this year's sales.

4. **D.** This answer is correct because under either method, the balance in the prepaid asset account on December 31, Year 2 (12/31/Y2), should be the unexpired portion of the policy. On 12/31/Y1, an adjusting entry would be made by debiting "Prepaid insurance" and crediting "Insurance expense" for two-thirds of the original payment (the unexpired portion of the policy). This would result in one-third of the payment being expensed. This entry would then be reversed on 1/1/Y2. At the end of Year 2, an adjusting entry would again be made by debiting "Prepaid insurance" and crediting "Insurance expense" for one-third of the original payment (the unexpired portion of the policy). Because the reversing entry will not be made until 1/1/Y3, the prepaid asset account balance would be the same on 12/31/Y2 for this method as it would have been had the payment originally been debited to "Prepaid insurance" on 1/1/Y1.

Error Correction

5. **B.** The requirement is to determine the amount of the prior period adjustment. ASC Topic 250 provides that an error in the financial statements requires restatement of the financial statements with an adjusting entry to retained earnings for the earliest period presented. When Raft incorrectly expensed the machine in Year 1, earnings before tax were understated

by $210,000. Had Raft properly capitalized this asset, it would have recorded $20,000 depreciation expense per year in Year 1, Year 2, and Year 3. Depreciation expense is calculated on a straight-line basis as $20,000 [($210,000 − $10,000)/10 years] per year. Over the three years, Raft would have recorded a total of $60,000 of depreciation expense. Therefore, as of January 2, Year 4, expenses have been overstated by $150,000 ($210,000 − $60,000), and the tax effect of the adjustment is 30% × $150,000, or $45,000. Therefore, the prior period adjustment to retained earnings net of taxes is $105,000 ($150,000 − $45,000).

Accounting Changes

6. **C.** Changes in accounting estimates are reflected prospectively. The solutions approach is to determine the yearly amortization for Year 1 through Year 3, the book value of the patent at 1/1/Y4, and the Year 4 amortization expense.

Yearly amortization, Year 1 – Year 3:	$\frac{\$178,500}{15 \text{ years}} = \$11,900$
Book value at 1/1/Y4:	$\$178,500 - (3 \times \$11,900) = \$142,800$
Year 4 amortization:	$\frac{\$142,800}{7 \text{ years}} = \$20,400$

The remaining useful life of 7 years is the total useful life of 10 years less 3 years already amortized.

Financial Statements

7. **A.** *Extraordinary items* are material items that are both unusual in nature and infrequent in occurrence. Neither a sale of plant facility nor a foreign currency transaction is unusual in nature. Therefore, these two items would be reported as infrequent but not extraordinary. In addition, the gain on retirement of debt is not classified as extraordinary. Note that the sale of the plant facility is not classified as discontinued operations, because similar operations are carried on at another location.

8. **C.** *Comprehensive income* is net income plus or minus unrealized gains and losses that are recognized in comprehensive income for the period. Net income is equal to $110,000 ($800,000 − $600,000 − $90,000). An unrealized holding gain on available-for-sale securities is classified as other comprehensive income. Therefore, Choice (C) is correct because comprehensive income is calculated as net income of $110,000 plus the $30,000 unrealized holding gain on available-for-sale securities, which equals $140,000.

Inventory

9. **B.** The requirement is to determine the amount of inventory at year-end. If Loft uses the total of the inventory to apply the lower of cost or market method, it must compare the original cost of $610,000 ($210,000 + $400,000) to the market value of the inventory. The total replacement cost of the inventory is $520,000; the net realizable value is $650,000 (the ceiling), and the net realizable value less normal profit margin is $613,000 (the floor). Market value is the replacement cost, limited by the ceiling and the floor. Therefore, the floor value of $613,000 is used for the market value and compared with the original cost of $610,000. Therefore, the lower of cost or market is the cost of $610,000.

10. **C.** Ending inventory for Lin Co. can be estimated by using the gross profit percentage to convert sales to cost of goods sold (estimated). If gross profit is 30 percent of sales, then cost of goods sold is 70 percent (100% − 30%) of sales. In this case, estimated cost of goods sold is $140,000 ($200,000 sales × 70%). Estimated cost of goods sold is then subtracted from actual goods available for sale to determine estimated ending inventory:

Beginning inventory	$50,000
Purchases	$130,000
Goods available for sale	$180,000
Less estimated cost of goods sold	($140,000)
Estimated ending inventory	$40,000

Beginning inventory	$50,000
Purchases	$130,000
Goods available for sale	$180,000
Less estimated cost of goods sold	($140,000)
Estimated ending inventory	$40,000

Fixed Assets

11. **A.** Per ASC Topic 845, if the cash flows of the two assets are not significantly different, the transaction lacks commercial substance and is recorded at book value. Therefore, the land acquired is recorded as total of the cash paid ($50,000) plus the book value of the land surrendered ($100,000), or $150,000. The economic gain of $40,000 ($140,000 market value less $100,000 book value) is not recognized. The journal entry is

Land (new)	$150,000
Land (old)	$100,000
Cash	$50,000

12. **C.** This answer is correct because the equation for calculating sum-of-the-years' digits (SYD) depreciation is

$$\text{SYD depreciation} = \frac{\text{Years remaining}}{\text{SYD}} \times (\text{Cost} - \text{Salvage value})$$

Year 1: $\frac{4}{10} \times (1.00 - 0.15) = 34.0\%$

Year 2: $\frac{3}{10} \times (1.00 - 0.15) = 25.5\%$

And the equation for double-declining balance depreciation (DDB) is

$$\text{DDB} = \frac{200\%}{\text{Useful life}} \times \text{Book value}$$

Year 1: $\frac{200\%}{4} \times 1.00 = 50.0\%$

Year 2: $\frac{200\%}{4} \times (1.00 - 0.50) = 25.0\%$

Therefore,

Year 1: SYD < DDB (34.0% < 50.0%)
Year 2: SYD > DDB (25.5% > 25.0%)

Recall that salvage value is included in the SYD calculation and not in the DDB calculation.

Monetary Current Assets and Liabilities

13. **C.** The solutions approach is to set up a T-account for accounts receivable and then solve for the ending balance.

Accounts Receivable			
12/31/Y1	100,000	591,000	Year 2 collections from customers
Year 2 credit sales	611,000	45,000	Year 2 AR write-off
12/31/Y2	?		

The ending accounts receivable balance for 12/31/Y1 was given. This becomes the beginning balance for Year 2. The Year 2 credit sales would be recorded by debiting accounts receivable and crediting sales. The collections from customers would be recorded by debiting cash and crediting accounts receivable. The write-off of accounts receivable would be recorded by debiting the allowance account and crediting accounts receivable. The $17,000 of recoveries does not impact the ending balance of accounts receivable, as recoveries are put back into accounts receivable and then taken out as they are paid in Year 2. The ending balance can then be solved for by adding up the debit column of accounts receivable and then subtracting the credit column.

$100,000 + $611,000 − $591,000 − $45,000 = $75,000

14. **D.** This answer is correct because although the interest does not have to be paid until September 1, Year 3, proper accrual accounting requires that at the end of each year, an adjusting entry be made to accrue that year's interest expense. Therefore, at the end of Year 1, 4 months of interest would be accrued. At the end of Year 2, an additional 12 months of interest would be accrued, which makes the total interest accrued as of December 31, Year 2, equal 16 months.

Present Value Fundamentals

15. **C.** The desired fund balance on July 1, Year 6 ($1,200,000), is a future amount. The series of five equal annual deposits is an annuity in advance. Whether this is an ordinary annuity or an annuity in advance can be determined by looking at the last deposit. The last deposit (on 7/1/Y5) is made one year prior to the date the future amount is needed. Therefore, these are beginning-of-year payments, and this is an annuity in advance. The deposit amount is computed here:

$$\frac{\text{Future amount}}{\text{F.A. factor}} = \frac{\$1,200,000}{6.34} = \$189,274$$

16. **C.** The amount of cash received is equal to the selling price of the bond plus accrued interest if the bond is issued between interest dates.

Sales price (bonds were sold at par)	$1,000,000
Accrued interest for 2 months $\left(\$1,000,000 \times 10\% \times \dfrac{2}{12}\right)$	$16,667
	$1,016,667

17. **A.** The solutions approach is to make the entry necessary to record the amortization of the discount.

    Recall that the *discount on bonds payable* account usually carries a debit balance that reduces the carrying value of the bonds. Choice (A) is correct because the credit to the discount account increases the carrying value of the bond, and the debit to interest expense will decrease net income.

Present Value Debt Restructure

18. **C.** On 5/1/Y1, E & S recorded the land purchased at a cost of $500,000.

Land	$500,000
Cash	$100,000
Note payable	$400,000

The three payments made would result in debits to note payable totaling $90,000 ($179,000 payments – $89,000 interest), bringing the balance in that account down to $310,000 ($400,000 – $90,000). Because the land transferred to settle the debt had a fair value of approximately $310,000, there's no gain on restructure. There is, however, a loss on transfer of land of $190,000, because the fair value of the land is less than its carrying amount ($500,000 – $310,000).

Loss on transfer of land	$190,000
Note payable	$310,000
Land	$500,000

Present Value Pension

19. **D.** ASC Topic 715 requires that if the projected benefit obligation exceeds the fair value of plan assets, a liability must be recognized in the balance sheet.

20. **D.** This lease qualifies as a direct financing lease; therefore, interest revenue rather than rent revenue will be recognized. Had the lease qualified as an operating lease, rent revenue would have been recognized. The lessor's criteria for direct financing classification is as follows:

1. The lease transfers ownership to the lessee at the end of the lease.

2. The lease contains a bargain purchase option.

3. The lease term is greater than 75 percent of an asset's economic life.

4. The present value of the minimum lease payments is greater than 90 percent of the fair value of the leased asset.

In addition, collectability of the minimum lease payments must be predictable, and there may be no important uncertainties concerning costs yet to be incurred by the lessee. Because the question is silent in this regard, assume that the latter conditions are met. Recall that if one of the first four criteria is met, the lease is treated as a capital lease. In this case, because the lease term is for 80 percent of the asset's economic life, condition (3) is met, and the lease is properly treated as a capital lease.

Also, the amount of interest revenue will be smaller in Year 2 than the revenue in Year 1. This result occurs because the present value of the minimum lease payments or carrying value of the obligation decreases each year as lease payments are received. As this occurs, the amount of interest revenue on the outstanding amount of the investment will decrease as well. Over the course of time, the investment-reduction portion of each level payment increases and the amount of interest declines.

Deferred Taxes

21. **C.** For financial reporting purposes, income is recognized using the percentage-of-completion method. For tax purposes, income is recognized using the completed-contract method. In Year 1 and Year 2, financial income exceeded taxable income, resulting in a deferred tax liability. In Year 3, part of this temporary difference reversed; taxable income ($925,000) exceeded financial income ($825,000) by $100,000. This $100,000 amount is a reversal of a prior temporary difference; therefore, the deferred tax liability must decrease by the tax effect of the reversal, or by $30,000 ($100,000×30%).

Stockholders' Equity

22. **B.** A *property dividend* is a nonreciprocal transfer of nonmonetary assets between an enterprise and its owners. A transfer of a nonmonetary asset to a stockholder or to another entity in a nonreciprocal transfer should be recorded at the fair value of the asset transferred, and a gain (or loss) should be recognized on the disposition of the asset. The fair value of the property on the declaration date less the carrying value of the property equals the gain (or loss). Because the trading securities were purchased in the current year, they haven't yet been adjusted to fair value. Therefore, the carrying value at the date of declaration is $200,000, and the amount of gain to be recognized is $300,000 – $200,000 = $100,000.

23. **C.** The 30,000 stock appreciation rights (SARs) entitle the holders to receive cash equal to the excess of the stock's market price on the exercise date over $20. On 12/31/Y2, the estimate of total SARs compensation expense is $240,000 [30,000×($28–$20)]. Because the required service period is 3 years, this total expense will be allocated over a 3-year period. By the end of Year 2, the second year, two-thirds of the total estimated compensation expense should be accrued, resulting in a SARs liability of $160,000 (2/3×$240,000).

Investments

24. **C.** Under the cost adjusted for fair value method, the original stock acquisition is recorded at its cost. Subsequent to acquisition, that cost will be reduced by return of capital distributions, if any, and adjusted for any changes in fair market value. Under the equity method, the original stock acquisition is also recorded at cost. Subsequent to acquisition, that amount will be adjusted for changes in the investee's net assets (for example, earnings, dividends, and so on). Therefore, an increase in the market price of the common stock would require an increase in the investment account under the cost adjusted for fair value method but would have no effect on the account under the equity method.

Statement of Cash Flows

25. **D.** When presenting cash flows from operating activities under the indirect approach, net income must be adjusted for changes in current assets (other than cash) and in current liabilities. Further, noncash events must be removed from net income to complete the conversion of net income from an accrual basis to a cash basis. When prepaid expenses decrease, reported expenses exceed cash paid. The decrease in prepaid expenses must therefore be added to net income.

26. **C.** A stock option is a financial instrument that is recorded at its fair value and is remeasured to fair value at the end of each reporting period with the gains and losses reported in income of the period. On December 1, when Bann acquired the option, its fair value was $600. At the end of the reporting period on December 31, the fair value of the stock had increased by $3 per share ($43 − 40), and the fair value of the time value component of the option decreased to $400. Therefore, the fair value of the option at December 31 was ($3 × 2,000 shares + $400) = $6,400. The change in the fair value of the option was $6,400 − $600, resulting in a $5,800 increase in fair value. Net income is increased by the change in the fair value of the option in the amount of $5,800.

Personal Financial Statements

27. **B.** Per ASC Topic 274, a business interest that constitutes a large part of a person's total assets should be shown separately from other investments. The estimated current value of an investment in a separate entity, such as a closely held corporation, a partnership, or a sole proprietorship, should be shown in one amount as an investment if the entity is marketable as a going concern.

Interim Reporting

28. **B.** Per ASC Topic 270, a decline in inventory market price that is expected to be other than temporary should be recognized in the period of decline. A subsequent recovery of market value should be recognized as a cost recovery in the period of increase but never above original cost. Thus, Choice (B) is correct because the decline should be recognized when it occurs in the first quarter. The subsequent recovery should be recognized when it occurs in the third quarter.

Segment Reporting

29. **B.** ASC Topic 280 requires that selected data for a segment be reported separately if any one of three criteria is met. One of these criteria is met when a segment's operating profit (or loss) is greater than or equal to 10 percent of the greater of the absolute combined segment profit or loss. Thus, Klein has a reportable segment if the absolute amount of that segment's profit or loss exceeds $60,000 ($600,000 × 10%).

Partnership Accounting

30. **B.** The problem states that the bonus is 25 percent of partnership net income after deducting the bonus. The solutions approach is to write an equation and solve for the bonus, B:

$$B = \%(NI - B)$$
$$B = 0.25(\$300,000 - B)$$
$$B = \$75,000 - 0.25B$$
$$1.25B = \$75,000$$
$$B = \$60,000$$

Part IV
Auditing and Attestation

Five Types of CPA Engagements

- Audits
- Reviews
- Compilations
- Agreed-upon procedures
- Bookkeeping and basic accounting services

In this part . . .

✔ Go over the important topics for the auditing test, including reviews and complications.

✔ Test your AUD knowledge with 30 practice questions and find out how you did by reviewing the answers and detailed explanations.

Chapter 11

Taking a Closer Look at the Auditing and Attestation Test

● ●

In This Chapter

▶ Understanding the company and its internal controls

▶ Performing audit procedures and documenting your results

▶ Considering other types of engagements

● ●

The first step in any audit or attestation engagement is to gain an understanding of the client. The CPA needs to know what the company does and how its industry works. An auditor also assesses internal controls, which are the systems a company has in place to help generate accurate financial statements. The better the internal controls, the more a CPA can rely on the company's accounting systems. Finally, an auditor performs audit procedures, such as reviewing documents, tracing transactions through the accounting system, and discussing the financials with company management. Auditors document their findings in an audit opinion.

The auditing and attestation (AUD) test of the CPA exam tests your knowledge of these key areas. In this chapter, you become better prepared for this test by understanding the steps a CPA takes to complete an audit and the language used in an audit report.

Understanding the Engagement

To understand the engagement, a CPA considers the assertions a company makes about the financial statements it's presenting. For example, one assertion is that the asset account balances are properly classified as either short-term or long-term assets.

In this section, you make sure you have a handle on what an audit is and look at examples of typical audit procedures. You also go over what it takes to plan the audit and create an engagement letter.

Defining an audit

When a CPA performs an audit, he or she is providing an opinion. The opinion concerns whether the financial statements present information fairly, in all material respects, and in conformity with applicable reporting standards. An audit opinion comments on whether the financial statements are free of material misstatement. Consider these additional points:

- **Being materially correct:** The term *material,* which comes up throughout this book, refers to an issue or an amount that is relevant or important. An auditor doesn't provide an opinion about the financials being exactly correct. The CPA provides a high level of assurance but not an absolute level of assurance. Instead, the auditor gives an opinion as to whether the financials are materially correct.

- **Adherence to reporting standards:** Every entity has reporting standards for their particular set of financial statements. Regulators and industry standards require certain standards for financial reporting. As an example, public companies (those that issue securities to the public) must comply with SEC reporting standards. (Check out Chapter 8 for more on the SEC.) An auditor may state that the client has complied with SEC reporting requirements.

- **Financial statements:** The audit report addresses the company's financial position, the results of operations, and cash flows. Later in this chapter, you see the specific financial statements that are part of an audit.

- **Disclaimers and adverse opinions:** A CPA may disclaim an opinion or issue an adverse opinion. I explain disclaimers and adverse opinions later in the chapter.

Generally accepted auditing standards (GAAS) is a system of guidelines that CPAs use when performing audits. (You can find out about GAAS by visiting the AICPA website, www.aicpa.org.) GAAS requires an auditor to obtain an understanding of the company's internal controls and to assess fraud risk. *Fraud* is broadly defined as willful intent to deceive. For auditing purposes, *fraud risk* is the risk that a company employee will intentionally attempt to misstate the financial statements.

GAAS also requires the CPA to corroborate the amounts and disclosures in the financial statements. Auditors corroborate this information by gathering audit evidence. The client-produced accounting records aren't sufficient evidence to provide an opinion on the financial statements. The CPA must complete more procedures and gather more evidence. Here are several procedures for gathering audit evidence:

- **Inquiry:** Ask company management and staff about certain accounting transactions. If, for example, the accounts receivable balance is increasing faster than sales, the CPA may ask management why customers are paying more slowly. The client's answer may help explain the growing accounts receivable balance.

- **Physical inspection:** A CPA often physically inspects assets to confirm their existence. For example, an accountant often performs physical counts of inventory near the balance sheet date. The *balance sheet date* is the date on the balance sheet that's under audit. The balance sheet date is also always that last day of the company's fiscal year (December 31, for example). The CPA compares the items listed in the inventory records with the physical items she counts in the warehouse.

- **Observation:** Accountants gather audit evidence by simply watching employees perform tasks. Say that a company has a control in place for shipping. The shipping department ensures that each customer shipment matches details on the invoice that's also sent to the client. A CPA can visit the shipping department and see whether the employees are comparing the invoices to the shipping documents.

- **Third-party confirmation:** Generally, confirming information with a third party — someone outside the company — is considered more reliable than data from within the company. The third party has less motivation to manipulate data than the company being audited does.

  CPAs often send written confirmations to outside parties that do business with the client. For example, a CPA may send copies of invoices to customers and ask them to confirm whether the invoice is for items they actually bought. If the client owes money based on the invoice, the confirmation process helps corroborate accounts receivable.

The CPA firm should mail the confirmations and have the completed confirmations mailed to the CPA firm's office. This process prevents any manipulation by the client under audit.

✔ **Examination:** CPAs review records to determine whether transactions were handled correctly. Suppose the company has issued long-term debt using a corporate bond. The accountant reviews the loan document to confirm the interest expense due each year. The CPA can then check the cash account activity to confirm that the interest was actually paid.

To audit the number of common stock shares outstanding, the CPA reviews the number of shares held by the public according to the registrar's records. A *registrar* is an independent company that tracks the ownership of stock for a particular company. The registrar's records should agree with the common stock shares outstanding in the company financial statements.

✔ **Analytical review:** Analytical review considers trends and comparisons in the financial statements. Suppose that the CPA notices that the cash balance is declining during the year. The client is collecting cash more slowly. If the accountant notices that the accounts payable balance is increasing, that would be consistent with a declining cash balance. The company is collecting cash more slowly, so payables are increasing.

All the steps needed to audit a particular area of the company are listed in an *audit program*. You can think of an audit program as a checklist. In fact, auditors initial or input a checkmark on each step of the audit program as they complete work. If an auditor finds that an account balance needs to be changed, she proposes an *adjusting entry*. Head over to Chapter 1 for info on audit programs and adjustments.

Gaining knowledge of the client

For the AUD test, you need to know the difference between the auditor's responsibilities and those of the client. A CPA needs to be clear about what the client is asking him to do. That may require an audit or some other attestation service. An auditor also considers the assertions a company makes about its financials and how those assertions can be tested using audit procedures.

Going over the nature and scope of the audit

Both management's responsibilities and those of the auditor need to be clarified during the planning process. For example, the financial statements are the responsibility of management. The CPA's responsibility is to obtain audit evidence to provide an opinion on the financial statements.

The "nature and scope of the audit" also refers to the audit's objectives — and to audit limitations. An audit, for example, isn't designed to detect *fraud,* which is willful intent to deceive. Common audit procedures can't detect fraud. Also, the audit is limited to providing an opinion on whether the financial statements are materially correct. The audit doesn't verify that the dollar amount of every account balance is exactly correct. These guidelines generally apply to audits of both public and nonpublic companies.

During planning, the CPA needs to decide on a dollar amount large enough to represent a material misstatement of the financial statements. For example, the CPA may conclude that a $10,000 misstatement in the $250,000 accounts receivable balance is a material misstatement. The dollar amount of material misstatement can be the sum of many individual misstatements in accounts receivable (see the later section "Comparing risks related to sampling" for details), so the CPA firm keeps a running total of the misstatements noted during the audit. The CPA communicates to the audit staff that misstatements of $10,000 or greater for accounts receivable are to be considered material. Different financial statements may have different dollar amounts for considering misstatement.

Walking through assertions

Assertions are representations of management that are components of the financial statements. An assertion may be the dollar amount of accounts receivable, or it may state whether a liability balance is a current balance or a long-term one. When an auditor plans an audit, the procedures are designed to address each of the assertions in the following list.

These assertions address issues that may cause the financials to be misstated. Internal controls should be designed with these assertions in mind. For details on internal controls, see the later section "Comparing risks related to sampling."

The AUD test nearly always covers these assertions:

- **Occurrence:** The transactions recorded in the financial statements reflect events that actually occurred.

  If a company records sales and accounts receivable, the auditor may test the balances by sending a confirmation letter to the customer. The CPA firm can send a copy of the unpaid invoice and ask the client to confirm that she bought the product or service.

- **Completeness:** All the transactions that should be recorded are actually recorded.

  CPAs perform an audit procedure called the *search for unrecorded liabilities* to ensure that all material accounts payable are posted as of the balance sheet date. The CPA looks at checks that are paid shortly after year-end. The auditor then determines whether a payable needs to be set up for a check written after year-end. If, for example, the client pays a large balance for raw materials on January 5, the CPA wants to see whether the raw-materials balance was a payable as of December 31 (the balance sheet date). If the raw materials were received on December 29, the company should set up accounts payable on December 29.

- **Accuracy:** The amounts and other data in the financial statements have been reported accurately.

  Suppose the company has a $100,000, 7 percent corporate bond outstanding. To ensure that the interest expense calculation is accurate, the CPA recomputes the annual interest expense as $100,000 × 0.07 = $7,000. The auditor makes sure the interest expense calculated agrees with the amount recorded in the financial statements.

- **Cutoff:** Accounting transactions are recorded in the proper period.

  Revenue recognition is a company's policy for deciding when revenue should be posted to the financial statements (see Chapter 2 for details). Suppose an online seller of electronics has a policy to recognize revenue when goods are shipped to the client. A CPA may select large sales posted in the last week of the year and review the related shipping documents. If the items sold were shipped after year-end, the sales should not be recorded before year-end.

- **Classification:** Transactions are posted to the proper accounts.

  Say a company has a 5-year corporate bond outstanding. An auditor reviews the loan document and calculates how much of the principal will be paid back in the next 12 months. That amount should be posted to current liabilities, not long-term liabilities. The issue of current versus long-term is a classification issue.

- **Existence:** Balance sheet items (assets, liabilities, and equity) posted to the financial statements actually exist.

Note that the occurrence assertion deals with transactions in any type of account, whereas the existence assertion primarily addresses assets posted to the balance sheet. For example, if a company lists 1,000 shares of Acme Manufacturing common stock as an investment, the CPA can inspect an account statement from the company's investment firm to confirm existence.

✔ **Rights and obligations:** This assertion refers to ownership of assets and obligations to pay liabilities.

To verify that a company owns a piece of machinery, for example, an auditor can review the title for the machine. Having title to an asset indicates ownership.

✔ **Valuation:** The valuation assertion refers to the dollar amount of an item posted to the financials.

The *principle of conservatism* states that companies should avoid overstating the value of assets and equity and avoid understating the dollar amount of liabilities. These steps help prevent a firm from presenting a balance sheet that's overly optimistic. Assets, for example, are most often recorded at historical cost. An auditor could review purchase records to verify cost of an asset.

One challenge on the CPA exam is that some of the assertions are very similar. The valuation assertion, for example, is similar to the accuracy assertion. You may find that you can only narrow down your answer choices to two assertions. If you reach that point, pick one of the two and move on. Don't spend too much time debating over two very similar choices. Your time is better spent on another question that may be clearer to you.

Planning in more detail

When planning an audit, an auditor needs to consider whether certain preconditions are present. These preconditions make it possible for the CPA firm to efficiently perform an audit and help the auditor obtain sufficient audit evidence to support an audit opinion:

✔ The client uses an acceptable framework for financial reporting. On a basic level, the client uses a chart of accounts and reconciles bank accounts on a monthly basis. A *chart of accounts* is a listing of each account title and account number. The company also posts adjusting entries and uses the accrual method of accounting.

✔ The company accepts responsibility for designing and implementing internal controls.

✔ Management is willing to provide all relevant financial information and to make employees available to the audit staff.

Looking over an engagement letter

After both parties agree on the terms of the audit, the terms are documented in an engagement letter. An *engagement letter,* which is a written agreement between the client and the auditor, spells out the responsibilities of each party. The financial statements are the responsibility of management. The auditor, on the other hand, gathers sufficient audit evidence to support an opinion on the financial statements.

Here are some points that you find in an engagement letter:

✔ **The objective of the audit:** This includes the specific financial statements to be audited. If the audit will include comparative financial statements, the engagement letter lists the years compared. I discuss comparative financial statements later in the section "Reading an unqualified audit opinion."

✔ **The responsibilities of both the auditor and company management:** This includes management's responsibility to inform the auditor of any subsequent events. A *subsequent event* is an event of transaction that occurs after the balance sheet date but before the financial statements are issued. See Chapter 8 for info on subsequent events.

✔ **Agreements involving the work of internal auditors:** Check out the later section "Kicking around the work of internal auditors and outside specialists" for details on internal auditors.

✔ **A statement about the unavoidable risk that some material misstatements may not be detected, even if the audit is properly planned and performed in accordance with GAAP:** This risk exists because of the inherent limitations of both an audit and internal controls. *Audit risk* is the risk that an auditor will issue an unqualified audit opinion when the financial statements are materially misstated. This portion of the engagement letter explains audit risk.

✔ **Identification of the applicable financial reporting framework for the preparation of the financial statements and the expected form and content of the reports:** When I review the types of audit reports in the sections that follow, I refer to specific financial statements.

If an auditor is replacing another auditor, the CPA asks management for permission to contact the predecessor. Management should give the previous auditor permission to respond to all of the current auditor's inquiries. (Head over to the later section "Explaining the work of another auditor" for details.) If the CPA determines that management has limited the inquiry — or that the predecessor auditor isn't answering all of the inquiries — the auditor should consider not taking the engagement.

If the auditor worked on the client's audit in the prior year, the engagement is a *recurring audit*. A CPA and the company management should evaluate whether the terms of the engagement letter should be changed. If so, a new engagement letter is created and signed by the client. Here are some circumstances that may require a new engagement letter:

✔ A significant change has occurred in senior management or in the ownership of the company.

✔ The company has had a significant change in the nature or size of the business. A manufacturer that sells all its assets and becomes an investment company would require a new engagement letter. If Company A bought Company B and doubled in size, the new entity would require a new engagement letter.

✔ Significant changes have occurred in legal or regulatory requirements. Companies that issue stock to the public for the first time must start to comply with the requirements of the SEC. (Chapter 8 explains SEC regulation.)

In some cases, a law or regulation may require a specific layout, form, or wording of an audit report. The report wording may be significantly different from what GAAS (generally accepted auditing standards) requires. The auditor needs to evaluate whether the report format will cause confusion for the users of the audit report. Auditors also consider whether the legally required wording can be changed to be in accordance with GAAS or if a separate report can be attached. If not, the auditor should remove any reference to the audit being performed in accordance with GAAS. If law or regulation allows it, the CPA shouldn't accept the audit at all.

Reading a sample engagement letter

The AUD test will ask you about specific language in an engagement letter. Here's a standard engagement letter, presented by paragraph:

✔ **Objective and scope of the audit:** You have requested that we audit the financial statements of [company name], which comprise the balance sheet as of [balance sheet date] and the related statements of income, changes in stockholders' equity, and cash flows for the year then ended, and the related notes to the financial statements. We are pleased to confirm our acceptance and our understanding of this audit engagement by means of this letter. Our audit will be conducted with the objective of our expressing an opinion on the financial statements.

✔ **Responsibilities of the auditor:** We will conduct our audit in accordance with auditing standards generally accepted in the United States of America (GAAS). Those standards require that we plan and perform the audit to obtain reasonable assurance about whether the financial statements are free from material misstatement. An audit involves performing procedures to obtain audit evidence about the amounts and disclosures in the financial statements. The procedures selected depend on the auditor's judgment, including the assessment of the risks of material misstatement of the financial statements, whether due to fraud or error. An audit also includes evaluating the appropriateness of accounting policies used and the reasonableness of significant accounting estimates made by management, as well as evaluating the overall presentation of the financial statements.

✔ **Audit risk:** Because of the inherent limitations of an audit, together with the inherent limitations of internal control, an unavoidable risk that some material misstatements may not be detected exists, even though the audit is properly planned and performed in accordance with GAAS.

✔ **Considering internal control:** In making our risk assessments, we consider internal control relevant to the entity's preparation and fair presentation of the financial statements in order to design audit procedures that are appropriate in the circumstances but not for the purpose of expressing an opinion on the effectiveness of the entity's internal control. However, we will communicate to you in writing concerning any significant deficiencies or material weaknesses in internal control relevant to the audit of the financial statements that we have identified during the audit.

✔ **Management responsibilities:** Our audit will be conducted on the basis that management acknowledge and understand that they have responsibility for the preparation of the financial statements in accordance with accounting principles generally accepted in the United States of America. Management is responsible for the design and implementation of internal controls. The company will provide us with access to all relevant information, as well as any additional information we request. The firm will give us access to persons within the entity from whom we deem it necessary to obtain audit evidence.

✔ **Confirmations:** As part of our audit process, we will request from management written confirmation concerning representations made to us in connection with the audit.

✔ **Reporting:** We will issue a written report upon completion of our audit of [company name]'s financial statements. Our report will be addressed to the board of directors of [company name]. We cannot provide assurance that an unmodified opinion will be expressed. Circumstances may arise in which it is necessary for us to modify our opinion, add an emphasis-of-matter or other-matter paragraph(s), or withdraw from the engagement.

✔ **Sign and return:** Please sign and return the attached copy of this letter to indicate your acknowledgement of, and agreement with, the arrangements for our audit of the financial statements, including our respective responsibilities.

Under the signature line, the letter states, "acknowledged and agreed to."

Kicking around the work of internal auditors and outside specialists

Internal auditors are employees of the company being audited. They perform evaluations on business operations to improve risk management and internal controls. Internal auditors report to senior management, which means that the work of internal auditors can help improve corporate governance.

Internal audit departments may perform procedures that are similar to that of an external auditor. For example, an internal auditor may observe a process to determine whether internal controls are operating effectively.

Suppose a clothing store has a process for handling returned merchandise. Customers returning goods must fill out a form explaining why the goods are being returned. The customer must turn in the return form and the original purchase receipt before receiving a refund. This control is to ensure that all refunds are legitimate.

An internal auditor may take a sample of refund payments to verify whether a return form and purchase receipt are on file for each refund payment. If the sample work reveals that documentation is missing for some of the items sampled, the internal auditor may need to test more items and let management know that the control may not be effective. Check out the later section "Understanding sampling basics" for details on sampling.

If the internal auditor's work will have any bearing on the CPA firm's audit, the CPA must consider the competence, objectivity, and work competence of the internal auditor.

Another outside specialist is an *actuary*. Actuaries use math and statistics to assess probability. In the auditing field, actuaries are brought in to assess probability related to insurance and pension plans.

For a company pension plan, an actuary will use several factors (worker age, salary levels, investment rate of return) to compute the firm's future liability for pension payments to retired employees. The business needs to contribute enough dollars into the pension fund to meet the firm's future pension payment obligations. The actuary assesses whether or not the company's pension contributions are sufficient. The CPA firm will rely on the assessment performed by the actuary.

Actuaries also assist with life insurance company audits. The actuary will assess the age, gender, and health history of those who are insured. The actuary will use that analysis to assess, on average, when insured people will pass away. The CPA firm will rely on that analysis to determine whether the insurance company has enough assets to pay death benefits to each insured person's beneficiaries.

Assessing the Company and Internal Controls

Internal controls are put in place to help a company achieve several goals. These controls allow a business to operate efficiently and to create accurate financial reports. Controls also ensure that a company will comply with applicable laws and regulations.

An auditor makes a judgment on internal controls. The judgment on internal controls helps the auditor decide the nature, timing, and extent of substantive testing. *Substantive testing* is defined as audit procedures performed to test the financials for material misstatement. The material misstatement may be in account balance or in an accounting transaction.

For example, suppose the auditor reviews internal controls over inventory. The client performs a well-planned inventory count at the end of each month. The company also keeps accurate documentation of the count. The auditor may decide to perform less work on inventory or to change the type of procedures performed on inventory. In this case, the extent of the audit procedures would decline, and the nature of the procedures performed would change.

In most cases, the auditor insists on performing an inventory count on the balance sheet date. Because the client performs well-documented inventory counts each month, the auditor is willing to reply on a physical inventory count 5 days after the balance sheet date. The timing of the procedures is changed.

Every company has an internal control environment. The auditor needs to assess this environment so he can judge the reliability of the internal controls. Here are the components of a control environment:

- **Control activities:** The company performs these procedures to implement internal controls. Control activities include checking information for accuracy and completeness. These activities also include proper segregation of duties (see Chapter 5).

- **Risk assessment by management:** This addresses how management judges the effectiveness of internal controls. For example, the auditor considers how often management reviews internal controls and whether management is willing to make changes.

- **Documentation and communication:** This component considers how controls are documented. For example, all companies should have a written manual of accounting procedures, including control procedures.

- **Supervision:** The CPA considers how management trains employees on the controls. Implementing controls effectively should be a part of each employee's performance evaluation.

- **Control environment:** The CPA also judges how management communicates the importance of controls to the company. This component has to do with management's attitude about the importance of controls.

The following sections go over these components in more detail so you can confidently answer questions about them on the test.

Resolving materiality, risk assessment, and fraud

A CPA needs to determine materiality, which refers to a dollar amount of financial-statement error that's important or relevant to a financial-statement reader. In this section, you see a discussion of tolerable error and how that concept relates to materiality. I also explain how the tolerable error is applied to balance sheet accounts and wrap up with a discussion of fraud risk.

Starting with materiality

Materiality means that the event or transaction is large enough to be relevant and meaningful to the financial-statement reader. If the item isn't material, an auditor doesn't insist that management take action regarding an adjustment or disclosure. Misstatement of net income before taxes is often used to judge materiality.

Judging materiality involves asking whether a person relying on the financial statements would change her mind if she were aware of the misstatement. The level of materiality is a relative term, not an absolute one. An auditor may consider other firms in the same industry when evaluating materiality.

Suppose financial-statement readers have a high level of concern about possible misstatement in the financials for recycling companies. If the CPA is assessing materiality for a recycling company, then he or she may set the dollar amount of materiality lower. Financial-statement readers are sensitive to a lower dollar amount of misstatement.

Here are the steps an auditor performs to address materiality:

- **Preliminary judgment about materiality:** The CPA estimates the maximum dollar amount the financial statements could be misstated without affecting the decisions of a financial-statement reader.

  Suppose, for example, that a CPA is auditing Legacy Chairs, a manufacturer that does $5 million in annual sales. The auditor determines that a misstatement of $50,000 or less in net income wouldn't change the opinion of the financial-statement reader. The CPA plans audit procedures based on the judgment about materiality.

- **Tolerable misstatement:** *Tolerable misstatement* (or *tolerable error*) is the level of materiality assigned to a particular account balance. If the misstatement is below the tolerable amount, the account balance is fairly stated. The tolerable error is less than materiality for the company under audit.

  Say that the CPA is auditing accounts receivable for Legacy Chairs. Tolerable error is assessed at $10,000. The auditor would plan audit procedures to identify exceptions that added up to $10,000 or more. If the CPA firm found seven exceptions with a total dollar amount of $15,000, the total would be material to the account balance.

- **Posting an adjusting entry:** Suppose that the CPA selected a sample of accounts receivable balances and sent confirmations to customers. The CPA asked the customers to confirm the dollar amounts they owe, based on a sample of invoices sent to customers. In this example, the misstatement in accounts receivable is $15,000. The CPA would ask the audit client to adjust the accounting records to correct this misstatement. Specifically, the auditor might propose to debit (reduce) sales and credit (reduce) accounts receivable by $15,000.

- **Performing more audit procedures:** If audit procedures reveal exceptions above the tolerable-error dollar amount, the CPA needs to perform more procedures. The auditor sends confirmations to more customers to confirm accounts receivable. A CPA may also spend more time asking company employees about the accounts receivable process. The exceptions noted in the accounts receivable balance may indicate that the company's employees aren't processing invoices correctly. The auditor needs to determine the full extent of any errors.

Judging the balance sheet

Auditors apply tolerable error primarily to balance sheet accounts. When planning an audit, the CPA firm looks at each balance sheet account and makes a decision about the level of tolerable misstatement.

The reason tolerable error applies to balance sheet accounts and not the income statement relates to the nature of the double-entry accounting process. With *double-entry accounting,* every accounting entry requires at least one debit and at least one credit entry. Accrual entries, for example, impact both a balance sheet account and an income statement account. Here are two examples:

> ✔ **Accrued payroll:** Debit payroll expense (income statement account), credit accounts payable (balance sheet account)
>
> ✔ **Recognize insurance expense that was prepaid:** Debit insurance expense (income statement account), credit prepaid insurance (balance sheet account)

Just about every balance sheet account relates to an income statement account. If you audit inventory, you're performing work on an account that drives cost of goods sold. When inventory (an asset) is sold, the balance is posted to cost of goods sold (an income statement account). Accounts receivable drives sales and bad debt expense. Long-term debt impacts interest expense.

Because of this relationship, auditors make a judgment about tolerable error in the balance sheet. The CPA knows that the balance sheet auditing work will impact most of the income statement accounts. Although not necessarily a CPA exam test point, an auditor may tell you, "I audit the balance sheet, and the income statement audit comes from the balance sheet test work."

A *known misstatement* in an account balance is a dollar amount that the auditor can determine. *Likely misstatements* are not certain dollar amounts. If an account requires an estimate or judgment, the auditor and the company may differ on the account balance. Suppose that the company has a balance reserved to pay for a legal liability. That account balance is a liability. The auditor and the company may disagree on the amount reserved, based on the dollar amount of the lawsuit and the likelihood that the company will lose in court. An auditor may conclude that the reserve for legal liability is likely to be misstated.

Linking materiality to the income statement

You normally assess tolerable error in the balance sheet, and you typically assess materiality using net income in the income statement.

When making a judgment, an accountant should choose the more conservative approach. The principle of conservatism dictates that companies should avoid overstating assets and understating liabilities.

This concept relates to tolerable error in the balance sheet. Although the dollar amount of error is important, the increase or decrease in the account is also an issue. For example, an auditor is more concerned about an error that would overstate accounts receivable than an understatement. Again, the balance sheet is linked to the income statement. If accounts receivable is overstated, then sales may also be overstated. After all, if a company overstates the amount of money it's owed, the company is also overstating how much it sold.

The tolerable error in a balance-sheet account ultimately impacts the level of misstatement in the income statement. Materiality, on the other hand, is normally driven by net income in the income statement. Keep this connection in mind.

Performing risk assessment and fraud risk

One important risk assessment is the risk that key duties aren't segregated among different employees. (Chapter 4 defines segregation of duties.) Where possible, a company should segregate physical custody of assets from the authority to move or access the assets, and both of these duties should be segregated from the recordkeeping (accounting) function in the business. If these duties aren't segregated, the risk of fraud by employees is much higher. *Fraud risk* is the risk that an employee will intentionally misstate the financial statements.

A good example of segregation of duties relates to controls and passwords for a company's IT operations. An IT manager may keep the records of each user's username and password. However, that same IT manager shouldn't be able to use that information to access and make changes to data for each user.

Say, for example, that the IT manager is able to access and change the accounting records by using the accounting manager's username and password. The IT manager also has physical custody of assets. In this case, the asset is the company's IT technology (hardware and software). Suppose that the accountant is the record-keeper.

Maybe the IT manager wants to purchase an expensive piece of equipment for his own use. If the manager could access and change the accounting records, he could create a fake purchase order for the equipment he wants for himself. In this example, one person has authority over the assets and access to recordkeeping and could cover up a fraudulent transaction.

Reviewing an internal control environment

A CPA reviews the internal controls related to each type of account balance and accounting transaction. This review helps the CPA judge the reliability of internal controls. If internal controls are reliable, the auditor may perform less audit test work.

For an example of an internal control, consider a business that sells books online. Customers create their own usernames and passwords to log on to the site. Clients are assigned account numbers, which are linked to a credit or debit card. When a customer buys a book using her account number, the credit or debit card pays for the purchase. Here are some internal controls that might be important for this business:

- **Segregation of duties:** An IT manager should not have access to the accounting records. Suppose that someone in IT was able to access and post customer credit or debit card charges to a bank account she personally controlled. That same person was able to manipulate the accounting records to post those personal charges as legitimate customer purchases. This lack of segregation of duties would result in a theft that would not be detected easily. If a customer doesn't notice the charge and question it, the theft may not be detected at all.

- **Use of check digits:** *Check digits* are a set of numbers that are randomly added to an account number. The company's computer system can run a calculation on any account number that a customer attempts to use. The use of a check digit can prevent unauthorized people from creating fraudulent account numbers.

If the auditor finds that these controls are in place — and that the client applies them consistently — the CPA can rely on the segregation of duties and use of check digits as legitimate audit evidence. As a result, the auditor may perform less test work, because the CPA firm makes a judgment that the risk of financial misstatement is low.

Performing Audit Procedures

This section discusses how a CPA considers the nature, timing, and extent of audit procedures that may be performed for an audit. It also goes into detail on two areas of audit procedures that are heavily tested on the AUD test: audit sampling and auditing inventory.

Deciding on procedures for the audit

Auditors use *substantive testing,* also called *substantive test of details,* which is the process of gathering evidence to determine the extent of misstatement in the client's accounting records.

Tests of controls are audit procedures designed to verify whether a company procedure is being applied consistently. These procedures test how effective the control is in detecting and preventing material misstatements in the financial statements.

Using audit software

CPAs should consider using generalized audit software to perform audit procedures on a client's data. The advantage is that the CPA can test the customer's data without having to gain a great deal of knowledge about the company's hardware or software. Generalized audit software tests whether the company's computer system is producing the desired output.

Suppose that a large company sends out thousands of invoices a month. The firm offers discounts to customers based on the dollar amount of the purchase. Each invoice over $500 offers the client a 10 percent discount if he pays within 10 business days. Invoices over $500 list the discounted total owed as well as the full price.

Generalized audit software could be used to test the month's invoices and determine whether the discount was properly offered for all invoices over $500. This test doesn't require any special knowledge about the company's hardware of software. Most important, this specialized audit software may save the CPA firm time and costs on the audit.

Moving on to internal audit work and test of controls

Tests of controls are audit procedures designed to test the effectiveness of internal controls. Internal controls are designed and implemented to reduce the risk that the financial statements will be materially misstated.

Several of the audit procedures I explain in the earlier section "Defining an audit" can be a test of controls. Physical inspections of assets as well as observation are test-of-control procedures. Reperformance is another test of controls. As the name implies, *reperformance* means that the CPA performs the procedure of the control himself to determine whether the control operated effectively.

Suppose the company owns stock and recorded dividend income on stock holdings. The CPA would verify the dollar amount of dividends declared for the year and then multiply that amount by the number of shares owned. If the client owned 100 shares of common stock and the dividends-paid-per-share is $5, the CPA would multiply 500 shares × $5 = $500. He'd then compare the $500 with the dividend income that the client posted for that investment.

Introducing sampling

Audit sampling involves applying an audit procedure to less than 100 percent of the items that make up an account balance or class of transactions. An audit procedure evaluates some characteristic of the account balance or transaction.

Understanding sampling basics

Sampling is an audit tool that allows the CPA to review only a sample, or portion, of the items under audit. Because the accountant isn't auditing every item, the CPA firm is able to save time and expense. There is, however, *sampling risk* for a CPA firm that uses sampling. This is the risk that the results found using the sample don't reflect the results that would be found if the entire set of items were reviewed. The auditor strives to use a sample of items that has the same attributes as the entire set of items.

With *attribute sampling,* the auditor tests a procedure for an attribute. You can think of the attribute as a desired outcome. For example, suppose you make baseball gloves. At the end of production, each glove is inspected. When an inspector judges the gloves to be properly complete, he or she attaches a numbered inspection tag to the glove.

Inspected and tagged gloves are moved to the shipping department. Before the gloves are packed for shipping, a shipping department employee verifies that an inspection tag is attached. That employee initials a list of all issued (used) inspection tags. The gloves are shipped to customers with tags attached so that customers see that each glove was inspected.

An auditor may take a sample of inspection tag numbers. The CPA can check the inspection tag list to see whether a shipping department employee initialed the tag. That step is the attribute or desired outcome for each glove. If a glove shipped to a client doesn't have a shipping tag initial, the accountant would consider that a *deviation.*

Sample size represents the number of items selected for the sample, and *population* is the entire set of items that you're testing. If the rate of deviations found in the sample is much different from the deviation rate in the population, the sampling procedure has a high level of sampling risk. The amount of sampling risk varies inversely with the size of the sample. In other words, a larger sample size means less sampling risk. As you increase your sample size, your groups of items will have attributes that are closer to the attributes of the entire population.

In addition to sampling risk, CPAs work with *nonsampling risk.* These risks aren't related to sampling. The auditor, for example, may choose a sampling procedure that doesn't detect a material misstatement in the account balance under audit. In this case, the procedure does not relate closely to the potential error in the accounting records.

Auditors use the word *agree* to refer to a specific task that relates to audit work. In the context of performing an audit, the word *agree* means to compare two pieces of audit evidence to make sure they're the same.

Say, for example, that you're auditing cash. You're reviewing the client's bank reconciliation. You want to ensure that each client's bank deposit slip (which shows all the items deposited on a particular day) is posted to the cash accounting records. In audit language, you agree each deposit slip to a debit (increase) in the cash account balance.

Suppose that a large roofing company sends an invoice after a customer signs a contract for roofing services. At that point, the roofing company records a sale. The auditor wants to sample sales transactions to ensure that each recorded sale is supported by a signed customer contract. The auditor agrees a sample of sales invoices to ensure that a sales journal entry was recorded. However, this procedure may not identify sales that were incorrectly posted in the books. Instead, the auditor should have taken a sample of invoices and agreed them to a signed contract.

Comparing risks related to sampling

The preceding section, which introduces you to sampling, broadly defines sampling and nonsampling risks. Here, I define four additional types of sampling risk. Two types of risk relate to substantive testing, and two are connected to tests of controls. Keeping these risks straight for the AUD test can be challenging. Take some time to compare the different types of sampling risks.

Substantive testing is gathering evidence to determine the extent of misstatement in the client's accounting records. The CPA is concerned with two types of sampling risk related to substantive testing:

- ✔ **Risk of incorrect acceptance:** The risk that the sample supports the conclusion that the balance is not materially misstated when it actually is misstated

- ✔ **Risk of incorrect rejection:** The risk that the sample supports the conclusion that the balance is materially misstated when it actually isn't misstated

Suppose that you're testing to ensure that each shipping receipt agrees to a purchase order. This procedure helps to determine whether every incoming shipment of product was properly approved for purchase. Suppose that your sample supports the conclusion that incoming shipments are approved. The entire population of shipments, however, reveals that the numbers of shipments supported by a purchase order is materially incorrect. The number of unapproved shipments is relevant when compared to total shipments. The sample didn't reflect the results of the entire population, and the sample was incorrectly accepted.

Now suppose that the sample included a material number of exceptions. Many shipments weren't matched with a purchase order. For the entire population, however, the number of shipments missing a purchase order isn't material. If the auditor concludes that the balance is materially incorrect, that's an example of incorrect rejection.

Keep in mind that a material misstatement can be one item or the sum of multiple items that add up to a materially misstated amount. Suppose, for example, that a programming glitch causes each invoice to be generated with a $20 error that reduces the amount owed. So each invoice is $20 too low. If only a few invoices are wrong, the total amount isn't material. If however, a company issues thousands of incorrect invoices, the total dollar amount of misstatement may be material.

You can also implement sampling procedures for tests of controls, which test the effectiveness of internal controls. When using tests of controls, a CPA is concerned with control risk. *Control risk* is the risk that an internal control doesn't detect or correct a misstatement. CPAs are concerned with two types of control risk:

- ✔ **Risk of assessing control risk too low:** The risk that the assessed level of control risk, based on the sample, is lower than the true effectiveness of the control

- ✔ **Risk of assessing control risk too high:** The risk that the assessed level of control risk, based on the sample, is higher than the true effectiveness of the control

You can relate the sampling errors I discuss in this section to audit effectiveness and efficiency:

- ✔ **Inefficiency:** If you incorrectly reject an audit sample or assess the control risk as too high, the decision affects audit efficiency. Both of the conclusions would cause an auditor to perform more audit procedures — procedures that are unnecessary.

> ✔ **Ineffectiveness:** On the other hand, if you incorrectly accept an audit sample or assess the control risk as too low, the decision affects audit effectiveness. These conclusions would cause an auditor to rely on the already completed audit work when additional procedures are necessary.

Auditing inventories

The AUD section of the CPA exam heavily tests your ability to audit inventories. Inventory is often one of the largest asset balances on the balance sheet, along with accounts receivable. By definition, the inventory balance changes frequently during a month or year. The inventory balance increases when the firm purchases inventory or manufactures more goods, and when inventory items are sold, inventory decreases. The frequent changes in inventory can make the auditing process more difficult. The CPA is auditing a balance that may be changing every day.

The more assets (receivables, inventory, and fixed assets) a company has, the more financially healthy it is. The principle of conservatism dictates that the CPA should be concerned about overstatement of asset accounts. The CPA doesn't want an asset posted to the books unless it truly exists and the asset's cost can be verified. (Chapter 8 explains the principle of conservatism.)

To gather audit evidence to support the existence of inventory, CPAs often perform a physical count of inventory during an audit. Here's an overview of how an inventory count works:

> ✔ **Timing:** The CPA firm wants to plan an inventory count as close to the balance sheet date of the audit as possible. Ideally, the count is *on* the balance sheet date. That timing minimizes the number of transactions (and the dollar amount of change) between the balance sheet date and the inventory count.

> ✔ **Control over inventory:** When planning for the day of the inventory count, the CPA wants to prevent any inventory from entering or leaving the company's facility. The auditor works with the client to communicate the date of the inventory count to staff. If the inventory location is a retail store, the store is typically closed for the day. You may sometimes see stores closed for inventory counts at the mall.

> ✔ **Inventory records, tags:** The client prepares a detailed list of all of the items in inventory, a description of each item, the number of items, and the cost. The client prints the list for the auditors and company staff that will perform the inventory count. The inventory list is used to generate inventory tags. The client's staff prints the tags and attaches the tags to each inventory item.

> ✔ **Counting inventory:** Each person counting inventory is assigned pages of the detailed inventory list. The counter locates the physical inventory and compares each item's description, number of units, and cost from the inventory list to the tag on the inventory item. When a counter finds an inventory item, he removes the tag, keeping all tags for the auditors.

> ✔ **Exceptions:** If an inventory counter finds differences between the inventory list and the tag on the inventory item, he notes the exception. In some cases, a counter can't locate the physical inventory item during the count. An inventory counter may also note physical items that aren't tagged as inventory. That means that the inventory item isn't included in inventory account balance.

The CPA firm gathers all the data used to perform the inventory count. The counters ensure that all inventory listing pages and all the tags are collected and filed. The auditors also summarize all the exceptions. Here are some typical exceptions and how a CPA would account for them:

✔ **Physical inventory item not located:** If the physical inventory item isn't located, the inventory records are overstated. Inventory needs to be credited (reduced). Cost of goods sold (an expense account) is debited. The principle of conservatism states that if assets are overstated, they're most often expensed. (Head over to Chapter 8 for details on the principle of conservatism.)

✔ **Physical inventory item located, not on inventory listing:** If a physical inventory item isn't tagged, the inventory records are understated. No entry was made to increase inventory when the item was purchased or produced. Inventory needs to be debited (increased), and accounts payable needs to be increased.

✔ **Data on inventory tag is different from inventory listing:** In this case, the item description, number of items, or original cost per unit noted on the inventory tag doesn't match the inventory listing. The counter wrote down the exception on the inventory tag during the count. The accounting area needs to track down the purchase order, shipping receipt, or vendor invoice to determine the correct data for the inventory item. Inventory may be increased or decreased, depending on what the original records indicate.

✔ **Obsolete inventory:** *Obsolete inventory* no longer has any sales value to the company. The item may be obsolete because it has no more useful life. Perishable items (fruit and vegetables) at the grocery store are good examples. Technology changes may make a product obsolete. Traditional cameras, for example, are gradually losing market share to digital cameras and camera phones. Following the principle of conservatism, you'd address the overstatement by making an entry to reduce inventory and debiting cost of goods sold.

The auditor's goal is to verify that the balance of inventory matches the dollar amount of inventory counted, and the auditor's job is to propose accounting changes for the exceptions. Posting adjusting entries is company management's job.

Using estimates and subsequent events

Auditors need to assess the reasonableness of any account balances based on estimates. A *likely misstatement* is a misstatement based on the auditor's judgment about an account balance that's an estimate.

The *allowance method of estimating bad debt expense* (see Chapter 8) estimates bad debt based on the dollar amount of accounts receivable and on a percentage estimate of the balance that won't be collected. An auditor needs to make a judgment on that estimate. That judgment is based on the client's history of collecting accounts receivable and whether sales are growing or declining. The auditor may also consider the percentage of receivables that are due from new customers with no payment history.

Auditors also have to review *subsequent events,* which occur after the balance sheet date (the date of the audited financial statements) and decide whether the events should be disclosed. I cover subsequent events in Chapter 8.

Considering the Results of Your Audit Work

When the audit work is complete, the CPA prepares a report. A variety of types of reports exist, and the AUD part of the CPA exam tests them heavily. In fact, you need to memorize some of the report language to succeed on the AUD test.

In this section, you become familiar with the types of reports and the language they use, and you see a discussion of unqualified and qualified audit opinions.

Note: I use the terms *audit report* and *audit opinion* to mean nearly the same thing. Both terms refer to a one- to two-page report that explains the auditor's opinion on the financial statements. The AUD test uses both terms, which is why you see both terms used in this chapter.

Reading an unqualified audit opinion

An unqualified audit opinion is the most common type of opinion, so the AUD test has a heavy focus this topic.

Following are three paragraphs from an unqualified audit report. For test purposes, memorize this audit opinion so that you can write out the entire text from memory. The other report language on the exam is very often derived from this basic report.

- ✔ **Introductory paragraph:**

    We have audited the accompanying balance sheet of [company name] as of [balance sheet date] and the related statements of income, retained earnings, and cash flow for the year then ended. These financial statements are the responsibility of the company's management. Our responsibility is to express an opinion on these financial statements based on our audit.

- ✔ **Scope paragraph:**

    We conducted our audit in accordance with auditing standards generally accepted in the United States of America. Those standards require that we plan and perform the audit to obtain reasonable assurance about whether the financial statements are free of material misstatement. An audit includes examining, on a test basis, evidence supporting the amounts and disclosures in the financial statements. An audit also includes assessing the accounting principles used and significant estimates made by management, as well as evaluating the overall financial statements presentation. We believe that our audit provides a reasonable basis for our opinion.

- ✔ **Opinion paragraph:**

    In our opinion, the financial statements referred to above, present fairly, in all material respects, the financial position of [company name] as of [balance sheet date] and the results of its operations and its cash flows for the year then ended in conformity with accounting principles accepted in the United States of America.

A CPA may provide an audit report on *comparative financial statements*. A comparative financial statements report covers more than one fiscal year. If, for example, years 2014 and 2015 were audited, the unqualified audit opinion will be slightly different. If you're auditing XYZ Company and the balance sheet date is December 21, the first paragraph will refer to "the accompanying balance sheets of XYZ Company as of December 21, 2015 and 2014, and the related statements of income, retained earnings, and cash flow for the years then ended."

Adding explanatory language to an unqualified report

An auditor may add explanatory language to an unqualified audit report. The point of the extra language is to call the opinion-reader's attention to a particular issue. Here are some circumstances that may require explanatory language:

✔ **The auditor can't perform all the necessary procedures for the audit, so the audit is limited in scope.** In this case, the auditor adds an emphasis-of-matter paragraph. See the next section for details.

✔ **The audit opinion is based, in part, on the report of another auditor.** I discuss this language later in "Explaining the work of another auditor."

✔ **The auditor has substantial doubt about the entity's ability to continue as a going concern.** To be a *going concern,* a firm must be able to generate sufficient sales, income, and cash flow to survive over the long term.

✔ **A material change in an accounting principle — or in the method of the application of an accounting principle — has occurred.** Accounting principles are disclosed in the notes to the financial statements (see Chapter 8 for details). Suppose a company changes its inventory valuation method from first-in, first-out (FIFO) to last-in, first-out (LIFO). The audit report's explanatory language would note this change, saying something like, "As explained in Note 1, the company changed its method of inventory valuation from the first-in, first-out (FIFO) method to last-in, first-out (LIFO) method in year 2015."

✔ **A document containing the audited financial statements has information that is materially inconsistent with the audited financials.** The most common example occurs when the audited financial statements are included in an annual report. The auditor adds explanatory language to the audit report to explain the inconsistency. Check out the section "Creating reports on internal controls and other work" later in this chapter for more information.

Following are some specifics on reporting on scope limitations and work done by another auditor.

Reporting on a scope limitation with an emphasis-of-matter paragraph

A *scope limitation* occurs when the CPA can't apply all the audit procedures considered necessary to perform the audit. Scope limitations may be due to issues beyond the control of the client. Maybe the company lost some accounting records due to a computer problem. The limitation may also be client-imposed. If the company didn't give the CPA sufficient access to its customers, the CPA firm may not be able to confirm accounts receivable balances with clients. (See the earlier section "Defining an audit" for details on the confirmation process.)

Scope limitations may cause auditors to change their audit opinion on a client's financial statements. The auditor needs to make a judgment on whether the audit evidence collected is sufficient. If the scope limitation means that the evidence is insufficient, the auditor considers whether other audit procedures can gather sufficient evidence.

If the following two types of scope limitations are noted prior to the engagement, the auditor may still accept the engagement:

✔ Management imposes a scope limitation that the auditor believes will result in a qualified opinion.

✔ A scope limitation is imposed by circumstances that are out of management's control.

Suppose that the confirmation of receivables process was a scope limitation. The CPA can't perform other procedures to gather enough evidence for accounts receivable. The auditor may add an *emphasis-of-matter paragraph* to an unqualified opinion. This extra paragraph explains the scope limitation to the financial-statement reader. Here are some situations that call for an emphasis-of-matter paragraph:

- ✔ The company audited is a component of a larger business enterprise.

- ✔ The company had significant transactions with related parties.

- ✔ The auditor needs to emphasize an important subsequent event.

- ✔ An accounting matter affects the ability of the financial-statement reader to compare two or more years of financials. (*Note:* This point refers to accounting matters other than a change in an accounting principle. I address changes in accounting principles in the next section on explanatory language.)

If the scope limitation is client-imposed, like the confirmation of receivables example, and if the auditor concludes that the scope limitation is significant, a CPA may instead issue a qualified report or disclaim an opinion.

In some cases, a client asks a CPA firm to audit only one of the financial statements, usually the balance sheet. Auditing only one financial statement is not a scope limitation. In this situation, the auditor uses the same type of audit opinion language that you see earlier in "Reading an unqualified opinion."

Explaining the work of another auditor

A CPA may provide an audit report on comparative financial statements, covering more than one fiscal year. In some cases, a predecessor auditor audits the first set of financials, and a new, or *successor,* auditor audits the current year. If the audit opinion is based, in part, on the work of another auditor, the successor auditor makes changes to the current audit report in several places.

Suppose that another auditor performed the audit for Standard Furniture, which is a wholly owned subsidiary of National Furniture. Standard has assets of $300,000 and revenue of $200,000 for the year ending December 31, 2015. You're the CPA writing an audit report for National Furniture. Here are the changes to a standard audit opinion (you can find a standard opinion earlier in "Reading an unqualified audit opinion"):

- ✔ **Introductory paragraph:** Add the following to the introductory paragraph:

    We did not audit the financial statements of Standard Furniture, a wholly owned subsidiary, whose statements reflect $300,000 in assets as of December 31, 2015 and total revenue of $200,000 for the year ended. Those statements were audited by other auditors whose report has been furnished to us, and our opinion, insofar as it relates to the amounts included for Standard Furniture, is based solely on the report of the other auditors.

- ✔ **Scope paragraph:** This paragraph refers to "audits" instead of an "audit." Also, this section of the report changes the last sentence to read, "We believe that our audit and the report of the other auditors provide a reasonable basis for our opinion."

- ✔ **Opinion paragraph:** The first sentence is changed to read, "In our opinion, based on our audits and the report of other auditors . . ." This paragraph also refers to "the financial position of National Furniture and subsidiaries."

The predecessor auditor has a few tasks concerning audit opinions as well. Here are the steps required of the predecessor auditor:

- ✔ **Considering the prior-period report:** The predecessor auditor considers whether the audit report is still appropriate. The auditor reads the prior-period report and compares those financial statements with the current-period report (prepared by the successor auditor). If the predecessor auditor determines that a subsequent event requires the prior-period report to be changed, that auditor needs to inform the successor auditor and the client. Those changes may require adjustments to the financial statements or simply additional disclosures of the subsequent events. Subsequent events are also discussed in the "Looking over an engagement letter" section.

✔ **Sending the representation letter:** The predecessor auditor creates a representation letter and sends it to company management and to the successor auditor. Management confirms in writing that all material issues related to the financial statements have been disclosed. Because the financial statements are the responsibility of management, the auditor asks for a representation letter. Both management and the successor auditor confirm that there are no subsequent events that require the predecessor auditor to adjust or add disclosures to the prior-period report. As you can see, there are two steps in place to identify subsequent events. One step involves the predecessor auditor's review of the financial statements. The other requires management and the successor auditor to address the topic via a representation letter.

Going over other audit opinions: Qualified, adverse, or no opinion

Auditors sometimes have to issue audit reports that depart from the unqualified audit opinion language (see the earlier section "Reading an unqualified audit opinion"). The auditor may disclaim an opinion or even state that the financial statements aren't materially correct. Here are some examples that appear on the AUD test:

✔ **Qualified (or "except for") opinion:** This report states that, except for the effects of the matter(s) the qualification relates to, the financial statements are fairly stated and materially correct. The report states the specific exception. If, for example, the auditor wasn't able to perform a count of the physical inventory, that may cause the auditor to qualify the report. The auditor would attempt to find other audit procedures to gather evidence about the inventory balance. If the auditor couldn't gather sufficient evidence about the inventory balance, the report may be qualified.

✔ **Adverse opinion:** The adverse opinion states that the financial statements aren't fairly stated and materially correct.

✔ **Disclaimer of opinion:** As the name implies, the auditor isn't presenting an opinion on the financial statements.

You see more detail on these specific reports in the sections that follow.

Working with a qualified opinion

A qualified opinion is also referred to as an "except for" opinion. The auditor is stating that there's one area of the financial statements that doesn't warrant the unqualified opinion language. A CPA firm is also making a judgment on its ability to form an opinion on the financial statements being audited. Here are some situations that may lead to a qualified opinion:

✔ **Lack of audit evidence:** The auditor notes a lack of sufficient audit evidence to support an unqualified opinion.

✔ **Lack of disclosure in the financial statements:** In some cases, the CPA can reference information stated in another document, such as a report to shareholders or in a prospectus. A *prospectus* is a document that provides information to potential buyers of a company's initial public offering of common stock. If the auditor decides that the needed financial information isn't disclosed in another document, the CPA may issue a qualified opinion due to lack of disclosure.

- **Scope limitation:** A scope limitation prevents the CPA from applying all the audit procedures considered necessary to perform the audit. See the earlier section "Reporting on a scope limitation" for details on this limitation.

- **Contingent liability:** A *contingent liability* is a liability that may be incurred, depending on the outcome of a future event. Contingent liabilities are posted in the balance sheet when the liability is both probable and the amount can be reasonably estimated. Management provides the auditor with evidence to support the company's decision about contingent liabilities. For example, the auditor must evaluate whether the dollar amount estimate of the contingent liability is reasonable. If the CPA decides that the evidence isn't sufficient, the CPA firm expresses a qualified opinion.

- **Departure from accounting principles:** The auditor notes a material departure from generally accepted accounting principles (GAAP; see Chapter 8). When the CPA notes a GAAP departure, the CPA firm may issue a qualified or adverse opinion, depending on the seriousness and dollar amount of the departure. GAAP, for example, requires companies to use the accrual method of accounting. Using the cash method would be a departure from GAAP. (Chapter 4 explains cash basis and accrual basis accounting.)

The report should explain the reason for the qualified opinion in one or more explanatory paragraphs. The explanation goes before the final paragraph, which is the opinion paragraph. The opinion paragraph then uses the "except for" language to state that the opinion is qualified.

Suppose that a company expenses certain lease agreements. The auditor's evidence indicates that the leases should be capitalized, which would comply with GAAP. (See Chapter 8 for details on leases.) The auditor includes an explanatory paragraph that explains how the client handled the lease and the CPA firm's opinion on how the lease should be handled.

The paragraph then states the impact of the change to the financial statements. If the lease were capitalized instead of expensed, an asset account (for the lease asset) and a liability account (for the lease payments) would be set up. Expenses would be reduced, because the lease payments wouldn't be immediately expensed. Net income, as a result, would be higher. The opinion paragraph would include an "except for" comment related to the lease.

Say that the auditing firm wasn't able to obtain the audited financial statements for a foreign affiliate called Atlantic Building Materials — an overseas-based business that's an investment for the company being audited. Because of that scope limitation, the auditor decides to issue a qualified opinion. Here are some points related to the audit opinion language (for comparison, see the earlier section "Reading an unqualified audit opinion"):

- **Scope paragraph:** The second paragraph of the audit opinion begins with "except as discussed in the following paragraph."

- **Explanatory paragraph:** Add an explanatory paragraph:

    We were unable to obtain audited financial statements supporting the company's investment in Atlantic Building Materials . . .

    The paragraph states the company's dollar amount investment in the affiliate.

- **Opinion paragraph:** The last paragraph starts with "In our opinion, except for." The CPA again states the exception.

Suppose a CPA decides that the CPA firm needs to issue a qualified opinion due to lack of disclosure. The CPA firm adds a paragraph stating, "The company's financial statements do not disclose [the needed disclosure]. In our opinion, disclosure of this information is required by accounting principles generally accepted in the Unites States of America."

For a lack of disclosure, the opinion paragraph states, "In our opinion, except for the information discussed in the preceding paragraph . . ."

Dealing with an adverse opinion

If the financial statements don't conform to GAAP, an auditor issues an adverse opinion. The adverse opinion states that the financial statements aren't fairly stated and materially correct. An adverse opinion includes these components (for comparison, see the earlier section "Reading an unqualified audit opinion"):

- ✔ **Explanatory paragraph(s):** Just as with a qualified opinion, an adverse opinion includes an explanatory paragraph — possibly two paragraphs — after the scope paragraph. This addition explains the substantive reasons for the adverse opinion.

  The explanatory paragraph should discuss the principle effects of the subject matter that caused the adverse opinion. If the effects can't be reasonably estimated, that should also be addressed. If, for example, the company uses the cash basis of accounting, the paragraph would explain that the cash basis is a departure from GAAP. The CPA may go on to explain that the cash basis doesn't match revenue with expenses and creates financial statements that are misleading.

- ✔ **Opinion paragraph:** This final paragraph needs to specifically reference the explanation paragraph.

Suppose that Meadowview Jewelry values its inventory at fair market value rather than historical cost. Meadowview's fair market value is higher than cost. The CPA determines that this policy violates the accounting principle of valuing assets at historical cost. Here's how the language may look in the CPA's adverse opinion:

- ✔ **First explanatory paragraph (the problem):** This paragraph references the note in the financial statements that explains how the inventory is valued at fair market value and notes that depreciation is based on that fair market value. Here, the CPA explains that accounting principles that are generally accepted in the U.S. require that inventory be stated at an amount not in excess of cost.

- ✔ **Second explanatory paragraph (principle effects):** This paragraph explains the financial impact of posting inventory at historical cost. Inventory, in this instance, is overstated at fair market value, which also means that depreciation is overstated. This paragraph also explains the excess depreciation's impact on net income and retained earnings.

- ✔ **Opinion paragraph:** The opinion paragraph reads as follows:

  > In our opinion, because of the effects of the matters discussed in the preceding paragraphs, the financial statements referred to above do not present fairly, in conformity with accounting principles generally accepted in the United States of America, the financial position of . . .

This is the type of language you see in an adverse opinion.

Deciding to disclaim an opinion

When you *disclaim* an opinion, you give no opinion on the financial statements. Specifically, you can't form an opinion as to whether the financial statements are presented fairly and conform to GAAP. You need to provide all the substantive reasons for the disclaimer of opinion. The primary reason for a disclaimer of opinion is that you weren't able to perform audit procedures that were sufficient in scope to provide an opinion on the financial statements.

Here are some examples of the substantive reasons for the disclaimer of opinion. You'd list these comments in an explanatory paragraph, which would be positioned just above the opinion paragraph in the audit report:

- ✔ The company didn't make a count of physical inventory.
- ✔ Evidence of the cost of assets is no longer available.
- ✔ Company records do not permit application of audit procedures.

A second explanatory paragraph notes that the scope of the auditor's work wasn't sufficient to enable the auditor to express an opinion. Therefore, you state, "We do not express an opinion on the financial statements."

Creating reports on internal controls and other work

An annual report issued to shareholders usually contains other information, in addition to the audited financial statements. Suppose that the annual report includes a discussion of the sales and revenue generated by a new product. The CPA is obligated to read the other information and determine whether it's consistent with the audited financial statements. If the auditor determines that the other information isn't consistent, the CPA should add explanatory language to the audit report. The goal is to provide an annual report with consistent information for the financial-statement reader. See the earlier "Adding explanatory language" section for details.

Before releasing any confidential client information, the CPA generally must get the client's consent. For example, a CPA must get consent from the client before releasing information to the IRS.

Going Over Accounting and Review Engagements

CPAs work on other engagements that aren't audits. Generally, these projects are referred to as *accounting and review engagements*. This section of the AUD test requires you to change your thinking. When you conduct an audit, you provide an audit opinion (or audit report). The tasks described in this section are not audits, so these reports do not provide an opinion on the financial statements. The accountant does issue a report, but that report is not an audit opinion.

The AICPA defines an *attestation engagement* as an exam, review, agreed-upon procedure, or any type of assertion that's the responsibility of another party. A report on compliance with statutory requirements (laws or regulations) can also be structured as an attestation engagement.

The two most-tested attestation engagements are compilations and reviews. Planning compilation and review engagements is similar to planning an audit. (Check out the section "Planning in more detail" earlier in the chapter.) The accountant needs to be clear about what he or she is being asked to do and document those procedures in an engagement letter. As you move through this section, keep in mind what task the accountant is being asked to perform. That will help you understand the language in the accountant's report.

Meeting minimum SSARS requirements

CPAs working on accounting and review engagements must comply with the Statement on Standards for Accounting and Review Services, or SSARS. A committee within the AICPA issues SSARS standards.

Before delivering unaudited financial statements to a nonpublic client, a CPA must, at a minimum, comply with SSARS guidelines for a compilation engagement (I cover compilation engagements in the next section). To understand this guideline, note the following:

- *Unaudited financial statements* refers to compilations, reviews, agreed-upon procedures, and other engagements that are not audits.

- A *nonpublic client* is a company that hasn't issued securities to the public. Public companies (those that issue stock) must comply with regulations set by the SEC.

- The minimum requirements are the requirements for a compilation engagement. If, for example, you perform a review or agreed-upon procedures, you must comply with compilation engagement guidelines to meet this nonpublic client rule.

SSARS does not cover *consulting engagements,* the processing of financial data for clients of other CPA firms.

Working on a compilation engagement

The AICPA describes a compilation as the most basic level of service a CPA provides to a client with respect to the company's financial statements. In a *compilation engagement,* the CPA helps the client present financial statements in a format that meets regulatory and industry requirements. Put simply, the CPA is helping the client put the numbers in the right format for a financial-statement reader.

The CPA does not, however, provide any assurance that the financial statements are free of material misstatement. In other words, there may be material modifications to the financial reports that should be made, but the CPA isn't giving any assurance or opinion on that issue.

Here are some other points that explain a CPA's responsibility on a compilation engagement:

- The CPA must have knowledge of the client company and its industry.

- The accountant must read the financial statements and consider whether the financial statements are in a proper form. The proper form is one that meets regulatory requirements. The CPA also considers whether the financial reports are free of obvious material error. If, for example, a large cash balance is presented as negative numbers in the balance sheet, that's an obvious material error. A negative balance in cash should be presented as a loan from the financial institution (a liability).

- The CPA doesn't perform inquiries, do analytical procedures, or obtain an understanding of the firm's internal controls. The accountant doesn't assess the risk of fraud or perform any tests of the accounting records.

A compilation report includes these comments:

- "The compilation was performed in accordance with SSARS."

- "The accountant did not conduct an audit or review on the financial statements."

✔ "The CPA does not express an opinion on the financial statements or provide any assurance that the financial statements are in accordance with a given financial reporting framework."

Going over a review engagement

In a *review engagement,* a CPA performs procedures that will provide limited assurance that no material modifications need to be made to the financial statements. That is, no material modifications are needed to make the financial statements conform to the applicable reporting framework.

Here are some additional comments to clarify how reviews differ from compilations and audits:

✔ **Assurance:** A review provides limited assurance on the financial statements. An audit provides broader assurances, and a compilation provides no assurance on the financial statements.

✔ **Procedures:** The review requires a CPA to perform procedures, such as an analytical review. For example, the CPA may compare an increase in sales to the change in accounts receivable. If the company sells on credit, an increase in sales should also lead to an increase in accounts receivable. The point is to determine whether the changes in the account balances are reasonable. The compilation doesn't require any procedures to be performed. For a compilation, the accountant reads the financial statements and comments on formatting and any obvious errors.

For a review, a CPA gains an understanding of the client and the company's industry. A review requires analytical procedures and inquiries with client. The CPA performing a review needs to be aware of the possibility that he or she might fail to modify the financial statements when a material misstatement exists. An accountant who missed a material misstatement didn't perform the review correctly, rendering the review report inaccurate.

Keep in mind that a review doesn't include these procedures:

✔ Gaining an understanding of the client's internal controls

✔ Assessing fraud risk (*fraud risk* is the risk that company employees will work to intentionally misstate the financial statements)

✔ Performing tests on the accounting records or performing other audit procedures

The review report explains that the review was conducted in accordance with SSARS. The report points out that management is responsible for preparing the financial statements and that management designs and implements internal controls. The review report also states that the CPA isn't aware of any material modifications that should be made to the financial statements.

Moving through Professional Responsibilities

The AUD test covers several areas related to your professional responsibilities as a CPA. One important regulatory area that is heavily tested is the concept of independence. The test often provides scenarios and asks whether the CPA described in the scenario is independent of the client.

Another area of responsibility that is growing in importance relates to companies that issue securities to the public. The Public Company Accounting Oversight Board (PCAOB) has oversight over companies that issue these types of securities. This section discusses the auditor's responsibilities related to the PCAOB.

AICPA Rule 101 discusses independence. (You can read the full text of the independence rule by visiting www.aicpa.org and doing a search on "Rule 101.") The first line of Rule 101 explains that a member in public practice (in the practice of accounting) must be independent in the performance of professional services. Independence is required for attestation engagements (I define attestation engagements in the earlier section "Going Over Accounting and Review Engagements.").

Here are some instances in which independence is considered to be impaired:

- A CPA has a direct interest or an indirect material interest in the client. *Material* means large enough to be relevant.

- A CPA is trustee of a trust or administrator of an estate that has a direct or indirect material interest in the client. This statement includes any investment in the client by the trust or estate.

- A CPA has loaned money to the client or has taken a loan from the client.

- CPA firm partners, employees, and family members of either partners or employees jointly own more than 5 percent of the client.

- During the period covered by the financial statements, a CPA firm partner or employee was a company officer, director, manager, promoter, underwriter, voting trustee, or trustee of a company pension or profit-sharing plan.

Promoters and underwriters are involved in creating and selling a company's securities to the public. If any of the preceding guidelines apply to the CPA firm, the firm is not independent of the client. The CPA firm's independence is impaired. If the firm isn't independent, that firm should not perform attestation engagements for the client.

CPAs are allowed to provide bookkeeping services for an audit client. Bookkeeping services do not impair an auditor's independence.

The PCAOB was created by Congress to oversee the audits of public companies to protect the interests of investors. A public company sells securities (stocks and bonds) to investors. You can find out more about this entity at www.pcaob.org. One major goal of the organization is ensure that audit reports are "informative, accurate, and independent." The AUD test may ask questions related to PCAOB.

The PCAOB has standards for conducting audits and relating to auditor independence. Those standards are very similar to the standards already explained in this chapter. The PCAOB also has quality control standards. These standards are put in place to ensure that competent people perform the audit and that the audit staff is properly supervised. Specifically, the audit firm needs a system to train and evaluate employees. The CPA firm needs a process to review the work performed by the audit staff.

Chapter 12

Auditing and Attestation Practice Questions

•••

The auditing and attestation (AUD) test requires students to learn and use a great deal of technical language. Audit opinions (also called audit reports) document whether or not a set of financial statements are free of material misstatement. An audit opinion is signed by the CPA and provided to the client under audit. The language in audit opinions is very specific. Take time to understand and memorize that language.

Auditing and Review Services

1. A CPA is required to comply with the provisions of Statements on Standards for Accounting and Review Services (SSARS) when

	Processing financial data for clients of other CPA firms	*Consulting on accounting matters*
(A)	Yes	Yes
(B)	Yes	No
(C)	No	Yes
(D)	No	No

2. A CPA should **not** submit unaudited financial statements of a nonpublic company to a client or others unless, at a minimum, the CPA complies with the provisions applicable to

(A) Compilation engagements.

(B) Review engagements.

(C) Statements on auditing standards.

(D) Attestation standards.

3. If requested to perform a review engagement for a nonpublic entity in which an accountant has an immaterial direct financial interest, the accountant is

(A) Independent because the financial interest is immaterial and therefore may issue a review report.

(B) **Not** independent and therefore may **not** be associated with the financial statements.

(C) **Not** independent and therefore may **not** issue a review report.

(D) **Not** independent and therefore may issue a review report but may **not** issue an auditor's opinion.

4. When compiling a nonpublic entity's financial statements, an accountant would be least likely to

   (A) Perform analytical procedures designed to identify relationships that appear to be unusual.

   (B) Read the compiled financial statements and consider whether they appear to include adequate disclosure.

   (C) Omit substantially all of the disclosures required by generally accepted accounting principles.

   (D) Issue a compilation report on one or more but **not** all of the basic financial statements.

Auditing with Technology

5. To obtain evidence that user identification and password controls are functioning as designed, an auditor would most likely

   (A) Review the online transaction log to ascertain whether employees using passwords have access to data files and computer programs.

   (B) Examine a sample of assigned passwords and access authority to determine whether password holders have access authority incompatible with their other responsibilities.

   (C) Extract a random sample of processed transactions and ensure that transactions are appropriately authorized.

   (D) Observe the file librarian's activities to discover whether other systems personnel are permitted to operate computer equipment without restriction.

6. Carmel Department Store has an ERP information system and is planning to issue credit cards to creditworthy customers. To strengthen internal controls by making it difficult for one to create a valid customer account number, the company's independent auditor has suggested the inclusion of a check digit, which should be placed

   (A) At the beginning of a valid account number only.

   (B) In the middle of a valid account number only.

   (C) At the end of a valid account number only.

   (D) Consistently in any position.

7. An auditor may decide **not** to perform tests of controls related to the computer portion of the client's controls. Which of the following would **not** be a valid reason for choosing to omit tests of controls?

   (A) The controls appear adequate.

   (B) The controls duplicate operative controls existing elsewhere in the system.

   (C) There appear to be major conditions that would preclude reliance on the stated procedure.

   (D) The time and dollar costs of testing exceed the time and dollar savings in substantive testing if the tests of controls show the controls to be operative.

8. A primary advantage of using generalized audit software packages to audit the financial statements of a client that uses a computer system is that the auditor may

   (A) Consider increasing the use of substantive tests of transactions in place of analytical procedures.

   (B) Substantiate the accuracy of data through self-checking digits and hash totals.

   (C) Reduce the level of required tests of controls to a relatively small amount.

   (D) Access information stored on computer files while having a limited understanding of the client's hardware and software features.

Audit Sampling

9. Which of the following is included as part of the definition of audit sampling?

   (A) Inquiry and observation procedures.

   (B) Documentary evidence.

   (C) Evaluation of some characteristic.

   (D) Statistical techniques.

10. An auditor examining inventory may appropriately apply sampling for attributes in order to estimate the

    (A) Average price of inventory items.

    (B) Percentage of slow-moving inventory items.

    (C) Dollar value of inventory.

    (D) Physical quantity of inventory items.

11. An auditor plans to examine a sample of 20 checks for countersignatures as prescribed by the client's internal control activities. One of the checks in the chosen sample of 20 cannot be found. The auditor should consider the reasons for this limitation and

    (A) Evaluate the results as if the sample size had been 19.

    (B) Treat the missing check as a deviation for the purpose of evaluating the sample.

    (C) Treat the missing check in the same manner as the majority of the other 19 checks (i.e., countersigned or not).

    (D) Choose another check to replace the missing check in the sample.

12. Which of the following statements is correct concerning statistical sampling in tests of controls?

    (A) Deviations from control procedures at a given rate usually result in misstatements at a higher rate.

    (B) As the population size doubles, the sample size should also double.

    (C) The qualitative aspects of deviations are **not** considered by the auditor.

    (D) There is an inverse relationship between the sample size and the tolerable rate.

Engagement Planning

13. An understanding with the client must include the objectives of the engagement, management's responsibilities, and

	The auditor's responsibilities	Limitations of the audit
(A)	Yes	Yes
(B)	Yes	No
(C)	No	Yes
(D)	No	No

14. The primary responsibility for the adequacy of disclosure in the financial statements of a publicly held company rests with the

    (A) Partner assigned to the audit engagement.

    (B) Management of the company.

    (C) Auditor in charge of the fieldwork.

    (D) Securities and Exchange Commission.

15. In considering materiality for planning purposes, an auditor believes that misstatements aggregating $10,000 would have a material effect on an entity's income statement but that misstatements would have to aggregate $20,000 to materially affect the balance sheet. Ordinarily, it would be appropriate to design auditing procedures that would be expected to detect misstatements that aggregate

    (A) $10,000

    (B) $15,000

    (C) $20,000

    (D) $30,000

Evidence

16. Which of the following statements concerning audit evidence is correct?

    (A) Appropriate evidence supporting management's assertions should be conclusive rather than merely persuasive.

    (B) Effective internal control contributes little to the reliability of the evidence created within the entity.

    (C) The cost of obtaining evidence is **not** an important consideration to an auditor in deciding what evidence should be obtained.

    (D) A client's accounting data **cannot** be considered sufficient audit evidence to support the financial statements.

17. When auditing a publicly traded client, the auditor's program for owner's equity is **least** likely to include a step requiring

    (A) Analysis of the accounting for the proceeds of stock issuance.

    (B) Confirmation of outstanding shares with an independent registrar.

    (C) Reconciliation of the stock certificate book with the general ledger.

    (D) Tests of the computation of earnings per share.

18. As one of the year-end audit procedures, the auditor instructed the client's personnel to prepare a standard bank confirmation request for a bank account that had been closed during the year. After the client's treasurer had signed the request, the assistant treasurer mailed it. What is the major flaw in this audit procedure?

    (A) The confirmation request was signed by the treasurer.

    (B) Sending the request was meaningless because the account was closed before the year-end.

    (C) The request was mailed by the assistant treasurer.

    (D) The CPA did not sign the confirmation request before it was mailed.

19. An auditor will usually trace the details of the test counts made during the observation of the physical inventory to a final inventory schedule. This audit procedure is undertaken to provide evidence that items physically present and observed by the auditor at the time of the physical inventory count are

    (A) Owned by the client.

    (B) **Not** obsolete.

    (C) Physically present at the time of the preparation of the final inventory schedule.

    (D) Included in the final inventory schedule.

Internal Control

20. In an audit of financial statements, an auditor's primary consideration regarding a control is whether the control

    (A) Reflects management's philosophy and operating style.

    (B) Affects management's financial statement assertions.

    (C) Provides adequate safeguards over access to assets.

    (D) Enhances management's decision-making processes.

21. To verify that all sales transactions for which shipment has occurred have been recorded, a test of transactions should be completed on a representative sample drawn from

    (A) Entries in the sales journal.

    (B) The billing clerk's file of sales orders.

    (C) A file of duplicate copies of sales invoices for which all prenumbered forms in the series have been accounted for.

    (D) The shipping clerk's file of duplicate copies of bills of lading.

22. The safeguarding of inventory most likely includes

    (A) Comparison of the information contained on the purchase requisitions, purchase orders, receiving reports, and vendors' invoices.

    (B) Periodic reconciliation of detailed inventory records with the actual inventory on hand by taking a physical count.

    (C) Analytical procedures for raw materials, goods in process, and finished goods that identify unusual transactions, theft, and obsolescence.

    (D) Application of established overhead rates on the basis of direct labor hours or direct labor costs.

23. If the independent auditors decide that the work performed by the internal auditor may have a bearing on their own procedures, they should consider the internal auditor's

    (A) Competence and objectivity.

    (B) Efficiency and experience.

    (C) Independence and review skills.

    (D) Training and supervisory skills.

Reporting

24. Tech Company has disclosed an uncertainty due to pending litigation. The auditor's decision to issue a qualified opinion rather than an unmodified opinion with an emphasis-of-matter paragraph most likely would be determined by the

    (A) Lack of sufficient evidence.

    (B) Inability to estimate the amount of loss.

    (C) Entity's lack of experience with such litigation.

    (D) Lack of insurance coverage for possible losses from such litigation.

25. Which of the following best describes the auditor's responsibility for "other information" included in the annual report to stockholders, which contains financial statements and the auditor's report?

    (A) The auditor has no obligation to read the "other information."

    (B) The auditor has no obligation to corroborate the "other information" but should read the "other information" to determine whether it is materially inconsistent with the financial statements.

    (C) The auditor should extend the examination to the extent necessary to verify the "other information."

    (D) The auditor must modify the auditor's report to state that the "other information is unaudited" or "not covered by the auditor's report."

26. When a client will **not** make essential corporate minutes available to the auditor, the audit report will probably contain a(n)

    (A) Unmodified opinion.

    (B) Adverse opinion.

    (C) Qualified opinion.

    (D) Disclaimer of opinion.

27. Which of the following professional services would be considered an attest engagement?

    (A) A management consulting engagement to provide accounting information systems advice to a client.

    (B) An engagement to report on compliance with statutory requirements.

    (C) An income tax engagement to prepare federal and state tax returns.

    (D) Providing human resource utilization advice to the client.

Professional Responsibilities

28. In which of the following situations would a CPA's covered members' independence be considered to be impaired?

    I. The CPA maintains a checking account that is fully insured by a government deposit insurance agency at an audit-client financial institution.

    II. The CPA has a direct financial interest in an audit client, but the interest is maintained in a blind trust.

    III. The CPA owns a commercial building and leases it to an audit client. The rental income is material to the CPA.

    (A) I and II.

    (B) II and III.

    (C) I and III.

    (D) I, II, and III.

29. A CPA in public practice may **not** disclose confidential client information regarding auditing services without the client's consent in response to which of the following situations?

    (A) A review of the CPA's professional practice by a state CPA society.

    (B) A letter to the client from the IRS.

    (C) An inquiry from the professional ethics division of the AICPA.

    (D) A court-ordered subpoena or summons.

30. The AICPA allows an auditor to perform which of the following services for an audit client?

    (A) Performance of bookkeeping services for the client.

    (B) Authorization of transactions for the client.

    (C) Preparation of client source documents.

    (D) Preparation and posting of journal entries without the client's approval.

Chapter 13

Answers and Explanations to Auditing and Attestation Practice Questions

● ●

*H*ere are the answers to the auditing and attestation (AUD) questions in Chapter 12. As you review your answers, you'll notice the AUD test's heavy emphasis on audit opinions (also called audit reports). Make sure you memorize the report language for an unqualified audit opinion. That step will help you understand all the other types of audit reports.

Auditing and Review Services

1. **D.** SSARS requirements do not apply either to the processing of financial data for clients of other CPA firms or to consulting on accounting matters.

2. **A.** An accountant should not submit such information unless he or she has, at a minimum, complied with the provisions applicable to a compilation engagement.

3. **C.** Reviews require independence, and an accountant may not maintain independence when an immaterial direct financial interest is held in a client when performing attestation services.

4. **A.** This answer is correct because analytical procedures are not normally performed during a compilation.

Auditing with Technology

5. **B.** Examining a sample of assigned passwords and access authority will allow the auditor to test the effectiveness of the controls.

6. **D.** A check digit, while normally at the end of an account number, may be placed consistently in any position in the account when adequate computer programming exists (that is, the mathematical calculation of the check digit can be performed regardless of placement).

7. **A.** This answer is correct because if controls appear adequate, the auditor tests them unless (1) the costs of testing are expected to exceed the savings in substantive tests or (2) the controls are redundant to other internal control activities. Therefore, Choice (A) is not a valid reason for omitting tests of controls.

8. **D.** Generalized audit software allows an auditor to test the client's data, not the software or hardware. Because the software is generalized, it can manipulate data from various types of information systems.

Audit Sampling

9. **C.** This answer is correct because *audit sampling* is the application of an audit procedure to less than 100 percent of the items within an account balance or class of transactions for the purpose of evaluating some characteristic of the balance or class.

10. **B.** *Attribute sampling* expresses a conclusion about the population in terms of a rate of occurrence. Accordingly, determining the percentage of slow-moving inventory items would be an appropriate attribute sampling application.

11. **B.** Choice (B) is correct because an auditor would ordinarily consider the selected item to be a deviation.

12. **D.** The sample size increases as the tolerable rate decreases — an inverse relationship.

Engagement Planning

13. **A.** Professional standards require that both the auditor's responsibilities and limitations of the audit be communicated.

14. **B.** Financial statements are the representations of management, which is responsible for producing proper financial statements.

15. **A.** Choice (A) is correct because during the planning stage of an audit, it will ordinarily be difficult to anticipate whether all misstatements will affect only one financial statement. The auditor therefore generally is required to use the lower financial statement figure for most portions of planning.

Evidence

16. **D.** Auditors must obtain evidence beyond the accounting data.

17. **C.** Independent registrars maintain most stock certificate books, so the auditor is least likely to reconcile the stock certificate book with the general ledger for publicly traded companies.

18. **C.** Allowing the client to mail the confirmation directly violated the requirement that the confirmations remain under the auditor's control. The auditor is unable to ascertain whether the confirmation reached the proper party.

19. **D.** Tracing the test counts from the observation of physical inventory to the final inventory schedule determines that items observed by the auditor are included in the final inventory schedule.

Internal Control

20. **B.** This answer is correct because control risk should be assessed in terms of financial statement assertions.

21. **D.** This answer is correct because items actually shipped (as evidenced by bills of lading) represent the client's sales.

22. **B.** This answer is correct because periodic reconciliation of detailed inventory records with the actual inventory on hand by actual count will make shortages obvious. In addition to detecting shortages, employee awareness that a count will be conducted may prevent fraud relating to inventory.

23. **A.** The AICPA's professional standards require independent auditors to consider internal auditor's competence, objectivity, and work performance.

Reporting

24. **A.** This answer is correct because the lack of sufficient evidence is a scope limitation that may result in a qualified opinion.

25. **B.** The professional standards require that an auditor read the "other information" to determine whether it is inconsistent with the financial statements.

26. **D.** When the client imposes restrictions that so significantly limit the scope of the audit, the auditor generally will be required to disclaim an opinion on the financial statements.

27. **B.** A report on compliance with statutory requirements might be structured as an attest engagement in which the required "written assertion" relates to such compliance.

Professional Responsibilities

28. **B.** The Code of Professional Conduct prohibits situations II and III, while situation I is allowed. Situation I is acceptable because Interpretation 101-5 allows the CPA to maintain a checking account that is fully insured by a government deposit insurance agency in an audit client. The Code of Professional Conduct states that independence is impaired both by a direct financial interest in an audit client, regardless of whether it's placed in a blind trust, and by an indirect financial interest such as the earning of a material amount of rental income from an audit client.

29. **B.** A CPA may not disclose information to the IRS without the client's consent.

30. **A.** The AICPA allows performance of bookkeeping services for an audit client.

Part V
Regulation

Taxes withheld in 2013	$3,500
Refund received in 2013 of 2012 tax	$400
Deficiency assessed and paid in 2013 for 2011:	
Tax	600
Interest	100

Learning all the tax rules covered in the regulation test can be daunting to say the least. Head to www.dummies.com/extras/cpaexam for an article on how to use a bucket as a learning tool to clarify the tax rules in your mind.

In this part . . .

✔ Get a handle on the regulation test (often thought to be the most difficult of the four tests) with info on rules, regulations, and taxation.

✔ Practice answering 30 sample questions from this test and check your answers against the answers and detailed explanations provided.

Chapter 14

Taking a Closer Look at the Regulation Test

In This Chapter
▶ Understanding business law topics
▶ Working with individual taxation scenarios
▶ Going over taxation for businesses, trusts, and estates

The regulation (REG) test may be the most technically challenging test on the CPA exam. This test covers many topics that you might see in an undergraduate business law class, and it goes over the responsibilities a CPA has when performing both audit and tax work. A large section of the test covers business and individual taxation.

Addressing the CPA's Responsibilities

Like people in many other professions, a CPA has certain ethics requirements. In this section, you review ethics and walk through the licensing requirements for the CPA profession.

Understanding ethics requirements for a CPA practice

CPAs have to adhere to the AICPA's Code of Professional Conduct. The code includes both principles and rules a CPA must follow. Here's an overview of those principles:

✔ **Responsibilities, public interest, and acting with integrity:** A CPA needs to exercise professional and moral judgment. He should also act in a way that serves the public interest. For example, regulators, lenders, and investors use a company's financial statements to make decisions, so the accountant needs to generate clear and concise financial data for the public.

✔ **Objectivity and independence:** A CPA firm should be free of any conflicts that may affect the firm's relationship with a client. Here's an important phrase to remember for the REG test: A CPA must be "independent in fact and appearance." Accountants should avoid even the appearance of a lack of independence. The CPA, for example, should consider how she interacts with a client socially and how the public may perceive that relationship.

I largely cover the independence rules for AICPA's Code of Professional Conduct in the auditing and attestation services discussion in Chapter 11. Most importantly, an auditor must be independent of the company under audit. Other CPA services, such as consulting and tax, do not require independence.

✔ **Due care:** The CPA should observe the professional, technical, and ethical standards required in the industry, continually striving to improve his or her competence. Chapter 3 explains that CPAs are required to take continuing education courses to improve their competence. Many state boards require ethics courses as part of the continuing education process. Due care also means that a CPA must gather sufficient, relevant data to support any professional service he provides.

✔ **Scope and nature of services:** This principle refers to the type of work the CPA does and how extensive that work is. The accountant is required to supervise the quality control process within her firm. For example, if the CPA firm is proposing to audit a clothing manufacturer, the firm's staff must have the experience and qualifications to effectively perform the audit. The audit partner, for example, must have experience in the clothing manufacturing industry. The CPA should also avoid any conflicts of interest.

Customer information is considered confidential. A CPA should disclose client information only after getting approval from the client. Also, a CPA should generally not accept contingency fees. A *contingency fee* is a payment that will be paid only if a certain event or outcome occurs. For example, a CPA can't agree to perform an audit when the audit fee is contingent on the CPA's finding ways to cut the firm's expenses by 10 percent in the next year. There are exceptions to this contingency fee rule, which include certain tax preparation matters and court-designated accounting fees.

A tax preparer may incur IRS penalties if the preparer inflates deductions taken on a return above their true value. The preparer may also incur penalties if he takes a position on a tax return that is at variance (contrary) to the IRS or the U.S. Supreme Court.

Considering your legal duties and responsibilities

CPAs are involved when clients sell securities to the public. The Securities Act of 1933 requires that companies selling securities to the public disclose accurate financial information. Companies must disclose financial data when they issue stock to the public for the first time through an *initial public offering*, or IPO. The Securities Act of 1934 requires continuing disclosure after securities start trading in the marketplace. The Securities and Exchange Commission (SEC) implements the requirements of the Act of '33 and Act of '34.

Unless a particular security or transaction is exempt from the SEC registration, the company must fulfill all registration requirements. Registration includes audited financial statements, which CPAs provide. In addition, a CPA may be involved in reviewing the SEC's registration statement to verify that it's consistent with the audited financial statements.

There are legal consequences if the registration statement is misstated. A plaintiff may sue over a violation of the '33 Act if the plaintiff bought the securities and the registration statement misstates or omits a material fact. Because the registration statements contain financial data that is audited by a CPA, the CPA needs to review the financial data for consistency and accuracy.

If a CPA fails to discover the omission of a fact that is material to a registration statement under the '33 Act, a purchaser of the securities may recover losses from the CPA. The statute of limitations is 1 year from the date of the discovery of the omission and 3 years from the offering date of the securities.

Mulling Over Business Law Issues

The business law section of the REG test covers the agency-and-principal relationship. This section discusses this relationship as well as contract law, because many business agreements involve contracts. Finally, you see a discussion of the Uniform Commercial Code, or UCC.

Presenting the concept of agency

All companies have to work with the legal ramifications of hiring and managing employees. One set of rules that applies to the workplace is the concept of agency. Agency represents a legal relationship between an agent and a principal. The *agent* is authorized to act on behalf of the principal. The agent is also authorized to create a legal relationship with third parties.

Consider this scenario: Jimmy is hired by Piping Hot Pizza to deliver pizzas. Jimmy delivers a pizza to Sally, a third party. In this case, Bob is the agent acting on behalf of Piping Hot Pizza, the principal.

To create the agency relationship, all that's required is consent and a principal with *capacity*, the ability to do something. The relationship between agent and principal doesn't need to be in writing. If Piping Hot asks Jimmy to deliver pizzas, that request is considered consent. Because Piping Hot has the ability to make pizzas and hire drivers to deliver them, Piping Hot (the principal) has capacity.

Now consider what authority the agent has in his or her relationship with the principal. The REG test covers three types of authority in connection with the agency concept:

✔ **Actual authority:** The principal's words or actions cause the agent to reasonably believe that she has been authorized to act.

   Suppose Large Pharmaceuticals hires Jane to sell a blood pressure drug to doctors. If Jane the sales rep gets marketing materials and receives training from Large Pharmaceuticals, Jane the agent will reasonably believe that she has actual authority to sell the drug to doctors.

✔ **Apparent authority:** The principal's words or actions would lead a third party — who is a reasonable person — to believe that the agent has authority to act. This applies even if the principal and a potential agent never discussed an agency relationship.

   Suppose that Large Pharmaceuticals hires Joe, an independent contractor, to sell the drug to doctors. Joe sells products for several companies. Joe hands out business cards with a Large Pharmaceuticals e-mail address. From the third party's (doctor's) point of view, Joe has apparent authority to act on behalf of Large Pharmaceuticals.

✔ **Implied authority:** If an agent can be reasonably expected to carry out certain duties as part of her express authority, the agent has implied authority to do them.

   If Jane has express (specific, actual) authority to sell the drug to doctors, providing training on the drug to the doctor's staff would be an implied authority.

Going over agency liability issues

Some liability issues relate to the agency concept. First, consider situations in which agents may have liability to a third party:

✔ **Disclosure:** If the agency is undisclosed or only partially disclosed — that is, if the relationship between the agent and principal isn't quite clear to a third party — then both the agent and principal have liability to the third party.

✔ **Agent liable:** If the agent doesn't have actual, apparent, or implied authority (see the preceding section), the agent has liability to the third party.

✔ **Agent not liable:** If the agent has actual or apparent authority and the principal *has* been disclosed to the third party (along with the principal and agent relationship), the agent isn't liable for acts performed within the scope of his or her authority.

Indemnity is defined as providing security against damage. When you indemnify people in a legal sense, you're protecting them from loss or damages that relate to a potential legal liability. The following points relate to liability among agents, principals, and third parties:

✔ **Principal indemnified:** If an agent acts with apparent authority but without actual authority, the principal is liable to third parties who work with the agent. In this situation, the agent is liable to indemnify the principal for any damages or losses due to the agent's dealings with a third party.

Suppose an agent of a roofing company offers home siding to a roofing customer. To the customer, the agent has apparent authority to sell siding services. The customer could hold the principal (roofing company) liable for any siding agreement. The agent, however, would be liable to indemnify the principal, because the agent had no actual authority to sell siding.

✔ **Agent indemnified:** If the agent acts with actual authority, the principal must indemnify the agent for any payments the agent makes while working in his or her role. This is true for payments that are expressly authorized or deemed necessary to promote the business.

If the agent for the roofing company pays for fuel costs for the company truck while visiting customers, the agent is indemnified from personally covering those payments. The fuel costs were incurred for business purposes. Unless there's evidence to the contrary, there's an implied duty to compensate the agent for his or her services.

✔ **Principal holds third party liable:** A principal can hold a third party liable even if the third party's identity or even existence isn't disclosed to the principal.

Suppose a roofing company (a principal) provides building materials to an agent. The roofing company's understanding is that the building materials will be used for Client A. The agent instead uses the materials for Client B. The principal (roofing company) can hold the third party (Client B) liable for paying for the materials. This is the case even if the roofing company doesn't know the specific client for the materials.

The agent owes several types of duties to the principal, including a fiduciary duty (a duty of loyalty). The agent must act with reasonable care — that is, the agent shouldn't act in a negligent manner. An agent should be obedient, meaning that the agent should follow the instructions that the principal provides. Finally, the agent must be loyal — an agent should act in the best interests of the principal.

If the agent acts without authority, the principal has a choice. One choice is *ratification,* which means that the principal can be bound by the transaction and accept any liability that results from the transaction. The principal could also choose not to be bound by the action of the agent. For example, suppose the agent for the roofing company acts with no authority and accepts an offer from a third party to sell a building owned by the roofing company. With ratification, the principal can choose to accept the third party's offer or reject it.

Adding in tort liability

A *tort* is defined as a wrongful act that results in injury to another person. That injury may be a physical injury, or it may be damage to a person's property or reputation. A tort can lead to civil liability, as opposed to criminal liability. In civil cases, damages may be awarded.

The REG test asks questions about whether a principal is liable for an agent's torts. A principal can be held liable for the torts of an agent if the agent is working as an employee. In some cases, both the employer (principal) and employee (agent) are held liable for a tort. A big factor in deciding on liability is the amount of control an employer has over a worker.

The IRS website (www.irs.gov) has several publications that help companies determine whether a worker is an employee or an independent contractor for tax purposes. Just as with tort liability, the amount of control an employee has over a worker helps determine the proper classification. Employers are not held liable for the torts of independent contractors.

If the employer has the right to control an employee (agent), then the employer is liable for the torts of the agent. The employer who has liability for an agent's torts has liability for only the torts arising from work performed for the employer (principal). The employer also isn't liable for the following:

- **An intentional tort that the employer didn't authorize:** An *intentional tort* is a tort that was purposeful or intentional.

- **Criminal acts that the employer didn't authorize:** Say you manage a home healthcare business. An employee is assigned to help an elderly person with rehabilitation and to prepare meals. If the employee stole property without the employer's knowledge or authorization, that's simply a criminal act. The employer isn't liable for the stolen property.

The REG test may ask a question about torts in relation to workers' compensation. Typically, a state has a *workers' compensation* fund to pay benefits to workers who are injured while employed. Employers in the state contribute to the fund based on the number of employees they have. When a worker is injured on the job, he or she applies for the workers' compensation benefits.

Suppose that Paul works as a roofer for Treetop Roofing. Joe is an independent contractor who also works for Treetop. Paul, the employee, is injured on the job due to a tort that Joe committed. Paul obtains workers' compensation benefits and then successfully sues Joe for damages. Paul is required to reimburse Treetop for the workers' comp costs that the company paid him. This is the case regardless of whether the person who committed the tort was an employee or an independent contractor.

Another employee benefit that may be on the REG test is the Family and Medical Leave Act. The act provides that a worker can take up to 12 weeks of unpaid leave to care for a spouse who has a serious health problem.

Getting up to speed on contracts

A *contract* is a binding legal document that is enforced by a court of law or through binding arbitration. Each party of the contract makes a promise. If a party doesn't follow through on its promise, you have a *breach of contract*.

Suppose Unique Furniture agrees to make a custom dining room table for Jason, the client, for $2,000. Unique promises to make the table, and Jason agrees to pay $2,000. If Unique doesn't deliver a table that meets the terms of the contract, that's a breach of contract. On the other hand, if Jason receives a table that meets the contract's terms and then doesn't pay $2,000, that's also a breach of contract.

The legal authority related to contracts comes from several sources:

- ✔ Common law contributes to contract law. Common law, which comes from English law, is derived from customs and judicial precedent.

- ✔ Common law differs from statutory law, which represents laws passed by a legislative body.

- ✔ The rules of contract are also derived from the *Uniform Commercial Code*, or UCC, which I discuss later in this chapter.

Here are three types of contracts:

- ✔ **Express contract:** In this case, an actual contract is formed. Two parties make promises to each other. The contract can be written or oral.

- ✔ **Implied-in-fact contract:** The conduct of a party creates a contract. One party's actions lead the other party — who is a reasonable person — to believe that a contract exists.

  For example, suppose a patient visits the doctor. The patient intends to receive medical treatment in exchange for a fair and reasonable doctor fee. As a result, there's an implied contract between the patient and doctor.

- ✔ **Quasi-contact:** A quasi-contract is not an actual contract. Instead, a court may substitute a quasi-contract if the court deems that one party would be injured if some sort of contract were not put into place. In other words, the court believes that the contract should've been formed, even though it wasn't. The court may also put a quasi-contract in place if one party would be unjustly enriched without a contract in force. These types of agreements ensure that each party is treated fairly.

  Say that a doctor stops to help an elderly man who is unconscious on the sidewalk. The man didn't ask for medical aid and isn't aware that he's receiving it. The elderly man, however, does receive a benefit. In this case, the law imposes a quasi-contract. If a legal issue arises between the elderly man and the doctor, the courts will state that there is a contract between the two parties.

A *unilateral contract* occurs when one promise is exchanged for performance. If one promise is exchanged for another promise, a *bilateral contract* is in place.

An *executory contract* is one in which some duties haven't yet been performed. When all the duties related to the contract are complete, it's an *executed contract*.

The following section on contracts discusses an offer and acceptance. A warranty has some similarities to offer-and-acceptance rules in contract law.

An *express warranty* is created when a seller makes an affirmation of a fact or promise that forms the basis of the bargain with the buyer. This warranty, which can be oral or in writing, exists regardless of the seller's intent. For example, suppose you buy a new oven. The oven has a sticker that states, "1-year warranty." The seller of the oven has affirmed a promise. You as the buyer understand that a 1-year warranty is part of the bargain (the purchase of the oven). An express warranty exists.

Forming a contract

Three components are essential to forming a contract: mutual assent, consideration, and no defenses to formation.

Mutual assent means that there's an agreement through an offer and acceptance:

- ✔ **Offer:** An offer involves the intent to enter into a contract. The contract's terms must be definite and certain. The party making the offer must communicate that offer to the *offeree* — the party who receives the offer.

- ✔ **Acceptance:** The offeree must communicate acceptance to the party making the offer. The acceptance must be *unequivocal,* or clearly stated. When the offeree accepts, there's no need to restate any of the contract's terms. Only the person who receives the offer (the offeree) can accept it.

  The *mailbox rule* says that when the offeree mails acceptance, it's consider to be received.

If a party terminates an offer before the offeree accepts it, no contract is formed. The REG test covers several ways in which an offer can be terminated:

- ✔ **Offeror revocation:** The party who makes the offer can communicate the revocation to the offeree in several ways:
  - **Direct communication:** The offeror approaches the offeree directly, revoking the offer either orally or in writing.
  - **Indirect communication:** A reliable source for the offeree revokes the offer. In fairness to the offeree, the revocation must be clearly understood and actually accepted. *Indirect communication* doesn't mean the offeree accepts the offer by mistake.
  - **Effective publication:** If the revocation is published, it's considered effective.

In some cases, the offeror can't revoke the offer:
  - **A unilateral contract where performance has begun:** For example, if a painter agrees to paint your garage door for $300 and starts the work, you can't revoke your offer to pay him.
  - **An option contract:** An option contract takes place when one party pays consideration to keep an offer open. Say that George pays $2,000 to keep his right to buy a piece of land open for three more months. That option contract can't be revoked.
  - **A merchant firm offer:** If a merchant offers to buy or sell something and the offer is written and signed, the offer can't be revoked.

- ✔ **Offeree rejection:** The offeree can reject an offer in several ways:
  - **Express rejection:** This rejection is clear and specific. An offer is considered rejected when the offerer receives the rejection.
  - **Time lapse:** In some cases, the offer is rejected due to a lapse of time. This occurs when the offer is made with a time deadline.
  - **Counteroffer:** A counteroffer rejects the original offer while making a new offer.

- ✔ **Operation of law:** A law, or a change in law, can terminate a contract. The *subject matter* represents the item, product, or service that's the purpose of forming a contract. For example, the subject matter may be a used car or a service contract to repair a roof. If the subject matter is destroyed or if a law makes the subject matter illegal, the contract is terminated. The death or insanity of one of the parties to the contract also terminates the contract.

Consideration, which is broadly defined as a payment or reward, is another essential component of a contract. Contracts are enforceable only if there's a bargain of legal value. A *bargain* is a negotiation in which a person may be required to do something or not to do something. For example, a person may have to take an action, such as repair a car. On the other hand, a salesman leaving a company may sign a contract agreeing *not* to call on the clients of his former company for three months.

Put simply, both parties have to do something or give something in order for there to be a contract.

The bargain can be expressed in several forms. A payment of cash or giving up some other property can be expression of a bargain. Or a bargain can be expressed by committing time or by taking an action.

Legal value is defined as incurring a detriment or having a legal obligation to perform. *Incurring a detriment* means that you've given up something that has value. If you're an attorney and commit time to provide legal services, that has value. You're incurring a detriment because you can't use that time for another billable client.

Considering defenses and remedies

When something goes wrong with a contract, the situation is referred to as a *breach.* If a contract is breached, each of the parties may consider remedies to the contract.

The REG test covers a list of defenses to contract formation. In the following situations, a contract isn't properly formed, so the contract is voided:

- ✔ **Fraud:** *Fraud* is defined as willful intent to deceive. A related term is *scienter,* which refers to willful misrepresentation. If a party commits fraud or uses scienter to form a contract, the contract isn't properly formed, and the other party may sue for damages.

- ✔ **Innocent misrepresentation:** Innocent misrepresentation involves an honest mistake. If a manufacturer tells the other party that the company has the machinery to complete an order of hand towels but then determines that the machines can't do the job, that's innocent misrepresentation.

- ✔ **Duress:** The threat of unlawful harm is considered duress. If either party is under duress, the contracts should be voided.

- ✔ **Undue influence:** A party has undue influence if it can use its position of power to take advantage of another person.

- ✔ **Other violations of law:** Other unlawful situations can result in a voided contract. If one party is a minor or is intoxicated, that party can't enter into a contract.

If a party's actions cause a contract to be voided, you have a contract *breach.* A *remedy* is the discharge of a contract. Here are some situations in which a contract is discharged due to a breach:

- ✔ **Material breach:** This type of breach represents one party's failure to perform its duties under the contract. The other party has the right to compel performance or collect damages due to the breach.

- ✔ **Anticipatory breach:** A party has a clear indication that the other party won't perform its duties under the contract. Say, for instance, that Jean's Dresses orders 1,000 dresses to be delivered on May 1. Jean knows that the other party, Detailed Manufacturing, has the capacity to make 100 per day. On April 29, Jean finds out that none of the dresses she has ordered have been produced yet. Clearly, Detailed Manufacturing won't fulfill its side of the contract. In this case, Jane has the option of discharging the contract, suing for damages, or simply waiting to see whether the other party performs the contract.

Detailed Manufacturing can certainly withdraw from the anticipatory breach, meaning that it fulfills the contract. Maybe Detailed can find another manufacturer to produce Jean's order on time.

✔ **Minor breach:** In this case, the breach is immaterial or not consider substantial. Suppose that Detailed Manufacturing doesn't deliver 10 of the 1,000 promised dresses on May 1. All the other dresses are delivered on time. Jane, the other party, isn't entitled to a discharge but can sue for damages. If Jane sues for damages related to the 10 dresses, Detailed Manufacturing must pay the damages.

Besides discharging a contract, some other options exist when one party doesn't perform according to a contract. *Rescission* means that both parties are excused and the contract is voided. *Reformation* refers to changing the contract so that it reflects the original intent of both parties. You can think of reformation as making corrections to a contract.

The REG test may include some other specifics related to damages:

✔ **Compensatory damages:** These damages compensate a party for losses due to the unfulfilled contract. If company loses a customer order because the other party didn't fulfill a contract to manufacture a component part, the manufacturer may have to pay compensatory damages.

✔ **Specific performance:** A party may get a court order requiring the other party to fulfill the contract. If a business has a contract to buy a new office building and the seller doesn't fulfill the sale contract, a buyer may get a court order for specific performance.

✔ **Punitive damages:** These damages are assessed to a party that acts egregiously when intentionally refusing to fulfill a contract. Normally, punitive damages are assessed only when fraud is involved.

Understanding third-party contracts

You may see language on the REG test that refers to a promisor, promisee, and a third party. A *promisor* makes a promise to a *promisee.* A promisor, in this case, also owes a duty of performance to a third party. If the third party is an *intended beneficiary,* that party has rights under the contract. Specifically, the promisor and promisee must contract with the intention of generating a benefit for the third party.

A third party can become involved in a contract by obtained rights or duties. An assignor can assign rights to an assignee (the third party). A delegator, on the other hand, can ask a delegee (a third party) to perform a duty or obligation under a contract.

Generally, a party's rights in a contract can be assigned without consent of the other party. However, all parties must consent to assignment in the following three cases:

✔ **Personal services:** The contract requires personal services of the party that wants to assign the contract.

✔ **Contract language:** Language in the contract prohibits assignment without consent.

✔ **Assignment changes the contract:** Assignment would materially change the risks and obligations of the other party to the contract.

Using the Uniform Commercial Code (UCC) and credit relationships

You can think of the Uniform Commercial Code (UCC) as the basic rules of the road for businesses selling products and services to each other. Accountants need to understand and record sales transactions, which is why UCC is on the REG test.

Going over sales

Article 2 of the UCC applies to the buying and selling of *goods*, which the UCC defines as movable (tangible) things.

A *merchant* is someone who regularly deals in goods. Although UCC sales law applies to merchants (businesses) and non-merchants (individuals), merchants are held to a higher standard. An auto dealer, for example, is held to higher standard than an individual who's selling a car to a neighbor. The auto dealer will likely have much more knowledge and experience than the buyer. That may not be the case with the individual who's selling a vehicle to a neighbor.

As with contracts, UCC law for sales assumes that both parties are acting in good faith.

UCC sales law has rules for offer and acceptance that are slightly different from those you see for other contracts (see the earlier section "Getting up to speed on contracts"):

- ✔ **Merchant's firm offer:** A merchant's firm offer is irrevocable, even without consideration. In other words, a party can rely on a merchant's offer even if that party doesn't give up something of value (consideration) for the offer.

  The party must accept and sign the offer, and a written record must be filed. The offer must be kept open for a period not to exceed 3 months. For example, if Reliable Denim makes a written offer to Mountain View Jeans for 20,000 yards of denim at $5 a yard, Reliable must keep the offer open for a period of time.

- ✔ **Acceptance:** If the sale is between two merchants, the contract terms can be changed after the sale takes place. If the sales agreement involves a non-merchant, they can't. For a non-merchant, common law applies. Common law requires that the offer match or mirror the acceptance. (Check out the earlier section "Getting up to speed on contracts" for details.)

- ✔ **Consideration:** Consideration is broadly defined as a payment or reward. (See the earlier section "Forming a contract.") For UCC sales purposes, the consideration needs to be stated in the contract. The consideration can be modified as long as both parties act in good faith.

There are a few exceptions to the rule that consideration must be stated in the contract. One exception is an output contract. With an *output contract,* the buyer agrees to purchase the seller's entire output of goods for a stated period of time. Suppose that a denim manufacturer produces 20,000 yards of denim a month. If a buyer, West Coast Jeans, agreed to buy all 20,000 yards for 3 months, that arrangement would be considered an output contract. A second exception is a *requirement contact.* In this case, the seller agrees to supply a specific required output to the buyer for a stated period. If West Coast needed 15,000 yards of denim per month, a denim manufacturer could sign a requirement contract to meet that monthly need for a specific period of time.

As with other contracts, if one party commits fraud, the other party can use the fraud as a defense for not fulfilling its obligation in the sales commitment.

After the seller produces goods that conform to the requirements of the contract, the seller has the requirement of *tender of delivery.* The seller needs to hold the goods for the buyer and to notify the buyer so the buyer can plan to take delivery.

The REG test defines the *passage of title* as when a party (buyer or seller) assumes the rights and responsibilities for the goods identified the contract. The contract should also indicate the time and place when the goods pass from seller to buyer.

Risk of loss dictates which parties bear the risk of the goods' being damaged or destroyed. In a sales situation, the risk of loss period begins after the sale is complete but before the goods are delivered. For example, suppose that Chillwell Refrigerators has manufactured 50 refrigerators for a department store. The product is sitting in Chillwell's warehouse. Generally, the party with title to the goods has risk of loss. If Chillwell has title to the refrigerators and the goods are destroyed in a warehouse fire, Chillwell bears the risk of that loss. A company needs to insure goods against this type of loss.

Here are some conditions for risk of loss:

- ✔ The goods must conform to the contract. The seller also must segregate goods so that the buyer can identify them.

- ✔ If the seller isn't a merchant and uses a delivery carrier (like FedEx) to ship the goods from seller to buyer, then when the seller completes tender of delivery, the risk of loss transfers to the buyer. When someone who isn't a car dealer sells a car to another party, the seller isn't a merchant.

- ✔ If the seller is a merchant seller that doesn't use a delivery carrier, risk of loss transfers when the buyer takes possession of the goods.

- ✔ When a delivery carrier is used and the buyer and seller create a *shipping-point contract,* the risk of loss transfers to the buyer when the goods are delivered to the carrier. If FedEx is the carrier, this agreement means that the risk of loss moves to the buyer when FedEx picks up the goods from the seller. On an inventory question on the FAR test, you may see the term *FOB (free on board) shipping point* used to describe this agreement.

- ✔ If the seller and buyer set up a *destination-point contract,* the risk of loss transfers to the buyer when the buyer receives the goods. (The inventory portion of the FAR test uses *FOB destination* to describe this situation.)

All sales are final under UCC, unless the contract provides for some specific contingencies. A *sale on approval* means that the sale isn't final until the buyer approves it. A sale on return, also known as a *contingency sale*, is another special condition added to a contract. A *contingency sale* means that the sale isn't final until a particular event is resolved.

Suppose that Jane's Dress Shop sells goods on consignment. *Consignment* means that vendor and individual dress owners will loan Jane their dresses. If the item sells, Jane and the person who supplied the dress will share in the sales proceeds. If Jane doesn't sell the dress, it's returned to the owner. The original owner keeps ownership until the item is sold. Dresses on consignment aren't considered part of Jane's inventory. In this case, the event that needs to be resolved is the transfer of title (ownership) of the goods.

Plugging in sales warranties and sales liabilities

UCC sales law includes detail on warranties. An *express* (specific) *warranty* is created when a seller makes an affirmation of a fact or promise that forms the basis of the bargain with the buyer.

The REG test covers some information on implied warranties related to sales agreements (For help with this *implied* concept, check out the implied authority discussion in the earlier section "Presenting the concept of agency."):

- ✔ **Implied warranty of title:** In this case, the seller implies some information to the buyer. First, the seller implies that he has good title. *Good title* means that nothing will impede the buyer from getting title to the goods when they're purchased. In other words, there are *no encumbrances* to the transfer of title.

Say, for example, that Unique Windows is selling 20 windows to a homebuilder. Unique, the seller, implies that it has good title. However, the homebuilder finds out that the windows serve as partial collateral for a loan and cannot be sold until Unique pays the loan. The seller doesn't have good title, and the title is considered encumbered.

✔ **Implied warranty of merchantability:** This implied warranty says that you can reasonably assume that the product you buy from a merchant is fit for ordinary use. Suppose a builder buys 12-inch bolts for construction from Reliable Bolts. Bolts are designed to work at a certain stress capacity before they're at risk of failing (breaking). If the builder uses the bolts for normal construction use, without putting too much stress on them, this warranty implies that the bolts will work as designed.

This example illustrates a warranty that exists on a sale between two merchants. The builder and the bolt-seller both know the standard use for the product. If a seller wants to disclaim the warranty, the seller states that the goods are sold "as is" or "with all faults." The disclaimer may be on a sale between merchants or between a merchant and a non-merchant. To understand that concept, consider outlet stores that sell slightly flawed goods to consumers. Maybe a customer buys a pair of jeans that has some flaws in the stitching "as is" at a deep discount.

✔ **Implied warranty of fitness:** When a buyer relies on the expertise of a sales associate, there's an implied warranty of fitness. The seller is providing a product that fits the seller's intended use. For this warranty to apply, the seller must

- Understand why the buyer is making the purchase
- Know that the buyer is relying on his or her expertise

If Mark is buying skis for the first time and explains that to the sales associate, then an implied warranty of fitness exists. Again, this warranty can be disclaimed using "as is" or "with all faults."

You may hear about stories of product liability in the media: A company sells a product and is being sued for damages by the buyer. A party that sells a defective product has committed a *tort,* a wrongful act that results in injury to another person. The REG test covers two types of tort liability related to the UCC sales rules:

✔ **Strict product liability:** The seller, who is in the business of selling the product, sells a defective product. Because the product is unreasonably dangerous, the defective product causes an injury to the buyer. In this case, the injured party doesn't have to prove negligence. If a roofer puts a roof on a homeowner's house and loose shingles that fall off the house injure the customer, the roofer has strict liability.

✔ **Negligence:** A seller that breaches a duty of care, resulting in injury to the buyer, is guilty of negligence. Say that a car dealer sells a customer a car in good working order. However, the dealership didn't change a tire on the car properly, which leads the car buyer to have an accident. The car dealer has a duty of care to change the tire properly. In this case, the dealership was negligent.

The REG test may ask about buyer and seller remedies. *Remedies* represent the rights a buyer or seller has when the other party doesn't perform on a sales agreement. When something goes wrong with a contract, a *breach* occurs. Here's a summary of the remedies:

✔ **Seller remedies:** If a buyer rejects the goods or refuses to pay for them, the act is considered a breach of contract. The seller's remedies include stopping delivery of the goods to the buyer or reclaiming goods that have already been sent. The seller can also resell the goods to another buyer to recover the sales dollars that the buyer didn't pay.

✔ **Buyer remedies:** When a seller fails to deliver goods to the buyer, the seller has breached a contract. The buyer's remedies include rejecting goods that don't conform to the sales agreement. The buyer has the right to cancel the sales agreement or to require specific performance. *Specific performance* means that a party is required to perform a specific act. In this case, the buyer's remedy is that the seller delivers the goods described in the contract.

If the seller doesn't deliver the goods, the buyer may not be able to produce a product that a customer has ordered. Suppose you're a car manufacturer. If your engine supplier doesn't deliver car engines as promised, you can't make and deliver cars to your customers. The buyer's sales are at risk if sellers don't produce and deliver goods as promised.

✔ **Remedies available to buyers and sellers:** If either party has reasonable grounds to believe that the other party won't perform, it has the right to demand performance in writing. If the other party can't provide assurance, the situation is considered an *anticipatory repudiation*. The party concerned about lack of performance can wait a reasonable amount of time for performance and then recover damages, or it can recover damages immediately.

Putting in negotiable instruments and using titles

Commercial paper, which is a common test area on the REG test, is a contract between two parties. One party buys and owns the instrument, and the other makes a promise to pay money.

Because commercial paper can be bought and sold, it's considered a *negotiable instrument.* To help with the concept of negotiable instruments, consider a stock or bond investment. Stocks and bonds are traded between investors, and so is commercial paper.

Because commercial paper is a promise to pay money at a future date, it can be used as money. The holder of commercial paper is referred to as a *holder in due course,* which means the following:

✔ The holder takes the instrument *for value,* meaning that she gives up something to get the instrument. The holder typically gives up money, but the individual can give up some other type of asset, such as equipment or a vehicle.

✔ A holder in due course takes the instrument without knowledge of any known defects. This idea is important because the holder may sell (negotiate) the instrument to someone else.

✔ The holder takes the instrument without any defenses or claims.

The last two components of the holder-in-due-course rules exist so that commercial paper with problems or contingencies isn't sold to investors who are unaware of problems with the instrument. If a seller is aware of problems with the commercial paper, she knows that she can't sell that commercial paper to someone else and meet the holder-in-due-course definition. If the instrument doesn't meet the holder-in-due-course criteria, any agreement between buyer and seller is simply a contract. The instrument is not a negotiable instrument.

The REG test covers two types of commercial paper:

✔ **Note: a promise to pay:** A note involves two parties. A *payor* promises to pay money to a *payee.* For example, a certificate of deposit is an instrument in which a bank (payor) promises to pay an investor (payee).

✔ **Draft: on order to pay:** A draft includes three parties. A draft is an order from a *drawer* to a *drawee* to pay a third-party payee. The best example of a draft is a personal check. Bob, the drawer, orders his bank (drawee) to pay $50 to his utility company (payee).

As you read about negotiable instruments, look at the front and back of a personal check. You'll find the same type of language on a check.

Article 3 of the UCC defines negotiable instruments. A negotiable instrument has the following components:

- **An unconditional promise to pay, if the instrument is a note:** A draft has an unconditional order to pay. By *unconditional,* the UCC means that the instrument has no other conditions. The instrument should not include language such as "subject to."

- **A fixed amount of money:** Some business-law textbooks refer to this feature as a *sum certain.*

- **Payable to bearer or to order:** Your check likely says, "pay to the order of," because *order* refers to a specific party. Bearer instruments are payable to the person who holds the instrument. Bearer instruments, such as bearer bonds, require that the holder of the instrument write his name on the instrument before the issuer pays him.

- **Payable on demand or at a definite time in the future:** A ten-year corporate bond, for example, pays the principal amount of the bond in ten years.

- **No other undertakings:** In other words, there are no other promises besides the payment. Some exceptions exist. If the negotiable instrument is used as collateral, additional requirements are allowed.

- **Written and signed by the promisor, if the instrument is a note:** Drafts are signed by the *drawer.*

If a holder in due course makes a claim on the instrument, she is asking for payment. The other party (the *obligor*) is obligated to pay. If the obligor refuses to pay, his only defense is a real defense. (These defenses are similar to the contract defenses you see in the earlier section "Considering defenses and remedies.")

Here are some *real defenses* that you may see on the REG test:

- **Fraud in execution:** If the party was misled or lied to intentionally, that's considered a real defense.

- **Forgery, other illegalities:** If the negotiable instrument was forged or some other illegal act was conducted, the party has a real defense. Duress is also a real defense.

- **Material alteration:** If a negotiable instrument is altered so that the components of the instrument are materially different, the party has a real defense.

A *surety* is someone who provides a guarantee that a debt (obligation) will be paid. If a debtor induces a surety to provide a guarantee using fraud, the surety may not be released from paying the debt. If the creditor (lender) loaned the money to the debtor in good faith, the surety is obligated to pay the debt.

More than one surety can guarantee a debt. In this case, an individual surety is referred to as *co-surety.* The REG test may provide an example in which a co-surety pays more of a debtor obligation than he has to. This co-surety can implement the *right of contribution,* in which he demands that the other co-surety participants reimburse him for the proportionate share of the debt they owe.

Relating debtors to creditors

Bankruptcy is broadly defined as the legal status of a person who cannot repay debts owed to creditors. For the CPA exam, bankruptcy is a legal process in which the debtor is relieved of his or her debts and the creditors are given an amount of *satisfaction* (some possible repayment) on their portion of the debts. The bankruptcy process is available in the U.S. for individuals and businesses. Most types of businesses can apply for bankruptcy, including sole proprietorships, partnerships, and corporations.

Here are the three types of bankruptcy that the REG test covers:

- ✔ **Chapter 7 liquidation:** In a Chapter 7 liquidation, a trustee is appointed. A *trustee* takes administrative responsibility for the financial affairs of the bankrupt party. The trustee handles the distribution of assets to creditors.

- ✔ **Chapter 11 business reorganization:** In this form of bankruptcy, a plan to repay creditors is put into place. No trustee is appointed because no assets are liquidated.

- ✔ **Chapter 13 debt adjustment plan:** In a Chapter 13 plan, assets aren't liquidated. Instead, a trustee is appointed and a three- to five-year repayment plan is set up to repay creditors.

The next section goes into more detail on specific bankruptcy regulations.

Reviewing Chapter 7 and 11 bankruptcy rules

Both Chapter 7 and Chapter 11 bankruptcy filings provide an automatic stay to collection efforts. An *automatic stay* is an injunction that immediately halts collection actions by creditors. Note, however, that an automatic stay doesn't affect child support, alimony, and criminal prosecution. Here are two types of bankruptcy filings for Chapter 7 and 11:

- ✔ **Voluntary filing:** The debtor, who can file individually or with a spouse, initiates the filing. This filing kicks off an *order of relief,* which starts the legal proceedings in the court.

- ✔ **Involuntary filing:** The creditor performs this filing. The creditor must show that the debtor is generally not paying debts.

After the filing, the debtor must provide a series of documents to the court. Those documents include a list of all creditors as well as a listing of assets and liabilities and any property owned. The debtor also provides a monthly estimate of income and expenses and copies of *payment advices* (pay stubs and payments from clients if the debtor is self-employed). A debtor also provides copies of recent tax returns.

A creditors' meeting is set up with the trustee, the creditors, and the debtor. It takes place 20 to 40 days after the initiation of the order of relief. The purpose of this meeting is to allow the creditor to review the records that the debtor provided.

Bankruptcy estate property represents property that's included in the bankruptcy filing. On the REG test, you need to know what kinds of items count as property:

- ✔ **Included property:** Real and personal property are included. *Real property* is real estate (homes and land). *Personal property* includes vehicles (to remember this term, consider the items on which you pay personal property tax).

  Income earned from real or personal property is also included. Insurance proceeds, inheritance, and property from a divorce received in the 180 days before the filing are included property.

- ✔ **Excluded property:** Income earned after filing the petition is excluded. Bankruptcy law also provides certain dollar limitations for "items deemed necessary to live." Essentially, the debtor is given a budget for certain basic costs, such as costs for a vehicle and for medical expenses.

The following sections go into detail on each type of bankruptcy.

Digging into Chapter 7 bankruptcy

The purpose of a Chapter 7 bankruptcy is to allow the debtor a discharge from his or her debts. A trustee is normally appointed.

Objections to the discharge of debts prevent the discharge of any debts. If, for example, the debtor had debts discharged within the last 8 years before the current filing, debts cannot be discharged. If the debtor performs a fraudulent transfer of debt or conceals property from the trustee, debts can't be discharged. Debts can't be discharged if the debtor fails to keep books and records on his financial affairs.

Some debts can't be discharged in Chapter 7 bankruptcy. Here is a partial list of some of the more frequently tested debts:

- Taxes due within the last three years

- Alimony or child support (you can group these together as divorce-related payments)

- Any debt incurred by fraud or any other means considered illegal (also, all court-imposed payments, such as court damages, fines, and restitution payments)

Any illegal or improper behavior after the discharge of debts may cause the discharge to be revoked. Such behavior includes include obtaining a discharge by fraud or refusing to obey a court order.

Reaffirmation is the prevention of discharge of certain debts. These are debts that the debtor intends to pay back. A debtor may choose to reaffirm some debts to maintain a relationship with the creditor.

After the discharge of debts process is resolved, the bankruptcy rule moves on to the priority of payments. Secured creditors are paid for the full amount of their secured claims first. After secured creditors, priority creditors are paid, followed by general creditors.

A *secured creditor* has a security interest in a specific asset owned by the debtor. For example, when a bank makes a home loan, the bank takes a security interest in the home. If the borrower doesn't pay back the loan, the bank can take possession of the security interest and sell it. The sale would allow the bank to recover some or all of the loan amount.

A secured creditor wants to *attach* a security interest. For a security interest to be attached, these three conditions must be met:

- The debtor must have rights in the collateral.

- A creditor must extend value. The creditor must give something up (cash or property) to the debtor.

- A record of the security agreement between the buyer and seller must exist.

The bankruptcy court views some payments as being more of a priority than others. Here's a partial list of some payments in priority order, from highest to lowest:

- Child and spousal support

- Unpaid wages to employees that were payable within the last 180 days, up to a specific dollar amount cap

- Employee benefit plan payments due to employees, up to a specific dollar amount cap

- Personal injury claims

The last group to be paid, general creditors, is also *unsecured creditors*. An unsecured creditor's receivable is backed only by the borrower's ability to pay. An unsecured debt, such as a credit card balance, isn't backed by a specific asset. Unlike with a secured creditor, the unsecured creditor can't sell a specific asset to recover the amount of the loan.

If a secured creditor's debt repayment isn't completely satisfied by selling the related collateral, the creditor is still a part of the debt-collection process. The unpaid portion of the debt makes this creditor a general unsecured creditor. For example, suppose land is sold for $100,000 to satisfy a secured debt of $150,000. The creditor is now a general unsecured creditor for the remaining $50,000.

You may notice a trend as you run through bankruptcy law. In several situations, the law looks back to the period of time before the bankruptcy filing. For example, the rules take a look at wages owed before the filing, and certain property received in the 180 days before the filing counts as included property. The reason for these rules is to prevent a debtor from shifting around assets, income, or liabilities right before the bankruptcy filing to take advantage of creditors.

Continuing with Chapter 11 bankruptcy

The goal of Chapter 11 bankruptcy is to provide the business owner (the debtor) some options that allow the owner to restructure the business. *Restructuring* means that the owner uses the existing business assets to generate sales and earnings, and the owner uses the earnings to pay down debt. As a result, the trustee doesn't take possession of the debtor's assets in a Chapter 11 bankruptcy.

The trustee appoints a *creditor committee*. For an individual debtor, the committee consists of the seven largest unsecured creditors (an unsecured debt isn't backed by a specific asset). If the debtor is a corporation, the committee members are the seven largest holders of the company's equity. Stockholders own equity.

This committee consults with the debtor on how to administrate the bankruptcy process. The committee is responsible for monitoring how the debtor operates the business. Specifically, the business owner needs to use assets effectively to generate earnings so the debts can eventually be repaid. The debtor works with the creditor committee to create a repayment plan.

The debtor has the right to file a plan of reorganization within 120 days of the order of relief, which starts the legal proceedings. The debtor's reorganization plan must do the following:

- ✔ **Classify claim holders by type.** The plan lists secured creditors and each type of unsecured creditor (priority or general creditors). Chapter 11 bankruptcy has the same priority of payment system I explain earlier in "Digging into Chapter 7 bankruptcy."

- ✔ **Groups similar claims into classes.** All the secured creditors, for example, may be considered a class. The reorganization plan explains how claims within a particular class are treated.

- ✔ **Explain any impaired claims.** An impaired claim is a debt that won't be repaid completely or a claim in which a contractual right to repay is changed as a result of the reorganization.

A claim is considered accepted by class if at least two-thirds of the dollar amount of claims in the class vote for the plan. In addition, at least half of the number of claims within a class must also vote for the plan.

After a reorganization plan is filed and the creditors vote, the bankruptcy court decides whether to confirm the plan. The court confirms the plan if it's feasible and was proposed in good faith. The reorganization plan must also comply with the regulations of the bankruptcy court.

The court may decide to implement a *cram down exception*. In this case, the court confirms a reorganization plan that a class or classes of creditors have voted down. If the court judges the plan to be fair and equitable, it may put a cram down exception into place. The court forces the creditors to accept the plan, even though some have voted against it.

After the plan is approved, the debtor has to make the payments required in the reorganization plan. The plan also replaces the original contracts between each debtor and creditor with provisions in the reorganization plan.

Choosing a business structure and other regulations

The REG test asks about the different types of corporate structures someone can select when forming a business. Each structure has different rules about owner liability and its own method of taxation.

Picking a partnership structure

A *partnership* is defined as two or more people who enter into a business by creating a *partnership agreement.* A partnership is a separate legal entity, an entity that files its own tax return. The REG test refers to the revised uniform partnership act, which governs partnerships. This agreement documents how the partners allocate profits and losses and how a partner's capital account balance is calculated. Partner capital is comparable to the equity section of the balance sheet for a corporation. Both capital and equity refer to ownership in the entity.

Partners also have the right to participate in the partnership by voting on issues. Partners have a right to make decisions on important issues, just as stockholders have rights as owners of corporations.

A partnership is a *pass-through entity,* an entity in which the profit and loss flow through to the owners (see Chapter 4 for details). The partnership entity files a tax return, but the profit and loss on the partnership flows through to the personal tax returns of the partners.

Each partnership has at least one *general partner.* The general partners are responsible for the day-to-day management of the partnership. A general partner may manage the partnership himself or hire a manager.

A frequently tested area on the REG test concerns partnership liability. General partners have unlimited liability for the acts of the partnership. This includes other partners' actions on behalf of the partnership. *Unlimited liability* means that the general partner's personal assets are at risk, as is that partner's investment in the partnership. A limited partner's liability is limited to that partner's investment in the partnership.

Suppose a partnership owns a restaurant. Patrick is a general partner who manages the restaurant. Greg is a limited partner. After slipping and falling outside the restaurant, a customer sues the partners to recover the medical costs of his injuries. Patrick, the general partner, has unlimited liability for the litigation. The limited partner, Greg, has his liability limited to his partnership investment.

Ownership of a partnership is in partner *capital accounts.* Each partner has an individual capital account. The sum of all the capital accounts represents the entire capital of the partnership. Here are the transactions that increase and decrease capital accounts:

✔ **Partner capital increases:** Capital accounts are increased by capital contributions by the partners. When a partner contributes cash or other assets (like a vehicle or equipment), her capital account is increased. Her capital account is also increased by her share of the partnership profit. Each partner's share of profits and losses is documented in the partnership agreement.

▶ **Partner capital decreases:** A partner's taking assets out of the partnership is a *withdrawal*. The partner's capital is reduced by her share of partnership losses.

The partner's interest in the profit of a partnership can be assigned to someone else. If, for example, a partner wanted a child to receive income generated by the partnership, the partner can assign that interest. Ownership in a partnership, however, cannot be assigned. The rationale is that Partner A entered into a partnership with Partner B, so Partner A shouldn't be forced into a partnership with someone besides A.

Choosing a corporate structure

A *corporation* is a group of people authorized to act as a single entity. The corporation, in fact, is considered a person from a legal point of view. The owners of a company are shareholders, who invest assets in a company in exchange for common stock.

The equity section of a corporation consists of common stock, additional paid-in capital, and retained earnings (see Chapter 8 for details). Consider the transactions that would increase and decrease stockholders' equity:

▶ **Increase in stockholders' equity:** Issuing shares of stock to the public for the first time is an *initial public offering*. Investors pay cash (or contribute other assets) in exchange for stock. A public offering increases equity. Note that when stock is sold between investors, no additional funds come into the business. Companies raise funds when stock is purchased directly from the corporation. If a company generates earnings and keeps those earnings in the business, those retained earnings increase equity.

▶ **Decrease in stockholders' equity:** *Treasury stock* refers to stock repurchased by the corporation from shareholders. When the corporation buys back the stock, equity is decreased. When a company has earnings and pays a portion of the earnings to shareholders, the payment is a *dividend*. Dividends also reduce earnings.

The REG test focuses on the pros and cons of forming a corporation as a business structure.

Taking on security regulation

The REG test covers securities regulation, specifically the requirements of the Securities and Exchange Commission (SEC). Generally, the SEC regulates companies that sell securities (stocks and bonds) to the public. This is an important area for CPAs, because many businesses sell stock and bonds to investors. This section defines a security and discusses the Securities Acts of 1933 and 1934. These two acts cover most of the securities regulation that's covered on the REG test.

A *security* is defined as a passive investment. *Passive* means that the investor isn't actively involved in the operation of the business. Instead, the investor relies on the firm's management to make business decisions. The two most common types of investments are stocks and bonds (see Chapter 8 to read about accounting for stocks and bonds). The definition of a security also includes stock options, convertible securities, and certain partnership interests.

To succeed on the securities regulation section of the REG test, you need to know the differences between the Securities Acts of 1933 and 1934. The Act of '33 covers the regulation of securities when they're sold to the public for the first time. On the other hand, the Act of '34 regulates securities when they're trading between investors. The big emphasis on the REG test is the disclosure requirements for each of the acts.

An *initial public offering* (IPO) refers to a company's issuing of securities (usually common stock) to the public for the first time. A firm may have issued securities to investors in a private offering before the IPO. A private offering is made to investors who may be more sophisticated and have a higher net worth and annual income than typical investors. Proceeds from the private offering are used to get the company started. After a period of growth, the company may issue stock in an IPO.

Keep in mind that firms can issue more securities to the public to raise funds. Again, these stock shares are considered a public offering because they're being sold to the public for the first time. This isn't an initial public offering, however, because the public already owns some shares. If Barry's Bargain Basement issues 1,000,000 common stock shares in an IPO, he may issue 3,000,000 more shares in a later public offering.

Considering the Securities Act of '33

The SEC was created in response to the stock market crash of 1929. After the crash, legislators and securities industry officials determined that many investors had bought securities based on little or no accurate financial information. As a result, many investors were unaware of the financial risk they were taking. To address this concern, Congress passed the Securities Act of 1933, which requires that companies selling securities to the public register their securities with the SEC.

The term *registration* means that the issuer (the company issuing securities) discloses specific information and that the information is made available to the public. The SEC, however, doesn't ensure that the information is accurate. Here are some details on the registration process:

- **Groups involved in securities registration:** The *issuer* is the firm selling the securities to the public. The *underwriter* puts together the legal documents for the securities. A *dealer* sells the securities to the public for the issuer. Each of these parties must register with the SEC. Registration requires these parties to disclose information about their businesses.

- **Documents:** Two primary documents comprise the registration of a security:

  - **Prospectus:** A prospectus is a lengthy document that explains why the company is raising money, notes how it will use the funds, and includes a disclosure of the firm's audited financial statements. In Chapter 11, you see that an auditor is required to review any audited financial statements that are included in other documents, including a prospectus. The auditor reviews the prospectus to ensure that the audited financial statements are accurate.

  - **Registration statement:** The other required document is a registration statement. Typically, a registration statement is provided to investors before the prospectus is complete. The registration statement allows investors to educate themselves and consider placing an order to buy the securities before the prospectus is finalized.

Some types of securities are exempt from the Securities Act of '33, so these securities don't have to register with the SEC. These securities aren't sold using an SEC-required prospectus or registration statement. Although investors may be provided with information on these investments, the documents don't have to be submitted to the SEC. Here are some types of exempt securities that you may see on the REG test:

- **Intrastate sales:** These securities are sold only within one state. If you're raising money to build a factory in Ohio, for example, and you sell securities only to Ohio residents, your securities are exempt from SEC registration.

- **Commercial paper:** I discuss this type of security in the earlier section "Putting in negotiable instruments and using titles."

- ✔ **Insurance policies:** Insurance policies are exempt from SEC registration.

- ✔ **Securities issued by not-for-profit and religious organizations:** If a church issues bonds to raise money to build a new church, those securities are exempt from SEC registration.

Moving to the Securities Act of '34

Like the Act of '33, the 1934 Act was passed by Congress to protect investors and ensure that companies provide sufficient disclosure about securities. The Securities Act of 1934 regulates securities that trade between investors.

After a company issues a security to an investor, that investor may sell that security to someone else. If Harold sells a security to Maude, that's simply an exchange between two investors. The company issuing the securities doesn't receive any proceeds after the securities are issued for the first time.

The Act of '34 oversees *exchanges,* which are entities set up to allow buyers and sellers of securities to trade with each other. The New York Stock Exchange is one example. The '34 Act also contains additional registration requirements and reporting requirements.

The '34 Act requires these types of entities to register with the SEC:

- ✔ **Publicly traded companies:** Publicly traded companies are companies that have issued securities to the public. Again, the firm's public offerings are regulated by the '33 Act. After the securities start trading, they're covered by the '34 Act.

- ✔ **Private companies with minimum assets and shareholders:** Some companies that don't have publicly traded securities must register under the '34 Act. These companies are asked to register based on the dollar amount of assets they have and the number of private investors they've attracted.

- ✔ **Affiliates**: The term *affiliates* include exchanges as well as brokers and dealers. Brokers and dealers sell securities to the public.

Keep in mind that the REG test refers to brokers and dealers separately. The securities industry, however, uses the term "broker-dealer" as one phrase. If you work in the securities industry, realize that the REG test handles these terms differently from how your industry does.

One goal of the '34 Act was to expand on disclosure that had already been provided using '33 Act filings. Say, for example, that you bought 100 shares of the initial public offering for Susie's Shiny Shoes, a shoe manufacturer. Whether you hold the stock for years or sell them to someone else in three months, it's important for any investor to be updated on the financial position of Susie's Shiny Shoes. Investors rely on that updated information to make decisions about buying or selling the stock. That's the purpose of the '34 Act.

The '34 Act requires that specific financial reporting be submitted. The act also requires reporting of some key events and transactions. Here are some of those requirements:

- ✔ **Filing reports:** Companies file an annual 10-K report to the SEC. Each quarter, the firms file a 10-Q. You can find the templates used for both of these forms on the SEC's website (www.sec.gov). The information in these filings is similar to what you find in a prospectus or registration statement (see the preceding section on the '33 Act). The point is to require companies to constantly update investors and other stakeholders on the financial condition of the firm.

- ✔ **Tender offers:** The SEC website defines a *tender offer* as a broad solicitation to purchase a substantial percentage of a company equity. Any shareholder who will own 5 percent or more of the outstanding stock shares after a tender offer must file a report with the SEC.

- ✔ **Proxy solicitation:** A *proxy solicitation* occurs when anyone tries to obtain shareholder agreement for a proposal (or a set of proposals). The company or any individual can create a proxy solicitation. In the most common example, a company contacts shareholders and asks them to vote for members of the board of directors. In that case, shareholders have the right to attend the company's board meeting to vote their shares. The vast majority of shareholders fill out, sign, and return a proxy. That proxy represents their vote if they don't attend the meeting. A proxy solicitation requires an SEC filing.

- ✔ **A trade by an insider:** An *insider* is a person who owns 10 percent or more of the voting stock of a company. Company board members and senior officers (like the CEO or CFO) are also considered insiders. Insiders must report their trading activity to the SEC.

Keep in mind that companies can issue common stock that doesn't allow the shareholder to vote on company issues (or that limits voting). This is one of the few places on the CPA exam where voting versus non-voting stock is an issue. Unless you're told otherwise, assume that all common stock shares allow the shareholder to vote on important company issues.

Calculating Gift and Estate Tax

Taxpayers pay *estate tax* on the size (dollar amount) of their estate at death. A person's estate includes many types of assets, including bank account balances, investments, and property. An accountant helps individuals minimize the dollar amount of the estate at their death to minimize the estate tax.

Tax laws are in place to prevent donors from transferring their entire estates to other people before death. Gift tax law accomplishes this by taxing the transfer of assets. The donor of a gift is taxed on certain gifts to a *donee* (person receiving the gift). The donor is taxed, but the donee isn't.

Tenancy in common means that if two parties own property jointly, there's no right of survivorship if one of the owners passes away. If one owner dies with a will, ownership in the property will pass to the individual named in the will. If he dies without a will, ownership depends on *intestate succession*. State law will determine who the successor owner will be.

Checking out the gift tax calculation

The REG test may ask you to use the formula for computing a gift tax. Here's the basic gift tax formula:

$$\left(\begin{array}{c} \text{Gifts in the} \\ \text{current year} \end{array} \right) - \left(\begin{array}{c} \text{Annual exclusion} \\ \text{per donee} \end{array} \right) - \left(\begin{array}{c} \text{Unlimited exclusions} \\ \text{for the current year} \end{array} \right) = \text{Taxable gifts}$$

A taxpayer is allowed to exclude a dollar amount for a gift made during the year. For tax year 2014, the exclusion is $14,000. The taxpayer can donate to an unlimited number of donees and use the $14,000 exclusion for each donee. The *unlimited exclusion* refers to certain gifts that are not subject to gift tax, such as paying the medical or educational expenses for another person.

After you calculate the taxable gift balance, you multiply the balance by the gift tax rate for the year.

Suppose that Bobby gives $50,000 each to Carol and Jim in 2014. He also gives $30,000 to Joe for educational expenses. Here is Bobby's taxable gift balance:

$$(\$50{,}000 + \$50{,}000 + \$30{,}000) - (2 \times \$14{,}000) - \$30{,}000 = \$72{,}000$$

Bobby would multiply the $72,000 by the gift tax rate to calculate his gift tax liability. If his rate is 30 percent, his gift tax liability is $72,000×0.30=$21,600.

Note: To calculate the taxable gift balance in the preceding example, you could exclude the $30,000 education gift from the calculation. Because that gift is subject to the unlimited exclusion, you can set up the formula as follows:

$$(\$50{,}000 + \$50{,}000) - (2 \times \$14{,}000) = \$72{,}000$$

The $30,000 isn't included as a gift or as a subtraction. If this format is clearer to you, feel free to use this method. Also, keep in mind that Bobby (the donor) can give an additional $14,000 gift to Joe and use his annual gift tax exclusion.

Bobby can take advantage of the unified credit and use the credit to offset his $21,600 gift tax liability. If he uses the credit, he owes no tax. The *unified credit* offsets a taxpayer's gift and estate tax liabilities. As of this writing, a taxpayer can give away up to $5 million during his lifetime and not pay any gift tax. In other words, there are enough tax credit dollars available for the taxpayer to avoid any gift tax liability on up to $5 million in donations. If Bobby uses $21,600 of the credit to offset tax this year, that reduces his available unified credit in future years.

Spouses can split a gift made by one spouse for gift tax purposes. If Joe gifts $60,000 to a niece, Joe and his wife Sue can file paperwork and elect to split the gift. For gift tax purposes, each spouse gifts $30,000. The tax advantage is that each spouse can use his or her annual exclusion. Based on the 2014 exclusion amount, $28,000 of the total gift is excluded from tax ($14,000×2). The taxable amount of the gift is $60,000−$28,000=$32,000.

A *tax credit* can reduce a tax liability dollar for dollar. You can think of a tax credit as a gift certificate that reduces a tax liability. A tax deduction, on the other hand, reduces the calculation of a tax liability.

Remembering property transfers

The REG test may ask about property transfer rules. The word *title* means ownership. Companies have title to many types of assets, such as inventory, equipment, and vehicles.

A *deed* is a written document that transfers title or an interest in real estate. You may be asked about the criteria needed for a deed to be *valid,* or legally enforceable. A valid deed must include the following:

- Names of buyer (grantor) and the seller (grantee)
- Words evidencing intent to convey; in this case, *convey* refers to the transfer of ownership
- A legally sufficient description of the land
- Signature of the grantor (buyer)
- Delivery of the deed from seller to buyer

Taxing Individuals

The individual-tax section of the CPA exam contains the most facts, figures, and formulas. Students often dive into individual taxation without a study plan and get overwhelmed. Use this section's comments to create a plan of study that uses your time effectively.

Filing a return

This section explains the nuts and bolts of when to file returns and an individual's filing status.

Understanding when you must file

The first step for an individual is to understand the tax filing requirements. Generally, an individual taxpayer needs to file a return if her total income is equal to or greater than her personal exemption plus her standard deduction. For tax year 2014, personal exemption is $3,950, and the standard deduction for a single person is $6,200. In 2014, a taxpayer must file a return if his or her income is $3,950 + $6,200 = $10,150 or more.

There are exceptions for dependents and self-employed people. Those exceptions require taxpayers to file returns if their income is below this threshold.

Individual tax returns are due by April 15 of each year. An individual can file Form 4868 for an automatic extension. However, even if the individual files for an extension, all taxes are due on April 15 of each year.

Going over filing status

Your filing status impacts several dollar limitations on deductions and other tax calculations. Taxpayers use tax tables to calculate their tax liability. Tax tables differ, depending on your filing status.

Here are the filing status categories you may see on the REG test:

- **Single:** *Single* is defined as legally separated or not married. If a taxpayer is widowed and hasn't remarried, that individual uses the single filing status for each year after the year of the spouse's death.

- **Joint returns/filing jointly:** Filing status for a joint return is determined based on year-end. Couples who are married file jointly. If a spouse is widowed during the year and doesn't remarry, that taxpayer is considered married and files jointly for the year in which his or her spouse passes away. Similarly, if a spouse dies after year-end but before the tax return is filed, the widow or widower files a joint return.

- **Qualified widow or widower with dependent child:** A widow or widower who provides a principal residence for a dependent child for an entire year may qualify for this filing status. The taxpayer must file a joint return for the two years following the spouse's death to qualify.

- **Married filing separately:** A married taxpayer has the option of filing separately. In this case, all of the taxpayer's data on income and deductions is kept separate from the spouse's.

Reviewing head of household status

One last filing status is more complex than the others. The first type of taxpayer is someone who is married but lived apart from his or her spouse for the last six months of the year. The second category is for an unmarried or legally separated individual. This taxpayer also provided a home and some level of support for other people. Here are some details that relate to the second head of household category:

- ✔ The unmarried or legally separated person maintains a home for a dependent or dependents for more than half of the year.

- ✔ Qualified children and qualified dependents and relatives can be claimed as dependents. The Form 1040 instructions provide details on this topic.

- ✔ For the taxpayer to qualify for head of household filing status, a dependent relative usually must live with the taxpayer. A dependent parent, however, isn't required to live with the taxpayer. Suppose that Brian lives with his aunt and also cares for his mother. Bob's mother lives in a nursing home. In this case, both Brian's mother and his aunt qualify as dependents.

Visualizing the individual tax return

Many of the REG test tax-related questions are related to individual taxation. Individuals pay taxes using Form 1040. Here is the formula for taxable income on the 1040 tax return:

$$\text{Taxable income} = \text{Income} - \text{Adjustments}$$
$$= \text{Adjusted gross income} - \text{Standard or itemized deductions} - \text{Exemptions}$$

If you check out Form 1040 on the IRS website, you'll see the categories from the taxable-income formula. In fact, adjusted gross income is calculated at the bottom of page 1 of the 2013 Form 1040. The remainder of the items in the formula (deductions, exemptions, and taxable income) are computed on page 2 of the form. The formula takes taxable income and computes the tax liability of refund:

$$\text{Tax liability of refund} = \text{Taxable income} - \text{Credits} + \text{Other taxes} - \text{Tax payments}$$

Understanding the layout of the 1040 is a great way to pull together all the components of taxation for individuals. You can find most of the individual taxation test points on the REG test in the Form 1040 instructions. Both Form 1040 and the instructions are located at www. irs.gov.

Calculating income

On page 1 of the 1040 form, you calculate income. After calculating gross income, you make adjustments to arrive at adjusted gross income. *Gross income* is defined as any source that generated income for the taxpayer. You should consider any income a taxpayer receives, not just wages on a W-2 form. When income is posted on a tax return, it's *recognized*. Income is recognized when it's realized.

Chapter 8 defines a realized gain or loss on an asset sale. To realize a gain or loss, there must be both a buy and a sale. Income includes gains on sale and other sources of realized income.

The taxpayer can choose either the cash or accrual method for posting income to her tax return. (I explain the cash method and the accrual method in Chapter 4.)

Here are the categories of income that are most often included on the REG test:

✔ **Wages and salaries:** This includes wages and salaries paid. If a loan or debt is forgiven, the dollar amount is included in income. If the taxpayer is paid with some type of asset other than cash, the value of that property is included in income. Suppose you own a pizza shop and you provide $500 worth of food as payment for plumbing work. That $500 is considered income to the plumber. Finally, if you use company property for personal use, the value is considered a taxable *fringe benefit*. If an executive uses a company plane for personal use, the value of the trip (fuel and personnel costs) is taxable as income.

✔ **Dividend income:** A dividend is a distribution of a company's earnings to shareholders. Dividend payments are considered income to a shareholder.

✔ **Individual retirement account (IRA) earnings:** Earnings distributed from traditional IRA accounts are taxable. Contributions aren't taxed when the investor puts them in a traditional IRA, so the tax code assesses taxes when earnings are distributed. Roth IRA contributions are funded with after-tax dollars. These dollars have already been taxed, so earnings from Roth IRAs aren't taxed.

✔ **Pension and annuities:** Distributions from these plans are taxed as income. Taxpayers use an IRS worksheet to determine the taxable portion of these benefits.

✔ **Unemployment and Social Security income:** Portions of these payments are taxable.

✔ **Rental and other passive income:** *Passive income* is defined as income earned in business ventures in which the investor has little or no involvement. If you own and rent a vacation home, you may pay a company to rent and maintain the property. In that instance, you're a passive investor. Income from rental property and royalty income are the primary sources of passive income. Those activities are reported on Schedule E of the individual tax form 1040. Schedule E also includes income from partnerships, corporations, and estates and trusts.

✔ **State and local tax refunds:** When a taxpayer pays more tax than her tax liability, she receives a refund. Refunds of state and local taxes are taxable on your federal tax return if you use the itemized deduction. See the later section "Using itemized deductions."

✔ **Alimony and child support:** Amounts paid under a divorce or separation agreement are considered *alimony* payments. The same agreement may require *child support,* which is payment for the benefit of children of the divorced or separated parties. A taxpayer who receives alimony or child support includes the payment in income. An individual who pays alimony can deduct that amount from gross income to arrive at adjusted gross income. Payments of child support, however, can't be used to adjust gross income.

✔ **Business income:** Income earned in a business is posted to the personal tax return. Business income is calculated on Schedule C for the 1040 tax return. The calculation of business income on Schedule C is very similar to the income statement calculation I explain in Chapter 8.

✔ **Interest income:** Interest earned on corporate bonds and bonds issued by the U.S. Treasury and federal agencies (except U.S. series EE savings bonds) is considered income. Interest on bonds issued by municipalities, except industrial development revenue bonds, are tax-exempt. Municipalities issue industrial development revenue bonds to help develop businesses by building infrastructure (highways and roads). Because these bonds are issued to help businesses (for-profit entities), the interest is taxable.

Interest earned on an installment sale is also taxable. In an *installment sale,* the buyer pays the seller in installments over time. The sale agreement may require the buyer to pay interest on the amount still owed for the sale. That interest is taxable as income to the seller.

Here are examples of transactions that aren't considered income:

- **Wage and salary-related items not included in income:** *De minimus* is a Latin term that means minimal things. *De minimus* fringe benefits aren't taxable. If a company provides free coffee to employees, that benefit isn't taxable as income. Work-related meals and lodging aren't considered income. The traveling salesperson's expenses aren't additional income to the salesperson. Proceeds paid from a life insurance policy to a beneficiary due to the death of the insured aren't taxable as income. The employer-paid portion of health insurance premiums as well as qualified retirement, pension, and profit-sharing plans aren't considered income to the taxpayer.

- **Return of capital:** *Return of capital* occurs when a company returns an investor's original investment dollars. When a corporate bond matures, for example, the principal amount (face amount of the bond) is returned to the investor. Return of capital is not income. Stroll over to Chapter 8 for more on bonds.

- **Stock dividend:** Companies can choose to pay a portion of earnings to shareholders as dividends. Normally, dividends are paid in cash. Companies, however, have the option of paying *stock dividends,* which are in the form of additional shares of company stock. When the stockholder receives the shares, no income is recognized. If the shareholder sells the shares, he'll pay taxes on the sale proceeds.

- **Stock split:** A *stock split* occurs when a company issues more shares of stock but also reduces the price per share of all stock outstanding. For example, consider a two-for-one (2:1) stock split. Suppose the market price is currently $40 per share. If an investor owns 100 shares, she'll receive an additional 100 shares of stock. So the investor's ownership increases to 200 shares. The market price of the stock, however, will be cut in half to $20 per share. With a stock split, there's no net change in the dollar value of the stock holdings. That's because 100 shares at $40 has the same value as 200 shares at $20. Both holdings are worth $4,000. A stock split doesn't generate income.

- **Tax-exempt interest:** Interest on municipal bonds (state and local governments) isn't included in income. In addition, interest on U.S. series EE savings bonds is not income.

Qualified and non-qualified are two important terms to remember. A *qualified retirement plan* meets certain IRS criteria. As a result, these plans offer some tax advantages. Qualified plans, for example, may allow for plan contributions that are excluded from tax. A non-qualified plan doesn't have the same tax advantages.

Dealing with gains and losses

Capital gains and losses are calculated on Schedule D of the individual tax return (Form 1040). The gains and losses appear in the income section of Form 1040. To calculate capital gains and losses, you need to know which assets are considered capital assets and which are not:

- **Capital assets:** If a taxpayer puts together a personal balance sheet of his own assets and liabilities, the assets he includes are considered capital assets. These assets are owned personally and aren't part of any business venture. Investment securities (stocks and bonds) and personal property not used in business, such as a personal vehicle, are capital assets. A personal residence, which is considered real property not used in business, is also a capital asset. An interest in a partnership is a capital asset. That interest is the partner's capital investment in a partnership.

- **Not capital assets:** Generally, assets used in business aren't capital assets for an individual taxpayer. This includes inventory and accounts receivable, which are both assets but are owned by the business. Property owned by the business isn't considered a capital asset to an individual. Property includes land, equipment, vehicles, and goodwill.

Here's the formula to calculate a capital gain or loss:

$$\text{Capital gain or loss} = \text{Amount realized} - \text{Adjusted basis}$$

The *amount realized* may be cash, or it may be another asset. If two companies exchange equipment, for example, the amount realized is typically based on the value of the asset received. (Check out Chapter 8 for details.) For this discussion, keep in mind that the fair market value of the asset received is considered the amount realized.

An asset may also be exchanged for a service. Suppose a restaurant buys a new oven from Universal Ovens and agrees to provide catering services to pay for the oven. The fair market value of the catering services is the amount realized by the seller, Universal Ovens. The amount realized from a sale may also be cancellation of debt. If the restaurant buys a new oven and forgives a debt owed by Universal Ovens, the value of the debt is the amount realized by Universal Ovens.

In each case, any selling expenses incurred reduce the amount realized by the seller. Shipping costs incurred by the seller, for example, would reduce the amount realized.

Both a buy and a sell must occur to generate a capital gain. If you own an asset and hold it, there's no capital gain until you sell the asset. If the asset you own increases in price, the difference between your adjusted basis and the fair market value is an *unrealized gain*.

Adjusted basis for assets purchased is typically the purchase price. Accountants also refer to this as recording assets at *historical cost*. Note the following points regarding historical cost:

- **Capital improvements:** Adjusted basis is increased by capital improvements. A *capital improvement* is an asset with a useful life of a year or longer. This asset increases the value of another asset, usually real property. If, for example, you add landscaping and a parking lot to your building, that cost is considered a capital asset that increases the value of your building.

- **Accumulated depreciation:** Accumulated depreciation reduces adjusted basis. The sum of all of an asset's depreciation expense over the useful life is posted to accumulated depreciation. (Head over to Chapter 8 for more on this topic.)

- **Stock dividend:** A stock dividend doesn't change adjusted basis. That is, it doesn't change the total dollar value of the investor's stock holdings.

For property that is transferred as a gift, the adjusted basis for the receiver of the gift is the donor's original basis. This can create a large capital gain for the receiver of the gift when the asset is sold. (The earlier section "Calculating gift and estate tax" covers the taxation of gifts.)

Suppose the donor purchases 100 shares of IBM common stock. Fifty years later, the donor gifts the 100 shares to Larry. Larry's cost basis is the donor's cost from 50 years ago. Given the potential increase in the stock price, Larry may incur a large capital gain when he sells the stock.

If the fair market value of the asset gifted is less than the donor's cost, the receiver's adjusted basis is the fair market value. Suppose a donor buys GE common stock at $50 per share. The donor gifts the stock when fair market value of GE stock is $45 per share. The receiver's cost basis is the $45 per share fair market value.

Adjusting the records to arrive at taxable income

Accountants take the adjusted gross income figure at the bottom of page 1 of Form 1040 and make additional changes to the amount. Those changes allow the CPA to compute taxable income. You see the calculations at the top of page 2 of the 1040 form. This section explains those calculations.

Using itemized deductions

Itemized deductions are calculated on Schedule A of Form 1040. The REG test asks questions about the types of deductions a taxpayer lists on Schedule A. Here are the categories:

- **Medical and dental expenses:** This refers to medical-related costs incurred during the year.

- **Taxes paid:** Taxpayers can deduct state, local, and other taxes paid. This includes taxes paid for any tax period. The taxpayer can, for example, deduct 2012 state taxes paid in 2015 on the 2015 Schedule A. The deduction is allowed for state taxes paid during the tax year, regardless of the year that the taxes were originally due.

- **Interest paid:** Primarily, this line refers to interest paid on a home mortgage.

- **Charitable gifts:** This refers to gifts to charity, including non-cash assets donated.

- **Casualty and theft losses:** This line refers to losses incurred that weren't covered by an insurance policy.

- **Job expenses and miscellaneous deductions:** Some job-related expenses that aren't reimbursed by the employer are included here.

Including exemptions

Exemptions reduce adjusted gross income. The tax code allows for both personal exemptions and exemptions for dependents. A taxpayer's filing status helps determine exemption amounts on the tax return (head to the earlier section "Going over filing status" to find out more). Here are some details on exemptions:

- **Personal exemptions:** If two people file as married filing jointly, each taxpayer gets an exemption, assuming that neither person is claimed as a dependent on another person's tax return.

    An individual gets only one exemption on one tax return. Spouses filing as married filing separately each take one exemption. If a dependent is born during the tax year (or passes away during the year), an exemption can be taken for that individual.

- **Dependent exemption, qualifying child:** A child must meet a number of criteria for a taxpayer to take a dependent exemption on her return. First, the child must be related to the taxpayer. This includes grandchildren and foster children. Second, the child must be under 19 years old or under 24 if he's a full-time student. Disabled children of any age meet the age requirement. Finally, the taxpayer must provide more than half of the financial support for the child, and the child must live with the taxpayer for more than half of the year.

- **Dependent exemption, qualifying relative:** To be claimed as an exemption as a qualifying relative, the relative must be related to the taxpayer. This rule includes parents, siblings, and step-relatives. The rule also allows for claiming an exemption for non-relatives who live with the taxpayer the entire tax year.

    There's an income limit for qualifying relatives (although disabled relatives are excluded from the income-limit rule). For tax year 2013, the relative must earn less than $3,900. Finally, the taxpayer must provide more than half of the financial support during the year, and the relative can't be married.

Wrapping Up the Business Taxation

This section covers some taxation issues related to businesses. This is an important section. The method of taxation for a particular type of business is a factor when deciding on the form of your business.

Using a C corporation

The fiscal year-end for a C corporation is typically December 31. Tax rules, however, allow for a fiscal year-end that differs from the last day of the year. Many retailers, for example, have a spring year-end. Much of their sales and expense activity occurs around the holidays, so these companies prefer to end the fiscal year in February or March, when they finish accounting for a busy holiday season.

The tax form for a C corporation is Form 1120. You can easily download the form and instructions from the IRS website (www.irs.gov).

The filing date for C corporation tax returns is March 15 of the year following December 31. If the fiscal year ends on March 31, the tax return is due on the 15th day of the third month after year-end. In this example, that would be June 15. If the due date falls on a weekend or holiday, the tax return is due on the next business day.

Going over estimated taxes and tax rates

A C corporation is required to make *estimated tax payments* during the fiscal year. Other types of businesses are also required to make these payments. This system exists so that an entity pays its tax liability during the year instead of waiting until the tax return is filed. Estimated tax payments are due on the 15th day of the month following the end of the quarter. Payments for the second quarter (April through June), for example, are due on July 15.

The taxpayer should plan estimated tax payments so that the corporation pays at least 90 percent of the current year tax due or 100 percent of the tax due for the prior year — whichever amount is smaller. This rule applies to self-employed individuals and small businesses. Larger businesses have to pay 100 percent of the tax due for the current year.

Like most tax tables, the corporate tax rates are *graduated tax rates*. As a corporation's income increases, the rate of tax is higher. Graduated tax rates require the taxpayer to pay the given tax on the income related to the given tax rate. To illustrate the graduated tax rate concept, here is a portion of the tax rate schedule from the 2013 Form 1120 instructions:

Taxable income: $75,000 to $100,000, tax is $13,750 plus 34% of the amount over $75,000

If a C corporation's taxable income were $80,000, the company would pay

$$\$13,750 + (0.34 \times \$5,000) = \$13,750 + \$1,700$$
$$= \$15,450$$

Note: The $13,750 in the instructions represents the tax paid on income below $75,000. The 2013 tax tables indicate that the tax rate for income between $50,000 and $75,000 is 25 percent, and the tax rate from $0 income to $50,000 is 15 percent. Therefore, the tax on the first $75,000 is $(0.15 \times \$50,000) + (0.25 \times \$25,000) = \$13,750$.

If your C corporation income is $80,000, you pay tax on income at 15, 25, and 34 percent.

C corporations also incur an *accumulated earnings tax.* As the name implies, this tax is on excess accumulated retained earnings. Retained earnings represents income that the company retains to operate and grow the business. Companies can either retain earnings or pay them to shareholders as dividends. The purpose of the tax is to encourage corporations to pay earnings to shareholders. Check out Chapter 8 for info on retained earnings.

Understanding alternative minimum tax

The *alternative minimum tax,* or AMT, applies to many C corporations and individuals. AMT requires the taxpayer to make two tax calculations. The company puts together a standard tax return. Then the corporation calculates taxes using the alternative minimum tax form. The corporation pays taxes based on whichever form generates the higher tax liability.

AMT starts with the taxable income from the standard C corporation tax return (Form 1120). Certain items deductible on the standard tax return are added back to income. Here are two of the most tested items:

- ✔ **Depreciation of post-1986 property:** Essentially, this category represents accelerated depreciation on certain assets.

- ✔ **Tax-exempt interest income on private activity bonds:** Private activity bonds are a type of municipal bonds. State, local, and city governments issue municipal bonds. Interest income on municipal bonds is generally exempt from federal tax. AMT adds the previously tax-exempt income back into income.

Because AMT adds back items that are deductible on a standard return, the taxable income is higher. Higher taxable income results in an increased tax liability. Generally, AMT will generate a higher tax liability.

Reviewing C corporation distributions

One tested corporation tax deduction is the dividend-received deduction. This deduction encourages a business to own common stock in other businesses. As the name implies, dividends earned by owning common stock of other companies is subject to a tax deduction. The current deduction is 70 percent of the dividend income received. If the Premier Corporation earned $5,000 in dividend income from common stock, $3,500 (0.70 × $5,000) would be deductible on the C corporation's tax return.

A *dividend* is defined as a distribution of earnings to a shareholder. Dividends can be paid in cash or with other corporation assets, such as equipment or a vehicle. If the asset has appreciated in value, the corporation should use the appreciated value (fair market value) for the distribution. The corporation recognizes the difference between the cost of the asset and the fair value as gain. The distribution is treated as if the asset were sold to a third party.

Suppose that a company owns a piece of machinery with a cost of $30,000. Due to demand for the machinery, the value of the asset has increased to $42,000. If the machinery is distributed to a shareholder, the company recognizes a gain of

$42,000 fair market value − $30,000 cost = $12,000 gain

Applying a partnership structure

A partnership is a pass-through entity. The partnership entity files a tax return, but the profit and loss on the partnership flows through to the personal tax returns of the partners. This section goes into detail on the taxation of a partner's investment in a partnership.

Going over partnership basis

A partner's *basis* in the partnership is the partner's investment of capital into the partnership, less any withdrawals of capital or loans taken by the partnership. Basis is increased by the partner's share of profits and reduced by the share of losses.

Keep in mind that capital can be a cash investment or the investment of some other asset, such as equipment or a vehicle. Suppose that Diana is a partner in the Sightline Restaurant. Diana contributes $40,000 in cash and a large commercial oven worth $4,000. At this point, the balance in Diana's capital account is $44,000. If Diana withdraws $2,000 from the partnership, her updated capital balance is $42,000 ($44,000 less $2,000). The $42,000 is considered Diana's *adjusted basis* in the partnership.

If a partnership takes out a loan, each partner's basis is reduced by his or her proportionate share of the loan. The share of the loan assigned to each partner is stated in the partnership agreement.

The capital contributions and withdrawals activity should be kept separate from the partner's share of partnership income and losses. Note that profit and losses do change the partner's basis. However, contributions and withdrawals may not affect the partner's tax return (see the next section for details).

These profits and losses flow through to the partner's personal tax return. If, for example, Diana's share of Sightline Restaurant profit is $30,000, the $30,000 is posted as income to Diana's personal return. Her Form 1040 (personal tax return) would include the $30,000 plus any other income that Diana earns during the year. That might include W-2 income as an employee or income on a 1099 form for work performed as an independent contractor.

Checking out partnership withdrawals

The REG test may bring up liquidating and non-liquidating distributions. A *non-liquidating distribution* occurs when a partner withdraws some capital from the partnership but continues to have a capital balance. A partner can withdraw up to the dollar amount of the adjusted basis in the partnership and not incur any tax. That's because the withdrawal is considered a *return of capital*. The partner is simply taking money out that was invested previously.

Suppose that Jerry has an adjusted basis of $100,000 in his capital balance at Standard Plumbing, a partnership. Jerry can withdraw up to $100,000 without creating a taxable event. A *taxable event* means that a transaction generates a tax liability.

The return of capital concept applies to other asset and investment transactions. *Return of capital* means that when the investor sells an investment, she gets back the dollars she originally invested in the asset. The original investment dollars are excluded from the calculation of a taxable gain. The gain on an asset represents any amount received that's greater than the original cost.

Say you buy 100 shares of Microsoft common stock for $40 per share. Your cost basis is $100 \times \$40 = \$4,000$. Cost basis is similar to basis in a partnership. If you sell the 100 shares of stock for $5,000, then $4,000 of the sale is return of capital (original investment). Those dollars aren't taxed. You are taxed on the difference between the sales proceeds and the cost basis. In this case, the taxable gain on the sale is $5,000 sales proceeds − $4,000 cost basis = $1,000 gain.

The distribution could be cash or other assets owned by the partnership. If the partnership distributes an asset to a partner, that partner's capital account is reduced by the book value of the assets received. *Book value* is the cost of the asset, less any accumulated depreciation.

If Jerry receives a truck from the Standard Plumbing, a partnership, he considers the book value of the truck to account for the distribution. Suppose the truck has a cost of $25,000, with $17,000 in accumulated depreciation. The book value of the truck is $25,000 − $17,000 = $8,000. Jerry's basis in the partnership is reduced by $8,000.

If a partner receives a distribution in excess of his or her adjusted basis in the partnership, the distribution amount greater than adjusted basis is taxed as a gain. Using the truck example, suppose that Jerry's adjusted basis in the partnership is $6,000. If Jerry receives a truck with an $8,000 book value as a distribution, he incurs a $2,000 gain ($8,000 truck − $6,000 adjusted basis).

A *liquidating distribution* means that a partner is withdrawing his or her entire capital balance for the partnership. That situation may occur because the partner is selling his interest to someone else. A liquidation may occur when the partner retires or when the partner passes away. The partnership agreement may have a clause that triggers a liquidating distribution when a partner dies.

Here's the tax impact of a sale of a partnership interest or a partner withdrawal:

- ✔ If sales proceeds equal the adjusted cost basis, there's no gain or loss.

- ✔ When the sales proceeds exceed the adjusted cost basis, the partner incurs a taxable gain. If the cost basis is greater than the sales proceeds, the partner has a loss for tax purposes.

Keep in mind that a partnership interest is a capital asset, just like a stock or bond investment. As a result, the sale of the partnership interest generates a capital gain or loss.

Taxing Trusts and Estates

Trust and estate taxation questions require you to know several complex formulas. Because of the complexity, I've separated these topics from other types of taxation in this chapter. This section explains the concept of distributable net income. You then move to the tax calculation for trusts and then taxation of estates. Some of the information in this section overlaps with the earlier section "Calculating gift and estate tax."

Here are some important terms the REG test may cover:

- ✔ **Principal (corpus):** Principal is the assets that make up the trust or estate. The *principal* is also referred to as the *corpus*.

  Chapter 8 discusses principal and interest related to bonds. You can connect this definition of principal with the bond definition of principal (the amount a borrower repays at maturity).

- ✔ **Beneficiary:** The beneficiary is the person who receives the principal from the trust or the person who is entitled to the benefit of the corpus.

- ✔ **Fiduciary:** A *fiduciary* is a person put in a position of trust. A *trustee* is a fiduciary for a trust, and an *executor* is a fiduciary for an estate. A fiduciary has a duty to hold and invest the principal amount and also to allocate and distribute income generated by the trust or estate investments.

Suppose that Susie sets up a trust with Reliable Bank as trustee. Susie funds the trust with $20,000 of Don's Donuts common stock, which represents the principal amount of the trust. Her son David is beneficiary of the trust. Reliable Bank, the trustee, has a fiduciary duty to hold the shares of Don's Donuts stock and to distribute dividend income from the trust to

David, the beneficiary. This is a basic trust format, because trust documents can provide a variety of instructions.

Donors (those who gift assets) are assessed a gift tax; however, for trusts and estates, taxes are assessed on the beneficiary. This difference reinforces a key point: Suppose an individual decides not to use a trust or set up the documents for an estate plan. Instead, the taxpayer decides to transfer assets to people only by gifting assets while he or she is still alive. Instead of having the beneficiary pay taxes, the taxes are paid when the assets are gifted.

Introducing distributable net income

Distributable net income (DNI) calculates the taxable portion of the principal, income, and capital gains generated by a trust or estate. Trusts and estates complete IRS Form 1041. Here is the DNI formula:

DNI = Adjusted gross income + Tax − Exempt interest − Deductions − Capital gains

Here are definitions for each of the DNI terms:

- ✔ **Adjusted gross income (AGI):** This amount includes all the income generated by the trust or estate. AGI includes taxable interest earned on investments, dividend income, royalties, and fees earned. This amount is different from AGI for a personal tax return. See the earlier section "Adjusting the records to arrive at taxable income" for more on personal tax calculations.

- ✔ **Tax-exempt interest:** Income from tax-exempt municipal bonds is added to compute DNI, just as tax-exempt interest is added back to net income to compute the alternative minimum tax (AMT). In both cases, tax-exempt interest is added to compute taxable income.

- ✔ **Deductions:** Charitable contributions are deducted from the DNI formula. The trust or estate can also deduct business expenses, such as accounting and legal costs associated with the trust. Fees paid to the executor or trustee can also be deducted.

- ✔ **Capital gains:** Capital gains are added to the principal of the trust, not to income. If the trustee sells 100 shares of General Electric stock in the trust for a $3,000 gain, that gain is added to the principal of the trust.

Commenting on trust taxation

Here are the two types of trusts that are most often tested:

- ✔ **Simple:** A simple trust requires that the principal amount remain in the trust. All the income must be distributed to the beneficiary. A simple trust doesn't allow for a charitable deduction for tax purposes.

- ✔ **Complex:** If you set up a complex trust, you're allowed to distribute the principal as well as the income generated from the trust. However, you don't have to distribute all the income generated. The complex trust is allowed a charitable deduction.

The taxation of a trust is based on the distributable net income. The ability to move principal or income out of the trust doesn't determine taxation. For example, a complex trust may be taxed on income that isn't distributed to a beneficiary.

Working on estate taxation

The REG test focuses on estate issues that occur when the individual passes away. The event is referred to as *death of the decedent*. As with trusts, an estate is taxed on the income generated in the estate. When the individual passes away, Form 706 needs to be filed. The return is due with any tax liability payment within months of the decedent's death.

The executor or a person designated by the executor compiles the tax return. The executor has a choice to make on the value of the assets. The estate's assets can be valued on the date of death or six months after the date of death.

The estate tax return can be viewed as a two-step process. First, an accountant computes the tentative tax. Then the tentative tax is adjusted for any gift taxes paid and the unified credit to compute the net estate taxes due. You'll see that, at death, the estate tax calculation combines the estate tax with gift taxes already paid.

First, here is the formula for the *tentative tax:*

$$\text{Tentative tax} = (\text{Gross estate} - \text{Allowable deductions} + \text{Taxable gifts}) \times \text{Estate tax rate}$$
$$= (\text{Tentative tax base}) \times \text{Estate tax rate}$$

The *gross estate* is the entire value of the estate's property. This value is based on the valuation method chosen (date of death or six months after death). Estates have allowance deductions, such as tax and legal fees and fees to the executor.

The formula adds any gifts that are taxable. (See the earlier section "Calculating gift and estate tax" for info on the gift tax.) After you add the items to compute the tentative tax base, you multiply the tax base by the estate tax rate to compute the tentative tax.

The second formula, *net estate tax due,* takes the tentative tax and adds in the impact of any gift taxes paid and the unified credit:

$$\text{Net estate tax due} = (\text{Tentative tax} - \text{Gift tax paid}) - \text{Maximum unified credit}$$
$$= (\text{Gross Estate}) - \text{Maximum unified credit}$$

The *unified credit* offsets a taxpayer's gift and estate tax liabilities. As of this writing, a taxpayer can give away up to $5 million during his or her lifetime and not pay any gift tax.

Suppose that Joe passes away. His gross estate, consisting of investments and property, is $2,000,000. Joe's executor paid $30,000 in legal and accounting fees related to the estate. Joe donated $100,000 in taxable gifts. He also paid gift tax totaling $25,000. At the time of Joe's death, he had $500,000 of the unified credit that had not yet been used. Suppose also that the estate tax rate is 30 percent. Here is the calculation of the tentative tax and the net estate tax due:

$$\text{Tentative tax} = (\text{Gross estate} - \text{Allowable deductions} + \text{Taxable gifts}) \times \text{Estate tax rate}$$
$$= (\$2,000,000 - \$30,000 + \$100,000) \times 0.30$$
$$= \$2,070,000 \times 0.30$$
$$= \$621,000$$

$$\text{Net estate tax due} = (\text{Tentative tax} - \text{Gift tax paid}) - \text{Maximum unified credit}$$
$$= (\$621,000 - \$25,000) - \$500,000$$
$$= \$596,000 - \$500,000$$
$$= \$96,000$$

Keep in mind that most REG test questions on this topic won't ask you for this entire calculation. Instead, a question may give you some of these numbers and ask for a portion of one calculation.

Chapter 15

Regulation Practice Questions

• •

*T*he regulation (REG) test focuses on two areas of business: business law and taxation. Consider using flashcards to learn and memorize terms for the REG section. You need to digest many definitions, facts, and figures before you take this test, and flashcards can be a big help.

Agency

1. Lund Pizza Company gave specific rules to employees, including obeying all traffic laws while delivering pizzas. An employee, while delivering pizzas one day, negligently went through a red light and injured the driver of another car. Which of the following is correct?

   (A) The injured driver can recover from either Lund or the employee or both.

   (B) The injured driver can recover from the employee but not Lund because the employee caused the accident while breaking one of Lund's rules.

   (C) If the injured driver chooses to hold the employee liable, the employee can require that he first seek recovery from Lund.

   (D) If a lawsuit is filed against both Lund and the employee, Lund can require that the injured party first exhaust all remedies against the employee before Lund need pay.

2. Which of the following statements concerning agency law is **not** true?

   (A) The agent owes a fiduciary duty to the principal.

   (B) The agent's duties are by necessity based on contract law.

   (C) The principal does **not** owe his/her agent fiduciary duties.

   (D) The agent does **not** owe fiduciary duties to third parties with which the principal asks the agent to deal.

Bankruptcy

3. An involuntary petition in bankruptcy

   (A) Will be denied if a majority of creditors in amount and in number have agreed to a common law composition agreement.

   (B) Can be filed by creditors only once in a 7-year period.

   (C) May be successfully opposed by the debtor with proof that the debtor is solvent in the bankruptcy sense.

   (D) If **not** contested will result in the entry of an order for relief by the bankruptcy judge.

4. Dark Corp. is a general creditor of Blue. Blue filed a petition in bankruptcy under the liquidation provisions of the Bankruptcy Code. Dark wishes to have the bankruptcy court either deny Blue a general discharge or **not** have its debt discharged. The discharge will be granted, and it will include Dark's debt even if

   (A) Dark's debt is unscheduled.

   (B) Dark was a secured creditor which was **not** fully satisfied from the proceeds obtained upon disposition of the collateral.

   (C) Blue has unjustifiably failed to preserve the records from which Blue's financial condition might be ascertained.

   (D) Blue had filed for and received a previous discharge in bankruptcy under the liquidation provisions within 8 years of the filing of the present petition.

Business Structure

5. Kinder, Lau, and Sanders form a partnership under the Revised Uniform Partnership Act (RUPA). Which of the following is **not** true concerning the partnership itself?

   (A) The partnership is a separate legal entity.

   (B) The partnership may own property in the partnership name.

   (C) The partners have joint but **not** several liability for business debts.

   (D) The partnership may sue another business in the partnership name.

6. Which of the following decreases stockholders' equity?

   (A) Investments by owners.

   (B) Distribution to owners.

   (C) Issuance of stock.

   (D) Acquisition of assets in a cash transaction.

Contracts

7. To satisfy the consideration requirement for a valid contract, the consideration exchanged by the parties must be

   (A) Legally sufficient.

   (B) Payable in legal tender.

   (C) Simultaneously paid and received.

   (D) Of the same economic value.

8. Generally, which one of the following transfers will be valid **without** the consent of the other parties?

   (A) The assignment by the lessee of a lease contract where rent is a percentage of sales.

   (B) The assignment by a purchaser of goods of the right to buy on credit without giving security.

   (C) The assignment by an architect of a contract to design a building.

   (D) The assignment by a patent holder of the right to receive royalties.

Commercial Paper

9. An instrument complies with the requirements for negotiability contained in the Commercial Paper Article of the Uniform Commercial Code. The instrument contains language expressly acknowledging the receipt of $10,000 by the First Bank of Grand Rapids and an agreement to repay principal with interest at 15% 1 year from date. This instrument is

   (A) Nonnegotiable because of the additional language.

   (B) A negotiable certificate of deposit.

   (C) A banker's draft.

   (D) A banker's acceptance.

10. Calhoun has in his possession a negotiable instrument which was originally payable to the order of Bannister. It was transferred to Calhoun by a mere delivery by Travis, who took it from Bannister in good faith in satisfaction of an antecedent debt. The back of the instrument reads as follows: "Pay to the order of Travis in satisfaction of my prior purchase of a used IBM typewriter, signed Bannister." Which of the following is correct?

    (A) Travis's taking the instrument for an antecedent debt prevents him from qualifying as a holder in due course.

    (B) Calhoun is a holder in due course.

    (C) Calhoun has the right to assert Travis's rights, including his standing as a holder in due course, and also has the right to obtain Travis's signature.

    (D) Bannister's endorsement was a special endorsement; thus, Travis's signature was not required in order to negotiate it.

Corporate Taxation

11. Pope, a C corporation, owns 15% of Arden Corporation. Arden paid a $3,000 cash dividend to Pope. What is the amount of Pope's dividend-received deduction (DRD)?

    (A) $3,000

    (B) $2,400

    (C) $2,100

    (D) $0

12. Mem Corp., which had earnings and profits of $500,000, made a nonliquidating distribution of property to its stockholders during 2014. This property had an adjusted basis of $10,000 and a fair market value of $15,000 at the date of distribution. The property was subject to a liability of $12,000, which its stockholders assumed. How much gain did Mem have to recognize as a result of this distribution?

    (A) $0

    (B) $2,000

    (C) $5,000

    (D) $7,000

Hint: The result is the same as if the corporation sold the property.

Debtor-Creditor Relationships

13. Ford was unable to repay a loan from City Bank when due. City refused to renew the loan to Ford unless an acceptable surety could be provided. Ford asked Owens, a friend, to act as surety on the loan. To induce Owens to agree to become a surety, Ford made fraudulent representations about Ford's financial condition and promised Owens discounts on merchandise sold at Ford's store. Owens agreed to act as surety and the loan was made to Ford. Subsequently, Ford's obligation to City was discharged in Ford's bankruptcy and City wishes to hold Owens liable. Owens may avoid liability

    (A) Because the arrangement was void at the inception.

    (B) If Owens was an uncompensated surety.

    (C) If Owens can show that City Bank was aware of the fraudulent representations.

    (D) Because the discharge in bankruptcy will prevent Owens from having a right of reimbursement.

14. West promised to make Noll a loan of $180,000 if Noll obtained sureties to secure the loan. Noll entered into an agreement with Carr, Gray, and Pine to act as cosureties on his loan from West. The agreement between Noll and the cosureties provided for compensation to be paid to each of the cosureties. It further indicated that the maximum liability of each cosurety would be as follows: Carr $180,000, Gray $60,000, and Pine $120,000. West accepted the commitment of the sureties and made the loan to Noll. After paying nine installments totaling $90,000, Noll defaulted. Gray's debts (including his surety obligation to West on the Noll loan) were discharged in bankruptcy. Subsequently, Carr properly paid the entire debt outstanding of $90,000. What amounts may Carr recover from the cosureties?

	Gray	Pine
(A)	$0	$30,000
(B)	$0	$36,000
(C)	$15,000	$30,000
(D)	$30,000	$30,000

Regulation of Employment

15. Wilk, an employee of Young Corp., was injured by the negligence of Quick, an independent contractor. The accident occurred during regular working hours and in the course of employment. If Young has complied with the state's workers' compensation laws, which of the following is correct?

    (A) Wilk is barred from suing Young or Quick for negligence.

    (B) Wilk will be denied workers' compensation if he was negligent in that he failed to adhere to the written safety procedures.

    (C) The amount of damages Wilk will be allowed to recover from Young will be based on comparative fault.

    (D) Wilk may obtain workers' compensation benefits and also properly maintain an action against Quick.

16. Which of the following is true under the Family and Medical Leave Act?

(A) The employee has the right to up to 12 workweeks of unpaid leave to care for his or her spouse who has a serious health problem.

(B) The employee has the right to up to 12 workweeks of paid leave to care for his or her newborn baby.

(C) The employee has the right to up to 12 workweeks of paid leave for the employee's own serious medical problems.

(D) This Act covers employees of all corporations and partnerships.

Federal Securities

17. Donn & Co. is considering the sale of $11 million of its common stock to the public in interstate commerce. In this connection, Donn has been correctly advised that registration of the securities with the SEC is

(A) **Not** required if the states in which the securities are to be sold have securities acts modeled after the federal act and Donn files in those states.

(B) Required in that it is necessary for the SEC to approve the merits of the securities offered.

(C) **Not** required if the securities are to be sold through a registered brokerage firm.

(D) Required and must include audited financial statements as an integral part of its registration.

18. A requirement of a private action to recover damages for violation of the registration requirements of the Securities Act of 1933 is that

(A) The plaintiff has acquired the securities in question.

(B) The issuer or other defendants commit either negligence or fraud in the sale of the securities.

(C) A registration statement has been filed.

(D) The securities were purchased from an underwriter.

Other Tax Topics

19. Don and Linda Grant, US citizens, were married for the entire 2013 calendar year. In 2013, Don gave a $60,000 cash gift to his sister. The Grants made no other gifts in 2013. They each signed a timely election to treat the $60,000 gift as one made by each spouse. Disregarding the unified credit and estate tax consequences, what amount of the 2013 gift is taxable to the Grants for gift tax purposes?

(A) $0

(B) $32,000

(C) $34,000

(D) $60,000

20. The Simone Trust reported distributable net income of $120,000 for the current year. The trustee is required to distribute $60,000 to Kent and $90,000 to Lind each year. If the trustee distributes these amounts, what amount is includable in Lind's gross income?

    (A) $0

    (B) $60,000

    (C) $72,000

    (D) $90,000

Individual Taxation

21. Paul Bristol, a cash-basis taxpayer, owns an apartment building. The following information was available for 2013:

    An analysis of the 2013 bank deposit slips showed recurring monthly rents received totaling $50,000.

    On March 1, 2013, the tenant in apartment 2B paid Bristol $2,000 to cancel the lease expiring on December 31, 2014.

    The lease of the tenant in apartment 3A expired on December 31, 2013, and the tenant left improvements valued at $1,000. The improvements were not in lieu of any rent required to have been paid.

    In computing net rental income for 2013, Bristol should report gross rents of

    (A) $50,000

    (B) $51,000

    (C) $52,000

    (D) $53,000

22. Frank Lanier is a resident of a state that imposes a tax on income. The following information pertaining to Lanier's state income taxes is available:

Taxes withheld in 2013	$3,500
Refund received in 2013 of 2012 tax	$400
Deficiency assessed and paid in 2013 for 2011:	
Tax	600
Interest	100

    What amount should Lanier utilize as state and local income taxes in calculating itemized deductions for his 2013 federal tax return?

    (A) $3,500

    (B) $3,700

    (C) $4,100

    (D) $4,200

Professional/Legal Responsibilities

23. Holly Corp. engaged Yost & Co., CPAs, to audit the financial statements to be included in a registration statement Holly was required to file under the provisions of the Securities Act of 1933. Yost failed to exercise due diligence and did **not** discover the omission of a fact material to the statements. A purchaser of Holly's securities may recover from Yost under Section 11 of the Securities Act of 1933 only if the purchaser

    (A) Brings a civil action within 1 year of the discovery of the omission and within 3 years of the offering date.

    (B) Proves that the registration statement was relied on to make the purchase.

    (C) Proves that Yost was negligent.

    (D) Establishes privity of contract with Yost.

24. A preparer of a tax return may incur penalties under the Internal Revenue Code in all of the following cases **except** where the taxpayer

    (A) Substantially overvalues property donated to a charitable organization.

    (B) Claims a substantial deduction for unpaid expenses incurred by a cash basis taxpayer.

    (C) Claims a substantial deduction for a loss resulting from an accidental fire.

    (D) Takes a position at variance with the Internal Revenue Code and a US Supreme Court decision on the specific point.

Property

25. On July 1, A, B, C, and D purchased a parcel of land as tenants in common, each owning an equal share. On July 10, A died leaving a will. Subsequently, B died intestate. After A and B's death,

    (A) C and D will each own a 1/2 interest in the land.

    (B) C and D will each own a 1/4 interest in the land.

    (C) C and D will each own a 1/3 interest in the land.

    (D) The tenancy in common will terminate.

26. On July 1, Bean deeded her home to Park. The deed was never recorded. On July 5, Bean deeded the same home to Noll. On July 9, Noll executed a deed, conveying his title to the same home to Baxter. On July 10, Noll and Baxter duly recorded their respective deeds. In order for Noll's deed from Bean to be effective, it must

    (A) Contain the actual purchase price paid by Noll.

    (B) Be signed by Noll.

    (C) Include a satisfactory description of the property.

    (D) Be recorded with Bean's seal affixed to the deed.

Partnership Taxation

27. Beck and Nilo are equal partners in B&N Associates, a general partnership. B&N borrowed $10,000 from a bank on an unsecured note, thereby increasing each partner's share of partnership liabilities. As a result of this loan, the basis of each partner's interest in B&N was

    (A) Decreased.

    (B) Increased.

    (C) Unaffected.

    (D) Dependent on each partner's ability to meet the obligation if called upon to do so.

Sales

28. Which of the following factors will be most important in determining if an express warranty has been created?

    (A) Whether the promises made by the seller became part of the basis of the bargain.

    (B) Whether the seller intended to create a warranty.

    (C) Whether the statements made by the seller were in writing.

    (D) Whether the sale was made by a merchant in the regular course of business.

Secured Transactions

29. In order for a security interest in goods to attach, the

    (A) Debtor must sign a security agreement that adequately describes the goods.

    (B) Debtor must retain possession of the goods until the underlying debt has been satisfied.

    (C) Creditor must properly file a financing statement.

    (D) Creditor must have given value.

30. During 2014, Fred Good traded a tractor used solely in his construction business for another tractor for the same use. On the date of the trade, the old tractor had an adjusted basis of $3,000 and a fair market value of $3,300. He received in exchange $500 in cash and a smaller tractor with a fair market value of $2,800. Assuming Mr. Good recognized $300 gain on the transaction, what is his basis in the new tractor?

    (A) $3,300

    (B) $3,000

    (C) $2,800

    (D) $2,300

Chapter 16

Answers and Explanations to Regulation Practice Questions

. . . .

Here are the answers to the regulation (REG) test questions from Chapter 15. Consider the answer explanations carefully. The REG test includes a lot of definitions and facts that can be difficult to keep straight. You'll find that the differences between answer choices can be very subtle. Take some time to understand each answer explanation.

Agency

1. **A.** Even though the employee was breaking one of Lund's rules, they can both be held liable, either individually or together.

2. **B.** Although there's typically a contract between the principal and agent in an agency relationship, this isn't required. For example, a principal may authorize a friend to act as his or her agent, and the agent might consent to do it as a favor. Additionally, the agent owes the principal fiduciary duties regardless of what duties are imposed by an employment contract.

Bankruptcy

3. **D.** An involuntary petition in bankruptcy, if not contested, will automatically result in the entry of an order for relief by the bankruptcy court. Only if the petition is contested will the creditor(s) be required to prove either that the debtor isn't paying his or her debts as they mature or that during the 120 days preceding the filing of a petition, a custodian was appointed or took possession of the debtor's property.

4. **B.** The fact that the debt of a secured party wasn't fully satisfied from the proceeds obtained from disposition of the collateral won't result in a denial of a general discharge, nor will the remaining portion of the secured debt be nondischargeable. In such situations, the secured party has the same priority as a general unsecured creditor (lowest priority) concerning the unpaid portion of the debt.

Business Structure

5. **C.** Under the Revised Uniform Partnership Act, the partners have joint and several liability for all of the partnership debts. This is true whether the debts are based on contract law or tort law.

6. **B.** The requirement is to identify the item that decreases stockholders' equity. This answer is correct because distribution to owners (dividends) decreases stockholders' equity.

Contracts

7. **A.** Consideration must be legally sufficient to satisfy the consideration requirement to form a contract (for example, a party binds herself to do something she isn't legally obligated to do or surrenders a legal right).

8. **D.** In general, a party's rights in a contract are assignable without the consent of the other parties. However, the following are situations in which this general rule doesn't apply and consent of the other parties would be required for a valid transfer to occur: (1) The contract involves personal services, credit, trust, or confidence; (2) a provision of the contract or statute prohibits assignment; and (3) the assignment would materially change the risk or obligations of the other party. Because the assignment by a patent holder of the right to receive royalties wouldn't alter the rights of the other parties to the contract, a valid transfer could be made without the consent of these parties.

Commercial Paper

9. **B.** A negotiable certificate of deposit is an instrument that complies with the requirements of a negotiable instrument and contains an acknowledgment of receipt of money by a bank with an agreement to repay it.

10. **C.** Transfer of an instrument causes the rights that the transferor had to vest with the transferee. Because Travis is an HDC (holder in due course), Calhoun acquires the rights of an HDC. Unless otherwise agreed, any transfer for value of an instrument not then payable to bearer (that is, "order paper") gives the transferee the specifically enforceable right to have the unqualified endorsement of the transferor.

Corporate Taxation

11. **C.** The requirement is to determine Pope's dividend-received deduction for the $3,000 dividend received from a 15 percent–owned corporation. Dividends received from a less than 20 percent–owned taxable domestic corporation are generally eligible for a 70 percent DRD. Here, Pope's DRD would be $3,000 × 70% = $2,100.

12. **C.** If a corporation makes a nonliquidating distribution of appreciated property to a shareholder, the corporation must recognize gain just as if the property were sold at its fair market value. Here, Mem must recognize a gain of $15,000 − $10,000 = $5,000. A liability increases the recognized gain only when the amount of liability exceeds fair market value.

Debtor-Creditor Relationships

13. **C.** Fraud by the principal debtor on the surety to induce a suretyship agreement will not release the surety if the creditor extended credit in good faith. But if the creditor (City Bank) had knowledge of the debtor's (Ford's) fraudulent representations, then the surety (Owens) may avoid liability.

14. **B.** The right of contribution arises when one cosurety, in performance of debtor's obligation, pays more than his proportionate share of the total liability. The right of contribution entitles the performing cosurety to reimbursement from the other cosureties for their pro rata shares of the liability. Because Gray's debts have been discharged in bankruptcy, Carr may exercise his right of contribution only against Pine and may recover nothing from Gray. Pine's pro rata share of the remaining $90,000 would be determined as follows:

$$\frac{\text{Dollar amount guaranteed by Pine}}{\text{Total amount of risk assumed by remaining cosureties}} \times \text{Remaining obligation}$$
$$= \frac{\$120,000}{\$120,000 + \$180,000} \times \$90,000 = \$36,000$$

Regulation of Employment

15. **D.** Wilk may obtain workers' compensation benefits and also maintain an action against Quick (the third party that caused the injury). If Wilk recovers against the third party (Quick) after obtaining workers' compensation benefits, a part of the recovery equal to the benefits received belongs to the employer (Young Corp.).

16. **A.** The employee has the right to up to 12 workweeks of unpaid leave to care for his or her spouse who has a serious health problem.

Federal Securities

17. **D.** The sale of $11 million in common stock doesn't qualify as exempt securities or an exempt transaction without additional information on the number and nature of any unaccredited investors. Because an exemption doesn't exist, Donn is required to fulfill all the registration requirements, which include audited financial statements.

18. **A.** This answer is correct because in order to establish damages under the Securities Act of 1933, the plaintiff must establish that he has acquired the securities in question. There is no requirement under the Act that fraud or negligence be proven as long as there is a misstatement of a material fact or the omission of a material fact present in the registration statement.

Other Tax Topics

19. **B.** The requirement is to determine the amount of the $60,000 cash gift to the sister that is taxable to the Grants for gift tax purposes. Don and Linda (his spouse) elected to split the gift made to Don's sister, so each is treated as making a gift of $30,000. Because both Don and Linda would be eligible for a $14,000 exclusion, each will have made a taxable gift of $30,000 − $14,000 exclusion = $16,000. Thus, the Grants' total taxable gift is $32,000 (16,000×2).

20. **C.** The requirement is to determine the amount of trust distribution that is includable in Lind's gross income. The maximum amount that's taxable to trust beneficiaries is limited to a trust's distributable net income (DNI). When distributions to multiple beneficiaries exceed DNI, the trust's DNI must be prorated to the distributions to determine the portion of each distribution that must be included in gross income. Here, because the distributions to Kent and Lind totaled $150,000, the portion of Lind's $90,000 distribution that must be included in gross income equals $(\$90,000/\$150,000) \times \$120,000$ DNI $= \$72,000$.

Individual Taxation

21. **C.** Gross rents include the $50,000 of recurring rents plus the $2,000 lease cancellation payment. The $1,000 of lease improvements are excluded from income because they weren't required in lieu of rent.

22. **C.** The $3,500 of taxes withheld is deductible, as is the $600 of tax paid during 2013 for 2011. The $400 refund of 2012 taxes doesn't reduce the 2013 deduction but may be includable in income.

Professional/Legal Responsibilities

23. **A.** A purchaser of securities may recover losses from the CPA firm that failed to discover the omission of a fact material to the statements under the Securities Act of 1933. The statute of limitations for this civil action is 1 year from the discovery of the omission and 3 years from the offering date.

24. **C.** A preparer of a tax return wouldn't incur penalties under the Internal Revenue Code where the taxpayer reduces his or her liability by justifiably claiming a deduction for a substantial loss (for example, a loss resulting from an accidental fire).

Property

25. **B.** Under tenancy in common, there's no right of survivorship; therefore, C's and D's ownership interests will not be affected by the death of A or B. A's interest in the parcel of land will pass to the individual named in the will, while B's interest will pass according to intestate succession.

26. **C.** The necessary requirements for a valid deed are (1) the names of the buyer (grantee) and the seller (grantor), (2) words evidencing an intent to convey, (3) a legally sufficient description of the land, (4) the grantor's (and usually the spouse's) signature, and (5) delivery of the deed.

Partnership Taxation

27. **B.** Because partners are individually liable for their share of partnership liabilities, a change in the amount of partnership liabilities affects a partner's basis for a partnership interest. An increase in a partnership's liabilities increases each partner's basis in the partnership by each partner's share of the increase. A decrease in a partnership's liabilities is considered to be a distribution of money to each partner and reduces each partner's basis in the partnership by the partner's share of the decrease.

Sales

28. **A.** This answer is correct because any seller, not only a merchant seller, may create an express warranty by making any affirmation of fact or promise that forms part of the basis of the bargain. Such a warranty may be made either orally or in writing and will exist regardless of the seller's intent.

Secured Transactions

29. **D.** A security interest attaches when all of the following have been met, in any order: The debtor has rights in the collateral, the creditor extends value, and a record of the security agreement exists. Thus, the creditor must give value for attachment to occur.

30. **C.** This answer is correct because the basis of an asset received in a like-kind exchange where boot received is

Basis of asset given up	$3,000
Less boot received	−$500
Plus gain recognized	+$300
Basis of asset received	$2,800

Part VI

The Part of Tens

Knowing various formulas is essential to your success on the CPA exam. In addition to the ten formulas provided in this part, check out www.dummies.com/extras/cpaexam for some bonus formulas that are good to know.

In this part . . .

✔ Discover ten mistakes that can lead to incorrect answers on the CPA exam so that you can avoid them.

✔ Familiarize yourself with more than ten common formulas that are frequently used on the exam so you can get comfortable using them.

Chapter 17

Ten Common Mistakes on the CPA Exam

In This Chapter

▶ Reviewing answer choices effectively

▶ Applying accounting principles correctly

▶ Understanding types of taxation

This chapter covers ten areas on the CPA exam that can be challenging. Because these topics are difficult, CPA candidates often make mistakes on these types of exam questions. These concepts are nearly always tested, so make sure you understand them. If you're able to nail down these concepts, you'll avoid some pitfalls on the CPA exam.

Skipping Your Notes When You Review Your Answers

Because the exam is no longer in written form, you're allowed to use noteboards. *Noteboards* are a tool to jot down information as you take the exam on a computer. If you need to perform a calculation, write down those numbers on the noteboard. When you review your answer choices, use your noteboard to review. Using the noteboard is a time-saver in your review, and it prevents errors.

Exam candidates sometimes come up with a solution but click on the wrong answer choice. Using a noteboard can help prevent this basic mistake.

Here are some ways your notes can help you as you check your work:

✔ **Crossing out incorrect answers:** One noteboard technique is to write down the problem numbers and circle them. Under each number, write "A, B, C, D" on your noteboard. As you work a problem, cross out the letters of the incorrect answer choices. As you review answer choices, check your noteboard to verify that you clicked on the correct choice on screen. Crossing out incorrect answers is particularly helpful if you're deciding between two answer choices. During your review, you don't have to reread all four choices; you can glance at your noteboard to see which two answers you preferred.

✔ **Checking formulas and calculations:** Another good use of the noteboard is to review your math. Say a calculation on Question 10 requires you to calculate earnings per share. You write down and circle "10" on your noteboard and jot down the calculation for earnings per share:

$$\text{Basic EPS} = \frac{\text{Net income} - \text{Preferred stock dividends}}{\text{Average common stock shares outstanding}}$$

You realize that you also need to calculate average common stock shares outstanding, so you write down that formula:

$$\text{Average common shares} = \frac{\left(\begin{array}{c}\text{Beginning}\\\text{common stock shares}\\\text{outstanding}\end{array}\right) + \left(\begin{array}{c}\text{Ending}\\\text{common stock shares}\\\text{outstanding}\end{array}\right)}{2}$$

You then use the data from the question to complete the formulas.

When you get to Question 10 in your review, take a look at the calculations on the noteboard to see whether they're correct. Many people make the mistake of not reviewing calculations or trying to perform the math in their heads, which leads to mistakes. Recheck your work on the noteboards.

✔ **Making sure you used the right information:** Another reason for reviewing your work using a noteboard relates to the amount of information you're provided with in a question. CPA exam questions provide lots of information that isn't needed to answer the question. The noteboard helps you plow through all that data and use only what you need.

Not Knowing the Language in Audit Reports

The auditing and attestation (AUD) test has a heavy focus on audit report language. The most common audit opinion (or audit report) is an unqualified opinion. CPA candidates should memorize the exact report language for the unqualified opinion (see Chapter 11 for the text). All the other types of audit reports — and reports for reviews and compilations — take their text from the unqualified opinion and make changes.

Exam candidates who don't memorize the unqualified opinion miss the opportunity to answer many questions easily. Those candidates also have trouble understanding how the reports relate to each other. Nearly all of the reports share some language.

The last paragraph of an unqualified opinion essentially states that the financial statements are free of material misstatement. A qualified opinion is sometimes referred to as an *except for* opinion. The qualified opinion adds language to an unqualified opinion template, stating "except for the information in the following paragraph." If you understand the unqualified opinion language, you can change the language to create a qualified opinion.

Not Understanding Segregating Duties

Fraud, which is on the auditing and attestation (AUD) test as well as the regulatory (REG) test, is defined as willful intent to deceive. The most important strategy to prevent fraud is proper segregation of duties. An effective way to learn segregation of duties is to review and understand scenarios. When the exam provides a scenario and asks whether it can lead to fraud, mull over who is performing each role in the process.

You can read about topics related to segregation of duties, such as fictitious payees and the reliability of third-party audit evidence, in Chapters 11 and 14.

For example, suppose that Bob controls the invoicing process. He decides to create a bogus invoice — a bill for a product or service that doesn't exist. Because Bob also authorizes payment, he cuts a check payable to the bogus company. Because Bob controls the bogus company's checking account, he uses the funds for his own purposes. If he also controls the bank reconciliation process, no one at the firm may notice the payment to the fake company.

This situation is referred to as a *fictitious payee*. To prevent this fraud, three separate people should handle the following duties:

- ✔ **Authorization:** One person should initial and authorize spending. This includes payment approval of invoices that come into the company.

- ✔ **Custody of assets:** A second person has physical custody of the checkbook. Other people in the organization can't access the checkbook to write a check.

- ✔ **Recordkeeping:** You can think of the bank reconciliation as the "last line of defense" for catching many instances of fraud. If Bob writes a check payable to a bogus company that he controls, a separate person handling the bank reconciliation may notice that the company is not legitimate. That bank reconciler can follow up on the questionable payment.

Another aspect of segregation of duties is the issue of third-party audit evidence. A *third party* is an entity that's outside of the company under audit. CPAs always prefer third-party evidence because the third party doesn't have any bias that would influence the data it provides to an auditor.

When a CPA firm is auditing cash, the third-party bank statement is considered reliable audit information. The company, to ensure that the business's cash account transactions agree with the bank's records, performs a bank reconciliation. If the book (company checkbook) doesn't agree with the bank statement, the company needs to investigate those differences.

When you're provided with audit evidence, keep in mind that third-party evidence is the most reliable.

Applying Accounting Policy Inconsistently

Some people struggle in applying accounting principles for several reasons. First, exam candidates often don't recognize an accounting principle when they see it. Second, some people don't understand that an accounting principle needs to be consistently applied. Otherwise, the company needs to provide additional disclosure.

The difference between cash basis and accrual basis may be the most tested principle on the exam. The accrual basis requires companies to post accounting adjustments for accruals and deferrals. The accrual method drives many of the types of accounts used in financial statements. Many CPA questions ask you to compare the financial impact of using cash basis versus the accrual basis. CPA candidates who are unclear on this difference are not prepared to succeed on the exam.

Say, for example, that a client pays $2,000 in payroll to employees on January 5. The $2,000 represents payroll expense incurred during the last week of December. The client's fiscal year-end is December 31 (you can assume this on the exam, unless you're told differently). The cash basis states that you record the expense when the check is written. Using the cash basis, the expense is recorded in January. The accrual basis dictates that the expense should be recorded when it is incurred — regardless of when the cash moves. The accrual method would record the expense in December because that's when the work was performed.

A CPA candidate needs to know that the cash basis delays recording of the expense until the year after the expense is actually incurred. The accrual basis records the expense in December. Using the accrual basis, the company would debit accrued payroll and credit wages payable in December.

Another frequently tested accounting policy change relates to inventory valuation. Inventory valuation is an accounting principle. Inventory is often the largest single asset on the balance sheet. A change in the valuation method for inventory can mean a large change in cost of sales and net income.

Suppose Sally Farm Equipment sells expensive equipment to farmers. Sally has three items in her inventory at the end of August. Here's the cost of each item and the date when the item was purchased:

June 30 purchase $1,000,000, July 15 purchase $1,200,000, July 31 purchase $1,500,000

Sally uses the first-in, first-out (FIFO) method to value inventory. Suppose that Sally sells a piece of equipment on August 5 for $1,600,000. FIFO assumes that Sally sells the oldest items first (the first items into inventory). In this case, FIFO indicates that the $1,000,000 inventory item purchased on June 30 is sold first. Sally's profit is $1,600,000 − $1,000,000 = $600,000.

Now suppose that Sally changed her inventory valuation method to last-in, first-out (LIFO) on August 1. Sally now uses the LIFO method for the August 5 inventory sale. LIFO dictates that Sally sell the newest units first. The inventory cost is now the July 31 purchase of $1,500,000. Her profit is $1,600,000 − $1,500,000 = $100,000.

You see that the change in inventory valuation method can change cost of sales and net income dramatically. In this example, the change in valuation increases cost of sales by $500,000. Net income decreased by $500,000 using the new valuation method.

Because of the potential impact, companies are required to fully disclose a change in inventory valuation method as well as other changes in accounting principles. Specifically, the company must display the net income using the old method and the new method. Presenting the financial impact allows the investor to make an apples-to-apples comparison between the two methods.

Changing an accounting principle can be a red flag to financial-statement readers, auditors, and financial analysts. The change may indicate that the company is trying to manipulate its net income. By showing the financial impact of the change, financial-statement readers see the full impact of the change in accounting principle.

Not Reviewing Financial Ratios by Type

Exam candidates need to understand a variety of financial ratios. This process can be frustrating if you don't have a method to group the ratios into categories. Some people make the mistake of memorizing the ratios in no particular order. You find more on financial ratios in Chapters 4 and 5.

You'll have more success with ratios if you group them together by type. For example, some ratios explain *liquidity*, which is the ability to use current assets to pay for current liabilities. Liquidity ratios are all about short-term cash flow. *Profitability ratios*, on the other hand, measure profit. They also explain the rate of return a company earns, such as return on assets or return on equity. Solvency questions address a company's ability to generate cash and pay debts over the long term.

If you group ratios intro these categories, you'll have more success pulling the formulas out of your memory.

Forgetting to Consider the Type of Taxation

When most people think about taxes, they consider only income taxes. The CPA exam covers several types of taxation, including gift tax, estate tax, and income taxes. When you're looking at a tax question, you may make the mistake of not first considering the type of tax that needs to be calculated. For example, if the question deals with the dollar amount of gifts a taxpayer can give, the question is about the gift tax, not income tax. Understanding the type of tax will help you identify the information you need to answer the question. You can read about taxes in Chapter 14.

Not Memorizing the Tax Format on Form 1040

Individual taxation is the most heavily tested area of tax. The CPA exam requires candidates to know many rules about individual tax. An effective way to study for this area is to print the two pages of Form 1040, the individual tax return. When you come across an individual taxation topic, consider where that information is located on Form 1040.

For example, suppose a question provides information on medical expenses and the client's interest expense on a home mortgage. Medical expenses and interest expenses are just two of dozens of topics on the individual tax portion of the exam. All those facts and figures can be confusing. Now consider where the tax information is posted on the tax return. Both of these expenses are used to calculate itemized deductions, which are on page 2 of Form 1040. If you can visualize where the information is posted on the return, you have a better chance of getting the right answer.

Confusing Present Value and Future Value

The CPA exam asks questions about the future value of an amount, given a certain investment amount and an interest rate of the investment. You may also have to compute the present value of something, given its value in the future. These questions can be particularly hard to understand.

First determine whether the question is asking about present value or future value. Diving in and starting to compute an answer without answering this basic question for yourself is a mistake. If you're unclear about which value you're calculating, you'll use the wrong data to compute your answer.

Suppose a company needs to accumulate assets to purchase a machine in 5 years. The firm can invest $50,000 each year, given a 6 percent rate of return on the dollars invested. How much will the firm accumulate by the end of five years?

Because this problem requires an amount needed in the future, this is a future value question. If a question requires an amount invested each year, it's an annuity question. To answer this type of question, you need to use the future value tables for an annuity. If the question involves a single payment, you use the lump sum or single sum tables. You can easily find these tables online. Take a look at the tables to help you understand the math involved in creating the tables.

Using the future value table for an annuity of 1, the future-value factor for 5 years at 6 percent is 5.6371. Multiply the annual amount invested by the future-value factor:

Future value = $50,000 annual investment × 5.6371 = $283,550

The company can then decide whether $283,550 is enough money to purchase the machine at the end of five years. If not, the firm can change the annual investment amount until the future value meets its requirements.

Another very common test question is to consider the present value of a series of payments. The payments may not be equal. This time, suppose that a company buys a new machine for $20,000. The machine will operate more efficiently than the old machine the company was using. The business calculates that using the new machine will create a $10,000 increase in cash flow for the first three years. The test question provides a discount rate of 8 percent. Present value questions use a discount rate, because the payments are discounted to a present value. You can think of present value as working back toward the present day.

Calculate the present value of the cash inflows and outflows. As a first step, consider the cash inflows and outflows by year. The outflow is the $20,000 check the firm writes for the machine. Because that check is written in the present day, there's no need to assign a present value to the outflow. Years 1 through 3 each have a cash inflow of $10,000.

Next, pull the present-value factors for Years 1, 2, and 3 at a discount rate of 8 percent. Because each cash inflow is the same, you'll use the present value of an ordinary annuity. Again, you can find present-value tables online. The present-value factor is 2.577. Here's the present value of the cash inflows:

Present value = $10,000 annual cash inflow × 2.577 = $25,770

The cash inflows less the payment for the machine is $25,770 – $20,000 = $5,770. The firm is $5,770 better off. Taking the present value of cash inflows and outflows is a way to evaluate a business decision about cash flow. If the present value you calculate adds up to a positive number (positive net cash flow), you should move ahead with the decision.

The present value of cash flows is only one decision-making tool. Managers may use many forms of analysis for the same decision.

Failing to Keep the Big Four Type of Costs Straight

The CPA exam asks many questions that address managing costs. It's a mistake to go over the more-complex cost accounting topics without first understanding direct costs, indirect costs (overhead), fixed costs, and variable costs. You can think of these costs as the Big Four. These cost terms are the building blocks for the other cost accounting topics on the CPA exam.

Don't start a cost problem without first identifying whether each of the costs is direct or indirect. A *direct cost* can be tied directly to the product or service produced. Direct costs increase and decrease with production. *Indirect costs* can't be directly tied to production. Changes in the level of production don't directly impact these costs.

Keep in mind that direct costs can be fixed or variable. Indirect costs can also be fixed or variable. Here are four examples using a blue jeans manufacturer:

- **Direct variable cost:** The cost of denim used to make blue jeans is a direct cost. The cost also varies based on the number of jeans produced.

- **Direct fixed cost:** A contract to repair machinery used in production is a fixed cost. The machine repair cost isn't incurred unless you're producing blue jeans — it's a direct cost. Another good example is the salary paid to a foreman who manages production. The cost incurred for that individual is fixed and is also directly tied to production.

- **Indirect variable cost:** Utility costs are indirect costs. The rationale is that you need to heat and cool the factory, regardless of the level of production. The cost also varies.

- **Indirect fixed cost:** Salaries paid to home office employees, such as lawyers and accountants, aren't directly tied to production. The salary levels are also fixed.

The exam frequently asks candidates to classify costs into these four groups.

Another critical mistake is not considering whether the fixed cost is stated per unit or in total dollars. CPA candidates sometimes think that if a fixed cost is stated on a per-unit basis, the cost will always increase with production. In fact, the total dollar amount for fixed costs is capped.

Suppose, for example, that your factory lease payment is fixed at $10,000 per month. If you produce 20,000 baseball gloves, your fixed lease cost per glove (unit) is $10,000 ÷ 20,000 gloves = $0.50 fixed cost per glove. Keep in mind that any glove produced over 20,000 won't add any fixed cost.

To avoid confusion, view fixed costs only in total dollars. Fixed costs per unit implies that every unit produced will incur additional fixed costs, which isn't the case.

Not Considering Employer Responsibilities for Individual Contractors

Many people study the contract, agency, and sales regulations without fully understanding independent contractors. Exam candidates should keep in mind that independent contractors have a different status from employees. In some cases, an employer's liability for the actions of an independent contractor is the same as with an employee. In other cases, the employer's responsibility is different. If you're unclear about this difference, studying the contract, agency, and sales topics may be difficult.

The IRS website provides a definition of an *independent contractor* for tax purposes. Here's that definition:

- The payer (the company hiring the contractor) has the right to control or direct only the result of the work.

- The payer doesn't control what will be done and how it will be done.

Say a company hires a painter to paint a fence. The result that the contractor is hired to perform is a painted fence. The business allows the painter to control the type and color of paint used, how many coats of paint are applied, and how the wood on the fence is prepared before painting begins. The painter is likely to be classified as an independent contractor and not an employee.

Keep this definition in mind. It will help you understand some concepts in agency and sales law.

Chapter 18

Ten Important Formulas to Understand

In This Chapter

▶ Going over the breakeven formula and target net income

▶ Understanding accrued interest and the effective interest method

▶ Getting up to speed on financial ratios

The CPA exam requires students to know a variety of formulas. This chapter explains some of the more heavily tested categories of formulas on the exam. If you make a list of formulas to memorize and understand, make sure to include this information.

Breakeven in Total Dollars and Units Sold

The breakeven formula is a handy tool for a business owner and a frequent topic on the CPA exam. This is a what-if tool that a company can use to plug in sales and cost information. *Breakeven* is defined as the level of sales and costs that will generate a profit of zero.

You need to know the formula in total dollars and using a per-unit format. Here's the total-dollars formula:

Sales – Variable costs – Fixed costs = $0 profit

Notice that the profit in the formula is set to $0. The CPA exam will typically provide three of the four variables in the formula and ask you to solve for the missing amount. Suppose, for example, that Bob sells software. His variable costs total $30,000, and his fixed costs total $50,000. Compute the breakeven sales in total dollars.

First, calculate the total costs: $30,000 + $50,000 = $80,000. Sales of $80,000 minus $80,000 in total costs generates a profit of $0.

At $80,000 in sales, the company breaks even. The exam may also ask you to calculate breakeven on a per-unit basis. CPA candidates sometimes think that if a fixed cost is stated on a per-unit basis, the fixed costs will always increase with production. However, the dollar amount of fixed costs is capped, so be careful with the data you're provided on fixed costs. Always consider total fixed costs when working on a question.

Here's the formula for computing breakeven on a per-unit basis:

Sales per unit – Variable costs per unit – Fixed costs = $0 profit

In this case, suppose that Bob is reviewing data on a per-unit basis. Fixed costs, however, are presented in total dollars. Bob's product has a sales price of $50 per unit. Variable costs are $30 per unit, and fixed costs total $20,000. Compute the breakeven point in units.

Note that this question asks about units, not dollars. You may want to jot down that idea on your noteboard so you understand what the question is asking. First step, fill in the data in the formula:

$50 sales per unit − $30 variable costs per unit − $20,000 fixed costs = $0 profit

Next, subtract sales per unit from variable costs per unit, which is $50 − $30 = $20 per unit. Now it's time for some algebra:

$20 per unit − $20,000 fixed costs = $0 profit   (Add $20,000 to each side.)

$20 per unit = $20,000 fixed costs   (Divide both sides by 20.)

$$\text{Breakeven per unit} = \frac{\$20,000}{20}$$

$$= 1{,}000 \text{ units}$$

Bob will break even (cover all variable costs and fixed costs) at 1,000 units in sales.

After you understand breakeven, you can move to target net income. Instead of setting the profit in the formula to $0, you plug in a desired income, or *target net income*. Keep in mind that for this book, *profit* and *net income* mean the same thing.

Suppose that Bob wants to generate a $5,000 profit for the month. His sale price is $50 per unit, and his variable costs are $30 per unit. Fixed costs total $30,000. For this problem, calculate the number of units sold that will generate a $5,000 profit. Here's the formula:

$5,000 = (Sales − Variable costs) − Fixed costs

$5,000 = ((Units × $50) − (Units × $30)) − $30,000

$5,000 = (Units × ($50 − $30)) − $30,000

$35,000 = Units × $20

1,750 = Units

Bob needs to sell 1,750 units to earn $5,000.

Accrued Interest Paid by a Bond Buyer

Accrued interest is defined as interest that the buyer of a bond owes the seller. Accrued interest becomes an issue when a bond is sold between interest payment dates. This concept is nearly always tested on the CPA exam. Here's the formula:

$$\text{Accrued interest} = \left(\begin{array}{c}\text{Bond} \\ \text{face amount}\end{array}\right) \times (\text{Interest rate}) \times \left(\begin{array}{c}\text{Total amount of time} \\ \text{the seller has owned the bond} \\ \text{since the last} \\ \text{interest payment date}\end{array}\right)$$

The face amount of a bond is the amount that the issuer must pay the owner at maturity. The interest rate is the rate stated on the face of the bond certificate. Accrued interest exists because the *registrar* for the bond issue can pay interest only to one person — the owner of the bond, when the interest payment is due.

Say that a $100,000, 6 percent corporate bond issued by Bruno's Bargain Basement pays interest twice a year. The interest payment dates are June 1 and December 1 of each year. The annual interest payment is $100,000 × 0.06 = $6,000. The semiannual interest is $6,000 ÷ 2, or $3,000. Also, assume that each month has 30 days. (The CPA exam should explain whether you should use a 30-day month or actual days.) Corporate bonds pay interest twice a year.

Suppose that Joe sells this $100,000 bond to Bill on September 1. In this case, Joe sells the bond after three of the six months have passed. On December 1, Bill will receive the entire $3,000 semiannual interest payment, even though he owned the bond for only three of the six months. Bill pays the seller Joe three months of interest, or $1,500, when Bill purchases the bond. Both parties will then properly receive three months of interest.

Double-Declining Balance Depreciation

Double-declining balance (DDB) is an accelerated depreciation method. This method recognizes more depreciation expense in the early years than straight-line depreciation. The formula can be confusing because it requires several steps. Here's the formula:

$$\text{Double - declining balance} = \text{Book value} \times (\text{Straight line depreciation rate} \times 2)$$

Keep in mind that this depreciation method stops when the book value (cost less accumulated depreciation) reaches salvage value. At that point, the owner will sell the asset and receive the salvage value sales proceeds. Selling when the book value reaches salvage value allows the owner to minimize the cost of using the asset.

Suppose Dave owns a piece of equipment with a cost of $200,000. Straight-line depreciation is over 4 years. The asset has a salvage value of $10,000.

To use the DDB method, consider the straight-line depreciation as a percentage and then double that percentage rate. In this case, the straight-line rate is 25 percent per year. The DDB rate is $0.25 \times 2 = 0.50$. For Year 1, multiply the book value by the DDB rate, which gives you $200,000 \times 0.50 = 100,000$.

The DDB method for Year 2 uses a new book value. Book value is calculated as the cost less accumulated depreciation. Year 2 book value is $200,000 cost − $100,000 Year 1 depreciation = $100,000. For Year 3, book value would be reduced by depreciation expense in Years 1 and 2.

With DDB, you keep multiplying the DDB rate of 50 percent by the new book value each year. Suppose that the book value for a particular year is $30,000 and the salvage value is $28,000. For that year, your depreciation would be $30,000 − $28,000 = $2,000. If using the DDB rate generates more than $2,000 depreciation in that year, you wouldn't use the formula.

Multi-Step Income Statement

The basic income statement is Revenue − Expenses = Net income. The exam usually asks questions about a more-complex version called the multi-step income statement. Here's the three-step formula:

Sales − Cost of sales = Gross profit

Gross profit − Operating expenses = Operating income

Operating income − Non-operating expenses + Non-operating income = Net income

To succeed on these questions, you need to understand the categories for revenue and expenses. The test may give you a list of accounts and their balances. You're asked to assign the amount to the correct category. Keep these points in mind:

- ✔ **Gross profit:** Gross profit is sales less cost of sales. *Cost of sales* includes those expenses directly related to manufacturing a product or providing a service. Suppose you make wooden ladders. Your direct materials, such as wood and metal, are part of cost of sales. Direct labor costs that you pay for workers to cut and assemble ladders are also a direct cost. Gross profit is not net income; other expenses are incurred before you get to net income.

- ✔ **Operating expenses:** These expenses aren't directly related to generating a product or service. However, they're required to operate the business each month. Nearly all companies, for example, incur legal and accounting costs. Those expenses don't relate to making ladders, but you can't run the business without them.

- ✔ **Non-operating expenses and non-operating income:** This category represents either income or expense that doesn't relate to normal business operations. If the ladder company sells a piece of equipment for a gain, that amount is non-operating income. If the ladder firm incurs a loss when it sells a building, that loss is a non-operating expense. The ladder company isn't in the business of selling equipment or buildings.

Inventory Turnover

Turnover ratios have to do with the rate at which a company collects money. This chapter lists two turnover ratios: inventory turnover and receivable turnover. In general, the faster a business can collect money, the better. If you can bring in dollars quickly, you can operate your business with a lower cash balance. Reducing the assets tied up in cash allows you to invest capital elsewhere. Generally, a firm wants to increase its turnover ratios.

Here's the formula for inventory turnover:

$$\text{Inventory turnover} = \frac{\text{Sales}}{\text{Average inventory}}$$

Average inventory is (Beginning period inventory + Ending period inventory) ÷ 2. The exam may ask you to calculate the formula or to identify factors that will change the formula. Keep in mind that a higher turnover ratio is better than a lower one. The more you can sell while minimizing your inventory investment, the better off you are.

Suppose Jane's Dress Shop has annual sales of $2,000,000 per year. Her average inventory is $200,000 each year. Jane's inventory turnover is $2,000,000 ÷ $200,000 = 10. This number means that Jane sells her entire inventory 10 times per year. That also means that Jane invests $200,000 to restock her inventory 10 times per year.

Assume that Jane is able to sell $2,200,000 of merchandise and maintain the same level of average inventory. Here's the new calculation:

$$\text{Inventory turnover} = \frac{\$2,200,000 \text{ sales}}{\$200,000 \text{ average inventory}} = 11$$

Jane is able to increase sales by $200,000 without any additional investment in her average inventory. If instead, Jane has to increase inventory to $400,000 to generate the $2,200,000 in sales, her turnover ratio would be $2,200,000 ÷ $400,000 = 5.5 times. The increase in inventory cost sharply reduces the turnover ratio.

Receivable Turnover

There are typically two assets that require the largest investment of a firm's resources: accounts receivable and inventory. These areas both involve an investment of cash. Cash is paid for inventory. For receivables, the investment of cash is the choice to sell goods on credit and wait for payment. The company must get cash from other sources to operate until the receivable is paid. A business may borrow or issue equity to raise cash to operate.

Here's the receivable formula:

$$\text{Receivable turnover} = \frac{\text{Net credit sales}}{\text{Average accounts receivable}}$$

Credit sales means that you sell a product or service and don't immediately receive cash. Net credit sales subtract any allowance for doubtful accounts from credit sales. Average accounts receivable is (Beginning receivables + Ending receivables) ÷ 2.

The higher the receivable turnover rate, the better. A higher turnover rate can mean several things:

✔ **You're generating more net credit sales for each dollar of accounts receivable.** Suppose you increase net credit sales from $1,000,000 to $1,200,000. Average accounts receivable stays at $50,000. Your receivables turnover increases from 20 ($1,000,000 ÷ $50,000) to 24 ($1,200,000 ÷ $50,000). You're collecting cash faster, without having to invest more dollars in accounts receivable.

✔ **You're reducing accounts receivable while maintaining the same level of net credit sales.** Suppose you reduce accounts receivable from $50,000 to $40,000. Net credit sales stay at $1,000,000. In this case, your receivables turnover increases from 20 ($1,000,000 ÷ $50,000) to 25 ($1,000,000 ÷ $40,000). You have less invested in accounts receivable and maintain the same level of credit sales.

A business can reduce accounts receivable in several ways. A company can insist that clients make a cash deposit for all sales. A firm can also tighten credit policy by not extending credit to customers who pay slowly.

Effective Interest Rate Method

The effective interest method is a process to account for interest expense when a company issues a bond. A bond issuer incurs interest expense when a bond is issued. The issuer pays interest based on the coupon or stated rate on the face of the certificate. The face amount represents the amount of principal that the bond issuer must repay to the investor at maturity. If a bond issuer has a $100,000, 6 percent bond outstanding, the annual interest expense is $100,000 × 0.06 = $6,000. The bond investor would earn interest income of $6,000.

Interest expense and interest income calculations are more complicated when the bond is issued at a premium or a discount. Here's an explanation of both terms:

✔ **Premium:** A bond issued at a premium is issued at a price higher than the face amount of the bond. If the $100,000 face-amount bond is issued at $120,000, that price represents a premium. A premium bond means that the issuer has additional income. That income is the difference between the issue price and face amount. In this case, the income is $120,000 − $100,000 = $20,000. For the bond buyer, the $20,000 is an added expense because she paid more than she'll receive at maturity.

> ✔ **Discount:** A bond issued at a discount is priced below the face amount of the bond. If a $100,000 face-amount bond is issued at $98,000, it's issued at a discount. The difference between the issue price and the face amount represents an additional expense to the bond issuer. This bond issuer's additional expense is $100,000 − $98,000 = $2,000. For the bond buyer, the $2,000 is added income, because he paid less than he'll receive at maturity.

A premium or discount is *amortized,* which means that the premium on the bond is gradually posted to income for the issuer. A discount is gradually posted to expense for the issuer. For an investor, buying at a premium generates more expense, and purchasing at a discount creates more income. The effective interest rate requires several steps to calculate the amortization of premium or discount.

The CPA exam typically asks candidates to calculate one year's worth of interest income or interest expense. The exam may ask you about either a premium or discount bond. Here are two examples.

Suppose that Jim, an investor, buys a $100,000 face-amount, 4.5 percent bond at $104,100. The premium on the bond is $104,100 − $100,000 = $4,100. To compute the amortization of the premium, the test question explains that the bond is "purchased to yield" 4 percent. The term *purchased to yield* provides the *yield,* or total return to investor Jim. Because Jim paid a premium, his total return (4 percent) is less than the stated interest rate on the bond (4.5 percent).

At the end of Year 1, Jim's interest income is the purchase price times the 4 percent total return, or $104,100 × 0.04 = $4,164. Note that the interest income paid to Jim is $100,000 × 0.045 = $4,500. His interest income is less than the interest payment because he paid a premium for the bond. Jim has recognized one year of bond amortization.

Jim later buys a $500,000 face-amount, 6 percent bond at $377,107. The discount on the bond is $122,893. The test question states that the bond is purchased to yield 10 percent. Jim's total return is higher than the 6 percent stated rate on the bond. That's because he'll receive more at maturity ($500,000) than he paid for the bond ($377,107).

At the end of Year 1, Jim's interest income is the purchase price times the 10 percent total return, or $377,107 × 0.10 = $37,710.70. Note that the interest income paid to Jim is $500,000 × 0.06 = $30,000. His interest income is more than the interest payment because he paid a discount for the bond.

Special-Order Profitability

Special-order questions can be tricky. Often, an exam candidate looks at the price of a special order and quickly judges that the order won't be profitable. The candidate ends up rejecting an order that in reality would be profitable for the company.

The special-order concept assumes that a business has excess capacity to fill an order. These questions also assume that fixed costs have already been paid for with other (earlier) production. Those fixed costs are considered sunk costs that can't be changed. As a result, fixed costs aren't part of the cost calculation for special orders.

The only costs you consider for special orders are the variable costs to produce the product and any additional costs that are specific to the special order. Your formula for special-order profit is sale proceeds less variable costs less any additional costs required for the special order. Fixed costs are excluded from your calculation.

Here's an example: Baseline Sports Supply makes youth baseball gloves that typically sell for $70 per glove. During that last week of the month, Sports Palace places a special order for 1,000 gloves. Sports Palace is willing to pay $55 per glove. Baseline's variable cost per glove is $40, and the firm normally allocates $20 to each glove to cover fixed costs (lease on factory, insurance costs, and so on). The seller also wants a logo sewn into each glove, which will cost an additional $5. Calculate Baseline's profit on the Sports Palace order. Here's the formula for Baseline's profit on the special order:

$$\text{Baseline special order profit} = \$55 \text{ sale price} - \$40 \text{ variable cost} - \$5 \text{ logo cost}$$
$$= \$10 \text{ profit}$$

The special-order calculation excludes any fixed costs.

Individual Taxation Formula: Form 1040

To understand individual taxation, visualizing the formula for taxable income is helpful. You can review the formula by going over the Form 1040 on the IRS website (www.irs.gov). Here's the formula for taxable income in two steps:

Income – Adjustments to income = Adjusted gross income

Adjusted gross income – Deductions – Exemptions = Taxable income

Consider these points regarding the formula:

✔ **Income:** This value includes income generated from many sources. In addition to wages and salary, taxpayers post interest and dividends in income as well as income from self-employment.

✔ **Adjustments to income:** Total income is reduced by many items to arrive at adjusted gross income. If you're self-employed, a portion of your self-employment tax is deducted from income. Certain self-employment investment contributions and health insurance costs are also posted here.

✔ **Deductions:** The CPA exam may ask you about the differences between the standard deduction and itemized deductions. Every taxpayer can take advantage of the standard deduction. Itemized deductions are computed on Schedule A. If the total you calculate on Schedule A is more than your standard deduction, you can take the higher deduction on Form 1040.

✔ **Exemptions:** The top of page 1 of Form 1040 allows you to calculate the total number of exemptions. The form provides a dollar amount for each person deemed to be an exemption. The total exemption amount reduces adjusted gross income.

After you calculate taxable income, Form 1040 instructions provide the tax tables you use to compute your tax liability. That amount is posted as tax on page 2 of the form. The tax total may be reduced by credits. Credits reduce taxes dollar-for-dollar.

After you know the total tax owed, you deduct any withholdings that were sent to pay your taxes during the year. Taxpayers typically withhold tax from their wages. The employer sends the withholdings to the IRS. You also reduce your total taxes by any payments you made during the year. If you still owe taxes after these adjustments, you have a tax liability. If you've paid in too much using withholdings and estimated payments, you're owed a refund.

Liquidity and Solvency Formulas

The inventory turnover and receivable turnover formulas I cover earlier in this chapter are liquidity ratios. *Liquidity* refers to a company's ability to use current assets to pay current liabilities. For this book, *current* means 12 months or less. *Solvency,* on the other hand, refers to a company's ability to pay liabilities over the long term. A business must be able to generate revenue and convert that revenue to cash over a period of years.

Suppose a business issues a five-year corporate bond. The company must make annual interest payments and then repay the principal amount of the bond at the end of five years. Businesses also need to invest funds to make large purchases. If a firm needs to replace an expensive piece of equipment in three years, the company may invest each year to accumulate funds for the purchase price. These transactions require cash inflows from sales over multiple years.

Two other liquidity ratios that are frequently tested on the CPA exam are the current ratio and quick ratio. Here's the current ratio:

$$\text{Current ratio} = \frac{\text{Current assets}}{\text{Current liabilities}}$$

Current assets include cash and assets that will be converted into cash within 12 months. That includes accounts receivable. A company expects to collect receivables in 12 months. If not, the receivables should be written off as bad debt expense. Inventory is also a current asset. Firms expect to sell their inventory within 12 months. If not, then inventory is considered obsolete — not an asset that can be sold. Obsolete inventory should be written off as cost of goods sold (an expense account).

Current liabilities include accounts payable and the current portion of long-term debt. Suppose a company has a bond that matures in six years. The bond requires the issuer to repay $100,000 of the bond's principal amount each year. The $100,000 due within a year is considered a current liability.

You can compare the current ratio to the company's checkbook. Funds expected to be paid in cash are current assets. Think about current assets as deposits to the checkbook, and consider current liabilities to be checks that must be written within a year.

Ideally, a company should have at least one dollar of current assets to pay for each dollar of current liabilities. That means that the current ratio is 1 or greater. Say a company has $1,000,000 in current assets and $800,000 in current liabilities. The current ratio is $1,000,000 \div \$800,000 = 1.25$. The company has $1.25 in current assets to pay each dollar of current liabilities.

The quick ratio is similar to the current ratio. Here's the formula:

$$\text{Quick ratio} = \frac{\text{Current assets} - \text{Inventory}}{\text{Current liabilities}}$$

Notice that the quick ratio takes the current ratio and excludes inventory from current assets. The rationale is that inventory is the least-liquid of the current assets, meaning that inventory will take the longest time to convert to cash. That makes sense, because a company may hold inventory for six months or longer. Other current assets, like receivables, are typically collected in 60 to 90 days.

This chapter wraps up with a solvency ratio:

$$\text{Times interest earned} = \frac{\text{Operating income before taxes and interest}}{\text{Interest expense}}$$

Times interest earned measures a company's ability to use earnings to pay interest on debt. The higher the ratio, the easier it is for the company to make interest payments. If a company had operating income of \$2,000,000 and interest expense of \$500,000, the ratio would be \$2,000,000 ÷ \$500,000 = 4. The company's available earnings are 4 times the amount of interest expense it must pay.

Appendix

Linking to Wiley CPAexcel

A critical step in preparing for the CPA exam is to work through lots of test questions. You see four sets of test questions in this book, along with answers and explanations. This book also includes a one-month subscription to the Wiley CPAexcel Online Test Bank. If you like what the Test Bank offers and want to continue drilling on CPA exam questions and simulations, you can purchase a full subscription after the month is over.

This appendix gives you the skinny on what the Wiley CPAexcel Online Test Bank is and how it can help you, how to access your free one-month subscription, how to extend your subscription, and whom to contact if you have any trouble along the way.

Understanding What the Test Bank Has to Offer

Boost your understanding of the CPA exam with the ultimate online practice tool. Use the Wiley CPAexcel Online Test Bank to sharpen your skills, replicate the real test environment, identify and tag weak subject areas, and customize question sets. View your progress by topic and understand when you've reached passing threshold.

Your one-month free access includes the following:

- More than 4,000 questions with detailed answers
- 164 enhanced simulations
- Replicated Prometric (computer test) experience
- Tracking of your strengths and weaknesses
- Forms and formats of the most current exam
- Rationales, hints, and a full text explanation for every multiple-choice question
- Practice exams that fully replicate the real exam
- Filters to select question sets by subtopic, answered versus unanswered, and more
- Randomization to prevent memorization
- Unlimited custom practice sessions and tests

Accessing Your Free Subscription

To gain access to your free, one-month subscription, all you have to do is register. There's no obligation to purchase and no credit card required. Just follow these simple steps:

1. **Find your PIN access code.**

   - **Print book users:** If you purchased a hard copy of this book, you can find your access code inside the front cover as a scratch-off.

   - **E-book users:** If you purchased this book as an e-book, you can get your access code by registering your e-book at dummies.com/go/getaccess. Go to the website, find your book and click it, and answer the security question to verify your purchase. Then you'll receive an e-mail with your access code.

2. **Go to www.wileycpaexcel.com/dummies.**

3. **Enter your access code and click Next.**

4. **Follow the instructions to create an account and establish your personal login information.**

That's all there is to it! You can come back to the online program again and again — simply log in with the username and password you chose during your initial login. No need to use the access code a second time.

Your registration is good for one month from the day you activate your access code. After that time frame has passed, you can purchase Wiley CPAexcel to continue accessing practice questions (see the next section for info on how to purchase).

Purchasing Wiley CPAexcel to Continue Your Practice

If you like Wiley CPAexcel and want to continue using the CPA Test Bank or want the full CPA Review Course after the one-month subscription is over, you have the option of purchasing extended access to the service at a reduced rate. Wiley CPAexcel offers a discount to readers who have purchased this book. A discount code will be e-mailed to you when you register for your free subscription.

Where to Go for Help

If you have trouble with the access code or can't find it, please contact Wiley CPAexcel Customer Support at 1-888-884-5669 or +1 928-204-1066 or visit http://efficient learning.custhelp.com.

Index

About the Author

Kenneth W. Boyd, a former CPA, has over 29 years of experience in accounting, education, and financial services. Ken is the owner of St. Louis Test Preparation (www.stltest.net). He provides online tutoring in accounting and finance to both graduate and undergraduate students. His YouTube channel (kenboydstl) has hundreds of videos on accounting and finance.

Ken is also the author of *Cost Accounting for Dummies* and coauthor of *Accounting All-In-One for Dummies*. He was also the creator and presenter of creativeLIVE's *Small Business Finance Basics: Quickbooks and Beyond* (www.creativelive.com), and he works as a finance and accounting author for Lynda.com.

Boyd has written test questions for the Certified Public Accountant (CPA) Exam for ACT, Inc. Ken is married and lives in St. Louis, Missouri, with his wife Patty and his three children, Kaitlin, Connor, and Meaghan.

Dedication

I dedicate this book to my father, Bill Boyd, who is a hero to me. This book is also dedicated to my closest friend, my wife Patty, and to our children. Finally, this book is dedicated to the faculty and staff of three St. Louis schools: Chaminade College Preparatory School, St. Peter Catholic School in Kirkwood, and Visitation Academy. Thank you for educating my children.

Author's Acknowledgments

I want to thank Stacy Kennedy, Acquisitions Editor, for the opportunity to write this book. Thanks also to Matt Wagner of Fresh Books Literary Agency, who presented me to Wiley. I owe a huge debt of thanks to Barry Schoenborn and Joe Kraynak, who served as the Technical Writers for my first two books. Their wit, wisdom, and work ethic helped me become a better writer.

Many thanks to the Wiley team: Chrissy Guthrie, Senior Project Editor; Danielle Voirol, Senior Copy Editor; and Ron DeWitt, the Technical Editor. They worked very hard to make this book more accurate and easier to read. Without them, there wouldn't be a book.

Publisher's Acknowledgments

Acquisitions Editor: Stacy Kennedy

Senior Project Editor: Christina Guthrie

Senior Copy Editor: Danielle Voirol

Technical Editor: Ron DeWitt

Project Coordinator: Sheree Montgomery

Cover Image: ©iStock.com/Lonely__

Apple & Mac

iPad For Dummies, 6th Edition
978-1-118-72306-7

iPhone For Dummies, 7th Edition
978-1-118-69083-3

Macs All-in-One For Dummies,
4th Edition
978-1-118-82210-4

OS X Mavericks For Dummies
978-1-118-69188-5

Blogging & Social Media

Facebook For Dummies, 5th Edition
978-1-118-63312-0

Social Media Engagement For Dummies
978-1-118-53019-1

WordPress For Dummies, 6th Edition
978-1-118-79161-5

Business

Stock Investing For Dummies,
4th Edition
978-1-118-37678-2

Investing For Dummies, 6th Edition
978-0-470-90545-6

Personal Finance For Dummies,
7th Edition
978-1-118-11785-9

QuickBooks 2014 For Dummies
978-1-118-72005-9

Small Business Marketing Kit
For Dummies, 3rd Edition
978-1-118-31183-7

Careers

Job Interviews For Dummies, 4th Edition
978-1-118-11290-8

Job Searching with Social Media
For Dummies, 2nd Edition
978-1-118-67856-5

Personal Branding For Dummies
978-1-118-11792-7

Resumes For Dummies, 6th Edition
978-0-470-87361-8

Starting an Etsy Business For Dummies,
2nd Edition
978-1-118-59024-9

Diet & Nutrition

Belly Fat Diet For Dummies
978-1-118-34585-6

Mediterranean Diet For Dummies
978-1-118-71525-3

Nutrition For Dummies, 5th Edition
978-0-470-93231-5

Digital Photography

Digital SLR Photography All-in-One
For Dummies, 2nd Edition
978-1-118-59082-9

Digital SLR Video & Filmmaking
For Dummies
978-1-118-36598-4

Photoshop Elements 12 For Dummies
978-1-118-72714-0

Gardening

Herb Gardening For Dummies,
2nd Edition
978-0-470-61778-6

Gardening with Free-Range Chickens
For Dummies
978-1-118-54754-0

Health

Boosting Your Immunity For Dummies
978-1-118-40200-9

Diabetes For Dummies, 4th Edition
978-1-118-29447-5

Living Paleo For Dummies
978-1-118-29405-5

Big Data

Big Data For Dummies
978-1-118-50422-2

Data Visualization For Dummies
978-1-118-50289-1

Hadoop For Dummies
978-1-118-60755-8

Language & Foreign Language

500 Spanish Verbs For Dummies
978-1-118-02382-2

English Grammar For Dummies,
2nd Edition
978-0-470-54664-2

French All-in-One For Dummies
978-1-118-22815-9

German Essentials For Dummies
978-1-118-18422-6

Italian For Dummies, 2nd Edition
978-1-118-00465-4

Math & Science

Algebra I For Dummies, 2nd Edition
978-0-470-55964-2

 Available in print and e-book formats.

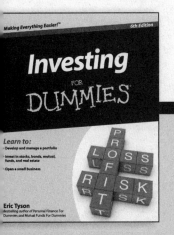

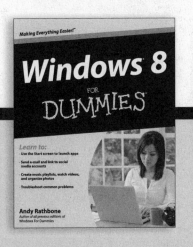

Available wherever books are sold. **For more information or to order direct visit www.dummies.com**

Anatomy and Physiology For Dummies, 2nd Edition
978-0-470-92326-9

Astronomy For Dummies, 3rd Edition
978-1-118-37697-3

Biology For Dummies, 2nd Edition
978-0-470-59875-7

Chemistry For Dummies, 2nd Edition
978-1-118-00730-3

1001 Algebra II Practice Problems
For Dummies
978-1-118-44662-1

Microsoft Office

Excel 2013 For Dummies
978-1-118-51012-4

Office 2013 All-in-One For Dummies
978-1-118-51636-2

PowerPoint 2013 For Dummies
978-1-118-50253-2

Word 2013 For Dummies
978-1-118-49123-2

Music

Blues Harmonica For Dummies
978-1-118-25269-7

Guitar For Dummies, 3rd Edition
978-1-118-11554-1

iPod & iTunes For Dummies, 10th Edition
978-1-118-50864-0

Programming

Beginning Programming with C
For Dummies
978-1-118-73763-7

Excel VBA Programming For Dummies,
3rd Edition
978-1-118-49037-2

Java For Dummies, 6th Edition
978-1-118-40780-6

Religion & Inspiration

The Bible For Dummies
978-0-7645-5296-0

Buddhism For Dummies, 2nd Edition
978-1-118-02379-2

Catholicism For Dummies, 2nd Edition
978-1-118-07778-8

Self-Help & Relationships

Beating Sugar Addiction For Dummies
978-1-118-54645-1

Meditation For Dummies, 3rd Edition
978-1-118-29144-3

Seniors

Laptops For Seniors For Dummies,
3rd Edition
978-1-118-71105-7

Computers For Seniors For Dummies,
3rd Edition
978-1-118-11553-4

iPad For Seniors For Dummies,
6th Edition
978-1-118-72826-0

Social Security For Dummies
978-1-118-20573-0

Smartphones & Tablets

Android Phones For Dummies,
2nd Edition
978-1-118-72030-1

Nexus Tablets For Dummies
978-1-118-77243-0

Samsung Galaxy S 4 For Dummies
978-1-118-64222-1

Samsung Galaxy Tabs For Dummies
978-1-118-77294-2

Test Prep

ACT For Dummies, 5th Edition
978-1-118-01259-8

ASVAB For Dummies, 3rd Edition
978-0-470-63760-9

GRE For Dummies, 7th Edition
978-0-470-88921-3

Officer Candidate Tests For Dummies
978-0-470-59876-4

Physician's Assistant Exam For Dummies
978-1-118-11556-5

Series 7 Exam For Dummies
978-0-470-09932-2

Windows 8

Windows 8.1 All-in-One For Dummies
978-1-118-82087-2

Windows 8.1 For Dummies
978-1-118-82121-3

Windows 8.1 For Dummies, Book + DVD
Bundle
978-1-118-82107-7

 Available in print and e-book formats.

Available wherever books are sold. **For more information or to order direct visit www.dummies.com**

Take Dummies with you everywhere you go!

Whether you are excited about e-books, want more from the web, must have your mobile apps, or are swept up in social media, Dummies makes everything easier.

Leverage the Power

For Dummies is the global leader in the reference category and one of the most trusted and highly regarded brands in the world. No longer just focused on books, customers now have access to the For Dummies content they need in the format they want. Let us help you develop a solution that will fit your brand and help you connect with your customers.

Advertising & Sponsorships

Connect with an engaged audience on a powerful multimedia site, and position your message alongside expert how-to content.

Targeted ads • Video • Email marketing • Microsites • Sweepstakes sponsorship

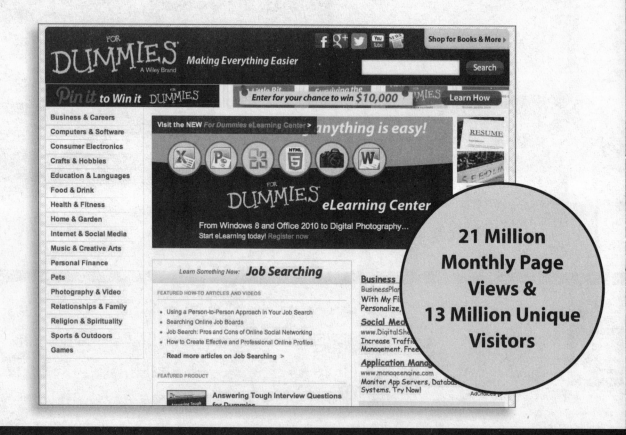

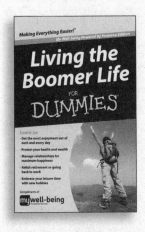

Dummies products make life easier!

- DIY
- Consumer Electronics
- Crafts

- Software
- Cookware
- Hobbies

- Videos
- Music
- Games
- and More!

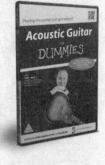

Dummies.com